# IN MY FATHER'S STUDY

## BEN ORLOVE

Foreword by Albert E. Stone

University of Iowa Press   Iowa City

University of Iowa Press,
Iowa City 52242
Copyright © 1995 by the
University of Iowa Press
All rights reserved
Printed in the United States
of America

Design by Richard Hendel

01 00 99 98 97 96 95 C 5 4 3 2 1
01 00 99 98 97 96 95 P 5 4 3 2 1

Library of Congress Cataloging-in-
Publication Data
Orlove, Benjamin S.
  In my father's study / by Ben
Orlove; foreword by Albert E. Stone.
      p.   cm. — (Singular lives)
ISBN 0-87745-490-6, ISBN 0-87745-491-4
(paper)
  1. Orlove, Robert.  2. Orlove,
Benjamin S.  3. Jews — New York
(N.Y.) — Biography.  4. Jews,
Russian — New York (N.Y.) —
Biography.  5. Jews, Russian — New
York (N.Y.) — Social life and customs.
6. Brooklyn (New York, N.Y.) —
Biography.  7. Brooklyn (New York,
N.Y.) — Social life and customs.
8. New York (N.Y.) — Biography.
9. New York (N.Y.) — Social life and
customs.  I. Title.  II. Series.
F128.9.J5O75  1995
974.7'004924 — dc20        94-37406
                                 CIP

# CONTENTS

en Orlove's *In My Father's Study* is in revealing and necessary ways a most unusual experiment in autobiography, perhaps the most singular so far in Singular Lives: The Iowa Series in North American Autobiography. Indeed, for many this story may not seem to be autobiography at all. Almost from the start, it can be read as biography, the life-story of an immigrant — a representative and appealing figure but quite unknown in the annals of American social history — written by his son. The writing, begun shortly after the father's death, exhibits little of either the filial piety and sentimentality or the scarcely veiled resentments and even outright hatred that often suffuse such activity. Instead, Ben has entered, through the actual doorway of his father Robert's California study, into half a century of his father's experiences, thoughts, and emotions. He does so with wry sensitivity and loving detachment. Moreover, Ben re-creates his own self along with a richly detailed family history. Though only one among other Orloves and Cohens, Ben emerges as the son who is a modest, masterful teller of two stories — *and* the artificer of his own identity.

Robert Orlove's life in America, like that of the others in his Eastern European Jewish family who settled and struggled in New York and Chicago, is only in detail and nuance different from the lives of many of the 35 million Europeans who moved to the United States in the great migration of 1840–1930. But every reader of this book will realize that nuance and detail make a world of difference. Ben Orlove's re-entry into his father's, uncles', aunts', and cousins' worlds constitutes a family history of notable density and immediacy. In economic terms, the Orloves brought from Europe expertise and industry as fur merchants and petty manufacturers. What Robert and his relatives achieved in this country was, however, not a successful family business. The precise situation is significant not only to the mature anthropologist who writes but to the former child who remembers the family squabbles, temporary partnerships, and frequent failures. "In short, they were a business family rather than a family business," he points out.

> If the goals of a family business are to avoid bankruptcy and show a profit, the goals of a business family are less well defined. The brothers worked hard, impelled not only by the need to earn money but by other desires as well: for approval from their father, for affection from their mother, for recognition of the family's name by other Jewish families in the fur trade. In this alternative view, the risks of failure were greater. After a bankruptcy, the members of a family business could cease being partners. . . . The members of a business family, though, would remain relatives and could never leave one another, could never end the accusations and counter-accusations of blame for their failures.

Major themes emerge from this reflection on family, business, success, and failure. First, Orlove's double narrative (a personal story enclosed at every point in family history) explores the fates of two marriage-related families in quite specific social circumstances. The Orloves were no Lehmans, the Cohens were no Rothschilds. Ancient rabbinic respectability within the faroff Pale counted for little in the land of dollars. Herein lies one value of this record: not only is the curtain of privacy and secrecy pulled aside to show the everyday experiences of one extended family but the daily drama occurs below the usual levels of social visibility or historical attention. Ordinary lives are treated with extraordinary attention and analysis not only because the writer is son, grandson, nephew, and cousin to his subjects but also because he has become an anthropologist. As a human scientist, Orlove shows on every page a capacity to stand outside as well as within the lives and characters of others who, unlike the Peruvian peasants he usually writes about, are of his own blood.

As the preceding quotation indicates, this family-and-self history is by turns passionate and cool, dramatic and analytic. In both modes the focus remains on relationships and character. Accusations and counter-accusations, approbation and affection, reputation and disgrace, success and failure, even suicide and nervous breakdown are described and mused upon. Such passions are, of course, commonly the burden of novels; one thinks, in this context, of Henry Roth's thirties masterpiece, *Call It Sleep*. Historians, too, have explored the darker sides of the immigrant experience. But Jewish-American autobiographers of the first or second generation — I am thinking of Mary Antin and Alfred Kazin, Kate Simon and Norman Podhoretz, among others — more typically hasten past the gritty circumstances of family quarrels and childhood disappointments on the way to the narrator's often triumphant escape from the paternal presence and ghetto beginnings. In part, Ben Orlove follows this path. His Brooklyn boyhood and adolescence are marked more by academic achievement than resentment and rebellion. Becoming the Harvard- and Berkeley-trained anthropologist is a muted process in this father- and family-centered account. Nonetheless, the social scientist's eye and imagination are steadily present in the patterns of insight and description, as well as in apt quotations from some passionate letters and diaries discovered in the father's study.

A chief reason for the son's downplaying his own successful career is the bleak fact that, for many years, the father's American experiences spell failure. Hence, the narrative stresses, nearly to the closing chapters, Robert's anomalous place in his business family. The fur business never meets the emotional needs of this sensitive, melancholy, insecure man who, as son and brother, business partner, husband and father, regularly fails to meet his own or others' expectations. His letters and diaries tell the son "why my father fled that world, and why he was so drawn to art. As I read about the disputes among my uncles and my grandfather, I could sense how he despised the petty connivings of the fur business, and how noble painting and drawing seemed to him. The calm solitude of his study, I realized, was a refuge from the tense intimacy of the fur shops, with their bickering, conspiracies, and outbursts of rage."

Fur business and "noble" art, though, are less remote from one another than one might suppose. For Robert Orlove worked "as a pattern-maker, one of the most highly skilled of the positions within the needle trades generally. He designed fur toys in the 1950s and early 1960s, much as he had designed fur hats in Chicago in the mid-1940s." So the father's flight from shop and street to the creative privacy and obscurity of his study, like his early retirement, was a logical expression of temperament. Part of the equation, too, was the complementary temperament of Katzy Cohen Orlove, Robert's dynamic, outgoing wife and Ben's mother. She early assumed the breadwinner's role in the family. His parents' personalities and careers intrigue Ben, leading to a series of thoughtful speculations about gender roles and the sometimes upsetting realization that his father might have been happier born a woman, while his mother could have been a successful American male. In such moments, Orlove's narrative reveals an affinity for his fellow anthropologist's autobiography, Margaret Mead's *Blackberry Winter*.

The father's study — a moveable center of the patternmaker's life and this son's re-creation — proved less a refuge than another locale for failure. Though practicing the arts of drawing, linoleum cuts, and collages, Robert Orlove soon discovered how far short his talent fell from his dreams. Copying his best friend's far more accomplished works, while tacitly allowing his family to believe these were his own creations, was one nagging secret. Only later in life did Robert Orlove resign himself to the role of museumgoer and friend of noted artists. With this adjustment, though, came the satisfying discovery that composing his own collages allowed him to express creativity and touch the lives of family and friends through mailing his witty and thought-provoking cards. The son's exploration of his dead father's crammed but orderly study contained some poignant, even mysterious, moments, but just as exciting and consoling was finding the boxes of a thousand such collages. The son alone realized the extent of the modest and private success his otherwise frustrated father achieved through art.

This son's account of the transformation of his sire from a reserved, insecure, unhappy young man and new husband into an urbane, well-read, and artistic older man is convincing and deeply satisfying. For the reader recognizes the varieties of success and failure early-twentieth-century America could offer its adopted sons and daughters. Furthermore, the father's tale incorporates (without displacing or overriding) the lives, affections, and attainments of wife and son. For the reader cannot fail to see how Ben's own development follows — never in detail but basically in hope and sensitivity — Robert's. Father, mother, and son are thus united in spirit, yet still distinct in temperament, by the epitaph Katzy and Ben agree on for Robert's gravestone: "a gentle man."

In fact, Ben's mother is, in her own way, as essential to the son's story as its ostensible subject. Passion, action, drive, intense family ties with "the Cohen girls" and her hesitant lover and husband — these are attributes celebrated in Katzy's life as they interacted with her husband's and son's personalities. As an aging widow in California, she sits sipping tea in her new home while her son sits in his absent father's study. There he sorts and studies the voluminous and sometimes shocking records of a lifetime (including, remarkably, a 1,600-word account of the first time he and Katzy made love). Both survivors recognize that Robert accumulated this mountain of memorabilia and arranged it carefully so that Ben could enter this room and, if he chose, share the writer's task of recreating and redeeming a disappointing life. No wonder the son occasionally hallucinates that the father still inhabits the room where, on a shelf, his ashes rest.

This unusual dual autobiography affords the curious reader its own special rewards, as all good life-histories do. It also reminds us of a larger truth about autobiography as art and humane science: a life-story is never, cannot be, exclusively about the self as actor and author. Each life and personal identity is a social construct and collective achievement. Though many American autobiographers hew — too narrowly as this book implicitly asserts — to the "I," other writers have demonstrated how in actual experience and memory the "I" is really a "we." Thus, telling another's story as a necessary way of telling one's own is also an American tradition. Ben Orlove has some signal ancestors and contemporaries, in fact. Gertrude Stein's *The Autobiography of Alice B. Toklas*, John Edgar Wideman's *Brothers and Keepers*, and (perhaps more pertinent still) Geoffrey Wolff's *The Duke of Deception* and his brother Tobias Wolff's *This Boy's Life* are exemplary multiple autobiographies in which the author merges with, respectively, lifelong friend and lover, brother as penitentiary prisoner, father, mother. Because Jewish culture is traditionally patriarchal and because so much American writing (by Jews and everyone else) dramatizes the archetypal relations of son and father, Ben Orlove has tapped into a remarkably rich vein of individual and collective experience in our multicultural society and history. He has emerged from his father's study with a record any son might be proud to claim as his own.

# ACKNOWLEDGMENTS

I t has been my good fortune to receive valuable help at each step in the writing of this book. I was encouraged by the response of the friends with whom I initially discussed the project, especially Lynne Cobb, Gary Hamilton, Craig McNamara, and Howard Ockman, and by the reactions of my colleagues to whom I nervously presented drafts of what are now chapters 4 and 5 at a brown-bag lunch at the University of California Davis Humanities Institute. Kay Flavell, Karen Halttunen, Roland Marchand, and Judy Stacey each sought me out afterward and provided me with kind words that remained in my mind as I began writing the other chapters. Their comments also helped me formulate a proposal to the Littauer Foundation, whose financial support I acknowledge with the gratitude that comes from knowing the difference that it has made in permitting some travel, many telephone calls, and massive amounts of photocopying. The Humanities Institute provided further assistance in the preparation of the manuscript; I am especially grateful to Ann Chamberlain for her efforts in transcribing my father's diaries. I am also grateful for the careful readings and helpful suggestions from the editors at the University of Iowa Press, especially Carolyn Brown.

Other people helped me maintain the momentum that I had picked up by midbook. I remember the long conversations with Barry Lenson and Gustavo Bonevardi, whom I came to know in the course of this book project, sons of friends of my father's, whose explorations of their own pasts have paralleled my own in surprising and moving ways. Carole Malkin's perceptive comments helped me recognize strengths and flaws that I might otherwise not have seen. My colleagues at Davis and at other northern campuses of the UC system have also been generous with their time in translating postcards, telegrams, passport requirements, and the various other documents that I have found in German, Latin, Russian, Swedish, and Yiddish, and in helping me establish points of fact on a wide range of historical questions. I had the good fortune to work with Jeffrey Escoffier, a gifted editor and colleague: his thoughtful comments on the first complete draft of this book led to a series of conversations from which I emerged with a stronger sense of purpose and resolve for the crucial stage of revision.

Unlike my anthropological articles and books about Latin America, which I have mostly written at the office, this book has been written at home, and it is my family whom I most wish to acknowledge, because they have been the ones who have most acknowledged me as I have written this book. They have seen me in many moods — distracted, troubled, elated, content — on occasion in my study as I actually was writing, more often during the breaks I would take, as I entered the kitchen for a cup of coffee, as I paced in the backyard, as I rushed into the living room to look at my father's prints on the wall. Judy, Jacob, Hannah, Raphael — I have been sustained by your patience, your solicitude, and, most simply and most profoundly, by your love.

# IN MY FATHER'S STUDY

# Chapter 1   R E M A I N I N G

I n the first months after my father died, I rarely went into his study. It was not that I avoided the apartment where he had lived; I went there several times a week to see my mother. After coming in, I would make myself a cup of coffee and then join her where she was sitting — on the sofa or at the dining table, or, if the weather was mild and she felt strong enough, outside on her front patio. We sometimes sat in silence, but more often we talked, ranging over a series of topics: her health, my children, the relatives who had written or called. My father came up in our conversations only infrequently and tangentially. Could I check on the top shelf of the pantry, my mother once asked, she couldn't reach up there and she thought that Robbie might have put the light bulbs there, the one in the hall had just blown out, but she didn't want to buy new ones if she still had some, she was sure that there were a few in the house somewhere, she had looked everywhere. We took pleasure in speaking of him as if he had not died but merely had stepped out of the house for a moment to mail a letter or to pick up the newspaper.

Another mother and son might have taken on the project of clearing out a study after the death of its occupant, sorting through old papers and photographs and reminiscing about the past. We had more pressing tasks at hand, though, since my father had taken care of all the domestic chores. He had bought the groceries, done the laundry, even cooked many of the meals. It was my mother who had been the invalid — everyone had expected her to die first. She had been much more limited by her emphysema than he had been by his weak heart. Accustomed to thinking of him as the healthy one, we had anticipated that he would recover from the heart attack that kept him in the hospital for nearly two weeks. We were shocked by his death following the second and third heart attacks, less than twelve hours apart.

My visits were the principal breaks in my mother's new isolation, as thorough as it was unexpected. She knew very few people in town because she and my father had moved from New York to California less than a year before. Other than exchanging greetings with the neighbor next door or chatting with Cuca, the Mexican woman who came once a week to clean her apartment, she hardly spoke with anyone other than me. On some of my visits, though, my mother would absent herself rather than engage in conversation. She might leave me in the living room while, with the slow pace that came from her age and infirmities, she would make a trip to the bathroom or go off to her bedroom to use her nebulizer, a machine that produced a fine medicated mist that penetrated deep into her lungs, but which was so noisy that it made conversation impossible. In these moments of solitude in her apartment, I would sometimes step into my father's study, where everything remained exactly as it had been on the day of the first heart attack that had taken him out of the apartment. I would look from the doorway, not so much at the room that he had only used for seven months, but at the pieces of furniture it contained, ones I had known all my life: the well-polished cherrywood desk, the long low bookcase, the black card table, the bureau that I had used as a child. I would occasionally go further into the room, walking to the card table with many items on it, the stack of magazines he had intended to read, the little notebooks he had made for himself from odd scraps of blank paper, a sheet of paper on which he had ruled lines to record the dates he received and replied to letters from my sisters — Carol in Israel, Judy in Connecticut — and from other relatives. I would pause in front of his desk to look at the line of small decorative objects on its top. Each one had a story, some of which I remembered. He had carved the tiny bust of his sister Gertrude, and he had also made the small heavy metal amulet with a vaguely Chinese look to it, a product of the period when he experimented with casting molten lead into plaster forms. A brightly colored wooden figurine, its face a ritual mask with enormous eyes, was a Pueblo Indian kachina that my father had the taste and foresight to buy in Chicago in the 1940s, when department stores sold them as dolls, before collectors, drawn to their powerful geometric forms and their exotic origins, drove their prices up. A small ivory carving of an old man, a monk with a high forehead and a raffish smile, was a netsuke, an ornamental Japanese button for kimono sashes, given to him by a friend who ran an art gallery near Union Square in Manhattan. He had collected owls because they symbolized wisdom and mortality, but who had given him this one of orange-brown glass, this other of painted metal? And what was that story about the strange round-bellied African carving, an unclothed figure with breasts and a penis? I was sure that I had once heard the story of how he had come to own it.

After a few brief and unsatisfactory inquiries, I stopped asking my mother about the origins of these objects. She often did not know them herself, and, in any case, she much preferred to tell stories of her own life rather than those of her husband's. With great animation she recounted anecdotes, particularly from the idyllic period when she and her five younger sisters were girls, after her family had moved uptown from the Lower East Side and before her father had died. We would talk more about her own past than about my father's, and I continued my private visits into his study. Sometimes I sat down at his table, the place in his study where he had spent the most time, and looked through the notes he had made. This sheet containing some abstract doodles and a comical sketch of some birds might have been a rough draft for a card, perhaps for someone's birthday. I could detect more clearly his intentions for a set of news articles and book reviews, carefully cut out from the *New York Times*. I remembered receiving such bundles of clippings from him, and here under the paper clip that held them together was a piece of paper with the name of the friend to whom he had planned to send them.

His desk drew me even more strongly than the table. As a child, I was fascinated with its shiny dark surfaces, its drop front, always left up and locked, and its four wide drawers, of which only the top one could also be locked. The bottom three drawers each had a pair of dark brass handles, much more impressive affairs than the simple knobs that we had on dressers and cabinets. Each handle consisted of two pieces, somewhat like a door knocker. The smaller piece, in the shape of the letter ∪, had small extensions on either end that fit into little protuberances on the larger, more ornate portion, which was attached directly to the drawer. The ∪-shaped piece usually hung straight down, suspended between the two protuberances, but it was free to swing up and down. I would sometimes watch my father reach down, slip his forefingers into the ∪-shaped pieces, and pull the drawer open. When I was still very small, I would occasionally try to imitate this simple act of his. The papers and books, though, made the drawers too heavy for me. With only my forefingers, I was unable to get a strong enough grip on the ∪-shaped pieces to pull the drawer open, but I could not fit all my fingers through the pieces to grasp them firmly. I would tug on the handles with my forefingers and middle fingers, the metal pressing sharply into my flesh as I attempted, unsuccessfully, to jerk the drawer open. I would content myself with an easier game, lifting one ∪-shaped piece all the way up so that it touched the top of the ornate portion, and then letting it swing down to strike the bottom with a dull metallic thonk. My efforts to examine the contents of these drawers had to wait for several years, until I was strong enough to open the drawers and old enough for my parents to leave me home alone. I found a few catalogs of art exhibits that my father had attended and a thick brown folder containing some sketches that he had made, but I was afraid to continue my explorations. I was sure that he would be able to tell that I had gone through his papers. Even if I took great care in putting them back neatly, I could not restore them to the perfect order in which he had left them.

And now I could inspect these drawers at my leisure. Their contents, I discovered, were principally boxes full of the elements that he would assemble into collages, pictures that he had cut out of magazines: one box of clocks, others of suns, of animals, of frames. I also found some items that he had preserved from his years in the fur business, including a few patterns for toys that he had designed. I remembered seeing these heavy pieces of cardboard on my visits to the shops in which he had worked in the fur district in Manhattan. He had explained the process to me: the cutters set the cardboard shapes against the rabbit pelts or velvet or plush before cutting the pieces out and passing them on to the machine operators who sewed them together, piles of toy dogs or teddy bears accumulating in a corner of the shop.

Now I could even open the locked portions of the desk, since my mother had given me the spare key. In the top drawer I found a jumble of old papers: report cards that my sisters and I had brought home, brief newspaper obituaries of my father's older brothers, certificates from an adult night school at which he had studied while he was looking for work during the Depression. I was particularly taken with the travel papers for the trip when he emigrated from Europe to America. He had been an infant in 1905 when the family fled from Russia to Germany during the Russo-Japanese War, and twelve years old when they left Germany in 1916, in the middle of World War I, for Sweden. Here, at seventeen, he was departing in 1921, along with his mother and younger siblings, for New York, to join his father and older brothers, who had already moved there. It took me a while to realize what an odd document the exit visa was, printed in Russian, Swedish, and French, signed by the provisional Russian Consul General in Stockholm, a representative of a government that had fallen from power several years earlier after its period of nine months' rule between the fall of the Czar and the triumph of the Bolshevik Revolution. It even took me a while to notice that the visa was issued not to Robert Orlove but to Salomon Orlowsky — my father had not yet chosen a new first name, nor had he dropped the final syllable of the last. I stopped reading the words and looked at the sepia-colored oval photograph, seven centimeters by five. I identified rather than recognized my father. I had to stop a moment to think, yes, this is what he must have looked like when he was seventeen. I examined the grave expression on his face, his head turned slightly downward, the serious look in his eyes, his lips slightly pressed together. Was he on the verge of tears, I wondered, or was I? The disruptions in his life suddenly overwhelmed me: his family scattered across different countries, the responsibilities for his mother and younger siblings thrust on him.

Unable to continue looking at the photographs and papers, unable to leave them, I sat motionless and lost myself in melancholy. After a long interval I sighed and looked up from the exit visa with the photograph, past the row of little sculptures on the desk, and out the window

*My father at age seventeen in Stockholm, 1921.*

ВЪ СТОКГОЛЬМѢ

Генер

Landed as Trans under Bond.

28 SEP 192

IMMIGRATION OF

*Salomon Orlowsky*

to the small tree in the patio outside, its branches shaking in the wind. I sighed again and slowly began to replace the photographs and papers. I locked the desk drawer and walked out of the study, returning to the living room and to conversations with my mother.

For most of a year I continued this pattern of infrequent forays into the study. I would find some paper—a letter or note or sketch—and slip into a long abstract reverie, more poignant than painful, from which I would emerge slowly, as if I were lying still in bed after I had

6

woken from a vivid dream rather than immediately getting up. I would replace the paper exactly as I had found it and leave the study quickly. Once, in describing to a friend my reluctance to alter the room and its contents in any way, I mentioned that if I really wanted to, I could try to purchase the apartment from the owners of the complex. I could then close off the study by hanging a maroon velvet cord from two brass posts that I would place in the doorway. The final step would be to put up a plaque by the door, announcing this room to be the study of Robert S. Orlove, a great man.

This image that had come to my mind not only captured the way I treated the room as a monument to him, almost as a shrine, it also showed my concern to make sure that no one else would come into this room, at least until I had completed my examination of its contents, a process that was advancing slowly and incompletely. I had been concentrating on my father's desk and table, even though the wide shallow closet at the back of the study contained his diaries, a long row of crimson volumes with the years stamped in gold leaf, and packages of letters from relatives, from friends, and from me as well — the correspondence that accumulated steadily while I studied in college and graduate school, while I carried out anthropological field work in Peru, while I taught in California, right up to the time when my parents moved from New York. It was not merely my sentimental attraction to the desk and worktable that kept me from going more frequently to the closet, from sliding its doors open. It was his immediate presence on the top shelf near the diaries, in the form of the urn that contained his ashes.

Having him cremated was an extreme violation of Jewish custom, one that disturbed my oldest sister Carol, and, I was surprised to find, that troubled me as well. I wondered whether this decision to be cremated was one of the many struggles of will between my parents. My mother was firm on the issue of being cremated herself, although I was not certain what her reasons were. She had always prided herself on being modern, and she had sided with her father, a secular and progressive man, in his disagreements with his parents and oldest sister, who followed every detail of Jewish religious law. Perhaps my mother simply wanted to get the job of losing her body done quickly, with the same impatient efficiency with which she cooked, ironed, walked. Above all, if she could not undo or even halt the withering of her flesh by age, she could at least prevent the further humiliation of its gradual decay in the grave. Though not finicky or squeamish, she hated rot in all its forms and even detested stickiness. I recall her once grimacing as she wiped up an egg that had fallen on the kitchen floor, furious at the egg white for slipping off the rag and back onto the linoleum. Whatever her reasons, she had already decided to have my father cremated, and any conversations she had with her children would not lead her to change her mind.

I was dismayed by the prospect of making the arrangements for his cremation, but that task was clearly my responsibility, and, as I thought it over, not a very difficult one; it would not take very long, and many other people before me had faced the painful task of planning a funeral or cremation. I was relieved to find that the funeral director was called Mr. Smith, in this informal California town where all adults move quickly to a first-name basis for conducting business. I could not imagine calling him Charlie or Tom or whatever his name was, and it was easier for me to refer to him as Mr. Smith than as the funeral director or the undertaker or the mortician, since none of those phrases came easily to me.

My interview with Mr. Smith began smoothly enough. He spoke to me for a few minutes about my father and then brought out the forms that we had to fill out. Many of the questions were entirely routine: his date of birth, his address. I assured Mr. Smith that it did not matter to me or my mother what garment would be placed on my father — a plain cotton shroud would be fine. What cut through my efforts at moving rather mechanically through this situation was a word that he used to refer to the ashes, "cremains." I was offended by the crass neutrality of this invented term, by its suggestion of advertising campaigns. The word stripped dignity away from my father, decency from Mr. Smith. I neither commented on it nor accepted it, but simply kept using the word "ashes" as we spoke, moving down the forms line by line, bringing the conversation toward its end. I was caught completely off guard by the final questions, ones that did not appear on the form. Yes, I said, my father did have a heart condition; yes, he had a pacemaker. Mr. Smith looked up at me, paused, and explained that it would have to be removed because pacemakers could explode in the ovens, damaging and even destroying them. For several weeks after that conversation I kept thinking of the portion on the left side of my father's chest where the pacemaker had been, just below his collarbone. At some moments, I thought that this spot was just as Mr. Smith had promised it would be, all sewn up; I imagined a few crude stitches of thick thread in his flesh. At other moments, I saw his chest unsewn, open, flaps of skin hanging above bone, above muscle, partly dried in the air. These two images would alternate in my mind, an exhausting obsession that continued even after the cremation had taken place.

It was not only the arrangement for the cremation that fell to me but the decision of what to do with the ashes as well. My mother did not seem to have any preferences in this matter. On a second visit to the funeral chapel a week or two later, I chose an urn for the ashes, selecting a small gray steel box from the array of other equally un-urnlike metal and wooden containers on a table in a corner of Mr. Smith's office. When the delivery man brought this urn to my mother's apartment, it was my responsibility to find a place to keep it. It took me no time at all to decide to put it in the study and just a few moments to select the spot, the bureau in the corner. Somehow this location seemed just right. It was an appropriately respectful choice, on the tallest piece of furniture in the room, and a convenient one: I would not have to go to the bureau in my search for other papers, since it only held the heavy winter clothes that my parents had not needed since they left New York. I quickly cleaned off the top of the bureau, found an attractive place mat in the linen closet, and placed the urn on it. As I looked back at the urn, I felt a strong sense of relief that my father's remains had returned from some undefined journey through the hospital morgue and the crematorium, that they could rest in his study, close to the window with the bright southern exposure.

The urn was not to remain in that spot for very long. Cuca, the cleaning lady, was shocked to discover that this metal box, rather than being just another one of the odd objects in the apartment, actually contained human ashes. After a week or two, she told my mother and me that she was sorry, but she could no longer go into his study to dust and vacuum. She could not bear to look at the urn, and it was even worse when she had her back turned to it. She would feel *una tremenda mano fría*, a huge cold hand, reaching out toward her.

It took me much longer to find a second spot as appropriate as the first. I walked around the apartment and looked at several locations outside the study — the cabinet above the refrigerator where my mother kept some little-used dishes, the back of the linen closet among the extra towels — but they all seemed wrong. I went back into the study. I could just put the urn in a bureau drawer, I thought, but that seemed disrespectful, as if the urn were something I was trying to hide. The closet seemed the only alternative, a spot where it would be out of Cuca's sight but still treated with honor. After trying, without satisfying results, to rearrange some items on the bookcase in the closet to make some room for it, I cleared some space on the right end of the high shelf. Carrying the urn disturbed me much more this time, even though I only had to take it a short distance; it could not have been even a dozen steps across the study from the bureau to the closet. How many more times would I have to move these ashes, I wondered. Even after his death, my father seemed destined to migration, to impermanence. It troubled me as well to bring the place mat across the room. Setting the urn on it the first time had been a simple spontaneous gesture of respect, a gesture that, when repeated, seemed trivial, mechanical, false, in fact grotesque. For the first time, too, I found myself having religious scruples. I felt as if I were playing at constructing some sort of pagan altar. I shifted the urn back and forth a few inches, hoping to find a better spot, and finally settled it back to the point I had originally chosen, and then shut the sliding door.

For a month or so I avoided the closet, but I eventually returned, impelled partly by curiosity, partly by a wish to prove to myself that I did not have any superstitious fears of ghosts. I found a great variety of papers, old letters from my father's brothers, some photographs of their children that my sisters had sent. I skimmed notebooks filled with collages. One contained pictures of clocks, many set in the sky as suns; in another, figures, some serious, some comical, were arranged under umbrellas; and a third consisted of twenty-six pairs, neatly labeled in alphabetical order, from Adam-and-Eve to two xebecs (a kind of sailing ship), two youths, and two zands (a sort of Persian angel, as best I can figure out). These collage notebooks, at once philosophical and light-hearted, gave me a strong sense of my father. I recalled him, cutting the pictures out of magazines, arranging them carefully on the page, but these collages did not induce the reverie that I had felt at his desk or table. I looked through these books and the other papers in a great hurry, torn between an impulse to examine the entire contents of the closet quickly, so that I would not have to return to it, and another impulse to leave the closet at once, to escape his presence. The sensation that he was watching me from his spot on the shelf high above me was particularly acute when I was putting the diaries back. I could never restore the perfect order that he had left: the sheets carefully returned to their envelopes, the books lined up evenly, the boxes in neat stacks. Even when I rearranged the papers again, placing them back with great care, I could not leave the area around the closet easily. I had been able to move gradually out of the zone of the urn's strongest presence when it was on the bureau, but now I had to close a door on it, inches in front of my father's face, as it were. I could not ignore the urn, I did not feel at ease when I could see it, and I was unable to imagine looking for another spot for it.

Almost by accident I developed a new form of visiting the study, the form that ultimately gave rise to this book. One afternoon, having overcome my reluctance to open the door to the closet and look through the papers in it, I had taken down a few volumes of his diaries. I was looking through them when my mother called, needing assistance — in looking up a telephone number, perhaps, or in deciding when she would need to refill one of her prescriptions. Rather than putting the books back in the closet, I left them on the table and went out to talk to my mother. Later that afternoon, when I was about to go home, I returned to the study, intending to replace the books on the shelf. It suddenly occurred to me that I did not have to put the books back, that I could take them home with me instead. I looked through them that night. Once my children had gone to sleep and I had made my regular evening call to my mother, my house seemed peaceful, the evening unhurried. I began reading his diaries, going through some sections word by word, skimming others. Instead of the complex portrait of his inner life that I had hoped to find, I read of his unrelenting despair. He doubted his skills as an artist, his ability ever to obtain work; he lamented his shyness with women. These diaries are really not what I want to read now, I realized, and I took them with me a few days later on a visit to my mother. After greeting her and talking with her for a while, I went to the study, excusing myself rather than waiting for a opportune break in the rhythm of our visit. I walked directly to the closet. The ashes did not trouble me this time. I looked right at the urn, nodded at it, and then turned to look through the papers for another set to take home with me. After a few minutes I selected a box containing the letters that my father's brother Max had written to him, and then I returned to my mother. Reading the letters on evenings later that week, I found them more to my liking than the diaries. I was fascinated by the details of the fur business in the 1920s, by the fierce disputes between my uncles and my grandfather, by the anecdotes that brought to mind stories that I had heard decades earlier. I returned the letters after I finished reading them and chose another box of papers, notes that my father had made about his own father. I had converted my father's study into a library in which I was the only librarian and the only borrower. I could read his papers at home, undisturbed by my mother's voice or by his ashes, and the thought of the papers no longer distracted me on my visits to my mother.

On one of my evenings at home, while I was reading through a series of notes that he had written about his mother, it suddenly occurred to me that I could write a book about my father. Each chapter would be based on a particular set of papers that I had found in his study. The idea stuck with me. I prepared the first chapter from Max's letters, another from a set of photographs I had found from 1921, all with inscriptions, and the project was under way. I began thinking about possible book chapters when I chose the papers that I took home, rather than relying on the more spontaneous curiosity that had been my sole criterion earlier. Doubts occasionally struck me, when the project seemed so huge that I considered abandoning it, but I always returned to it, never leaving it for more than a few weeks.

I continued to take the papers home with me, picking up a new set when I returned an old one, even after my mother, my sisters, and I agreed to bury my father's ashes. This postponed funeral turned out to be a substantial project, not only because I had to make plans with many relatives, but because of certain religious issues. My mother and I knew that we wanted to have his ashes buried in the Jewish section of the cemetery. Some members of the synagogue, though, viewed a cremated body as a violation of God's law and an intolerable presence in a Jewish graveyard, a source of ritual pollution, little better than a Jewish suicide or the remains of a gentile spouse of a Jew; others felt that members of the congregation, as integral parts of the community, had the right to bury their deceased family members, of whatever religion and in whatever state, in this section. I was concerned that no solution could be found, but I soon discovered that a number of years earlier a compromise had been worked out that divided the Jewish section into three subsections, a core surrounded by two concentric rings. The central area and the intermediate ring were reserved for the corpses that met the stringent criteria for burial, but anyone could be buried in the outer ring. This first intermediate ring, separating the core from the periphery, was the critical feature. As long as it was the width specified in the Talmud, and as long as it held only kosher corpses, it preserved the innermost zone from contamination by the bodies in the outermost ring. This system worked only because there were families that met the strict criteria for inclusion but were willing to have their dead buried close to, perhaps next to, some improper corpse. As things worked out, there developed a tendency to bury those with orthodox leanings in the center and those with ties to reform Judaism in the periphery. These two were separated and kept from conflict by a buffer zone, primarily of conservative Jews. Fortunately, there were still some gravesites available in the outer ring.

This potential obstacle overcome, I was ready to plan the funeral. I talked over possible dates with relatives and then made the arrangements with Vince, the caretaker at the cemetery. The shock came for me a few weeks before the funeral, when I took the urn from the closet to check how large it was and how much it weighed. Sitting at the table in the study, I found that the urn's cover did not fit tightly. Without thinking I lifted it off. Inside the urn I saw a small plastic bag that contained not only ashes but other substances as well, dark particles of grit and some small whitish lumps that I might have thought were sand and gravel if I had seen them somewhere else. For a brief moment I was confused, and I took a second, closer look. In sudden horror I recognized these things as actual distinct pieces of his body that had survived the fire, little bits of charred flesh, fragments of bone. I stuffed the bag into the urn and pushed the cover back on, shaking a little and feeling nauseated. It took me a long time to regain my composure, and then a while longer to remember my initial purpose of bringing the urn to

Vince. I stood up and went to my mother's kitchen cabinet. I looked through the cardboard boxes it contained, selected one, and put the urn into it. On my way back home I stopped by Vince's office at the cemetery and left the box with his assistant.

I saw the urn one more time, a few weeks later at the funeral itself. The rabbi, who had led a memorial service in the synagogue, was unwilling to be present at the interment of a cremated body, so he did not come to the cemetery. Earlier that day I had gone to the cemetery and arranged a semicircle of chairs near the gravesite, an unmistakable hole with a heap of freshly dug earth and a shovel next to it. My mother and the older relatives sat, others stood, and we read a few prayers. At a nod from me, Vince drove up in a little cart and handed me the urn. I felt calm as I settled the metal box into the hole, pressing it firmly into the earth so that it would remain in a vertical position. I was the first to pick up the shovel and scoop some earth into the grave. A few other relatives took turns at this task, and then we all stood silent for a long moment, looking at the half-filled hole. Quite willingly, and with a strong sense of relief, I walked back to it and began shoveling steadily until the grave was entirely covered. As I patted the earth down, an image came to my mind from a visit my parents had made to my house, when my father had felt a chill after settling himself on the sofa for a nap, and I had brought him an extra blanket and spread it over him, glad to hear his murmur of thanks before he fell asleep. I set the shovel down, stood up, and rejoined the other people. After a few more prayers, we left the cemetery and went back to my mother's apartment for a meal.

The funeral brought about a change: the grave provided my mother and me with a way we could jointly acknowledge my father's death. We continued to speak of him very little, but we made trips, usually brief and often entirely unplanned, to the cemetery, less than a mile from where she lived. On the different occasions when we were in my car—if I was taking her to get a haircut or driving her back home after she had come to my house—I might suggest, using the phrase we had developed, that we "go and see Robbie." On a few occasions she felt too tired to make this trip, but she usually agreed. In moments of physical strength she walked over to the spot where he was buried. More frequently, she just sat in the car, turning sideways in her seat so that her legs were outside the open door, and looked at the grave, its position on the edge of the Jewish section of the cemetery placing it not more than ten yards from the road. She often had something to say to him, invariably brief. "Robbie Orlove, did you have to leave me?" she once asked him, with an almost teasing tone in her voice.

I would also visit the cemetery on my own. From my father's grave under a large sycamore, I could look across the road to portions of the cemetery that still remained empty: a meadow with a reed-filled stream to one side and a hill beyond it. I would stand in the dappled shade while vague recollections, often of walks that my parents and I had taken in parks in New York, drifted through my mind. Late one night, when I was driving back home after dropping off the babysitter who had watched the children when my wife and I went out to dinner, I felt a sudden impulse to go to the cemetery. I parked and walked across the road to the grave. The shadows under the sycamore, the brilliant moonlight on the meadow, the distant barking of a dog, all seemed infinitely peaceful to me.

Although the burial had created the opportunity for these visits, it did not alter my pattern of reading my father's papers. I continued to go into the study only to return a set of papers I was finished with and to select a new one. Even though the urn was no longer in the room, other presences had entered the apartment and the study. As my mother's emphysema progressed, she required more and more assistance — in cooking, in dressing, in bathing — and eventually needed to have an aide present at all times — to support her arm as she walked from room to room, to help her in getting on and off the toilet, to attend to her if she woke disoriented in the middle of the night. The study became the bedroom of these live-in aides, first Valerie's room, then Shirley's, then Sharon's. I cleared my father's table, putting the papers that had been on it into a desk drawer, and piled up boxes on one side of the closet so that the aides would have some room for their own things: clothing, hair-curlers, romance novels, a Walkman.

My mother's last year was filled with barely averted crises, new combinations of medicines that eased her breathing but seemed to tax her heart or kidneys, lingering colds that threatened to develop into pneumonia, areas of red skin that nearly erupted into bedsores. She had better moments, when she would converse animatedly with visitors or read stories to my children, and sometimes she was strong enough for a drive, but these occasions became fewer and fewer, and there were many more times when she would simply sit on the sofa, keeping her strength in reserve for a meal or a walk to the bathroom. Her final downturn could have been far worse than it turned out to be. When a cold did develop into pneumonia, she was able to remain at home rather than go into a hospital because of a combination of fortunate circumstances: the presence of the live-in aides, the legal documents she had signed stating her opposition to respirators and other such equipment, the willingness of her doctor to make house calls. The pneumonia lasted only a week. She died in her sleep, having lived just long enough to see Carol on her annual visit from Israel.

I found the funeral and shiva, the customary week of mourning — the entire experience of grief, in fact — to be, if not entirely familiar, at least not the continuous series of surprises that they had been for me when my father died. My mother's funeral arrangements proceeded much more quickly than my father's. I was prepared to find Mr. Smith distasteful, and I could take relief in Vince's easy direct manner. With the plot next to my father's already reserved, I had no worries about the selection of a gravesite, and I made sure that the interval between the cremation and the burial was as short as possible.

One task, however, was completely new: closing up my mother's apartment, which fell to me, as the individual most familiar with its contents and as the executor of her will. Carol and her husband, Joe, stayed in Davis long enough to help me. We went through the apartment room by room and assigned a fate to the innumerable items that the apartment contained. We worked long days, conscious that we had a deadline, since the date of Carol and Joe's departure from California was less than a week away, fixed by airline reservations. Only infrequently did I come across a specific object that reduced me first to indecision and then to tears: a scallop-edged plate with a design of pansies, the last one that remained from the set of dishes we had used when I was a child, an old green shirt of my father's, its collar and cuffs too badly worn to be mended. Even these moments of more intense sorrow were brief. I would rejoin Carol and Joe and get back to emptying out the apartment, deciding to give the old sofa to Cuca and the patio furniture as well; to send these ice-cream glasses, only one missing from the original eight, to a niece; that drawing of Robbie's to a grandson; and to take the old sheets and towels to a charity.

As I think back to that time, I am struck by the great effort we made, working long days despite the summer heat, despite the encounters with decades-old fragments of our past. We certainly could have met our deadline more easily, choosing a few items for ourselves and sending all the rest to some charity or simply to the town dump. It even would have been possible to leave many of my parents' things behind. The managers of the complex were used to cleaning out apartments after their occupants died and the relatives had left. What allowed me to work so steadily, I realize, was my father's papers. On the first or second day of closing out the apartment, I began to bring the boxes from his study to my own house. As Carol and I went through our parents' apartment room by room, I sometimes thought of my own study and the boxes that I had just moved there, some stacked on a table, others arranged on bookshelves. That image kept me from being troubled by the need to make many decisions: about the pair of old night tables that had been by the side of my parents' bed as long as I could remember, about the drawerful of my mother's scarves, some fancy silk ones with prints, some warm woolen plaids. I could easily pick among these objects, keeping some, giving others away, or discarding them entirely, secure in the knowledge that the papers held all that I needed. Even though I would soon leave the apartment for the last time, I thought, I could always return to my study and the slow unpacking of the papers.

I was right. I spent a good deal of time with my father's papers in the months after my mother died, arranging the boxes on shelves, checking through each of them to get a general sense of their contents, and sometimes finding a letter or a note that would lead me to stop my organizing and to gaze off into space, lost once again in a reverie. By the winter after my mother died, I settled into a routine of spending two mornings a week in the study and an occasional evening as well. I kept my material in good order, one shelf for the manila folders of notes for future chapters, another for the completed drafts of other chapters, and a section of the desktop for the notes and drafts of the current chapter.

Even with a regular rhythm of work, I sometimes despaired of ever finishing the book. On several occasions, I imagined that one of my children might inherit an archive in which my father's papers and my own were mixed in a confusing disorder, and this burdensome legacy would pass from generation to generation, other papers accreting to it, until some disgusted Orlove in the future would simply throw out the entire mess, by this time grown to monstrous proportions. But the prospect of putting too much time into the project was as troubling as not putting in enough. The book project threatened to swallow me up. Despite my plans to work on the papers only in the morning, I sometimes remained longer, absorbed in photographs of my father's parents, in postcards sent back to Europe by the first relatives to arrive in America, in the entries in his diaries that described an artist whom he had met in his first years in New York. Stumbling out of the study in mid-afternoon, hungry from having missed lunch hours before, I would resolve to keep the book project down to the two mornings a week that I had set for myself.

And so the project continued. There was no end of dramatic surprises: booklets of food ration coupons from the last years of World War I in Sweden; the three-way correspondence linking my father, the State Department, and a cousin who had fled from Germany to France during World War II and sought permission to enter the United States. And there were more mundane bits of everyday life as well: an old Valentine's Day card that my mother had given my father, a list of books that he had checked out of the public library, a copy of my oldest nephew Adam's Bar Mitzvah speech.

I kept up the habit of writing that I had already established, picking up a set of papers, drawing on it for a chapter of the book, and then moving on to another set. I spent a few months on the notes that my father had written about his own father. I took nearly as long to sort through his correspondence with several artist friends. Once, while I was copying out some sentences that my father had written in a notebook, my eyes happened to rest for a few seconds longer than usual on the page on which I was writing. Suddenly, powerfully, my father's broad hand appeared, perfectly clear in every detail as it moved across the page, his strong fingers gripping the pen. For a moment I could not tell whether the hand that I watched as it wrote was my own or his. The hand that dropped the pen, at least, was mine, the hand that fell to my lap. I covered it with my other hand and leaned back in my chair, breathing heavily. Gradually, I returned to a calmer state. I sat up, looked at the clock and saw that an hour remained until noon. I rearranged the notes on my desk and got back to work.

*Remaining*

## Chapter 2  M O T H E R - B O O K

**M**y efforts to reconstruct the early years of my father's life from his papers have been made easier because he too had the impulse to write a book about a parent, as I discovered soon after I began to look through the closet in his study. My eye had been quickly drawn to a tall volume, more than a foot high, bound in black imitation leather. As I began to look through it, I realized that he had sought to write a book about his mother — or, to be precise, that he wanted to make such a book. He left the first page entirely blank, as publishers invariably do, and turned the second into a title page. In the lower left-hand corner he wrote N.Y. for the city and indicated the precise date by placing ⅛ in small digits between the 19 and 28 of the year. He decorated the page with a few restrained combinations of dots and lines. He titled his book *Mater nostrum*, meaning "our mother" in Latin, or, more literally, "mother of us," showing that he was writing specifically for his siblings. The title page also contained two other phrases, the first, *Sie hat ausgelitten,* in German, and the second, *sit tibi terra levis,* once again in Latin. On my first reading, these words lent a tone of seriousness to the work. Continuing in my assumption that they were part of a title page, I supposed that my father had intended them to be epigraphs. My curiosity about their meaning turned into surprise when a colleague of mine translated the first as "She has suffered all the way through." Another colleague with whom I happened to be talking a few weeks later did not hesitate before rendering the second as "May it be for you that the earth is light." He was familiar with these words, having seen them on a number of Roman tombstones. The phrases now seemed to be epitaphs rather than epigraphs. Taken together, they indicated my father's hope that his mother would find release from her trials when she was buried in her grave. The title was now his mother's name, or at least some variation on the "beloved mother" sort of phrase. It was as if the city and date marked the place and time of death, not of publication. Even the few bits of decoration were ones that could be carved in stone as well as printed on a page.

The responsibility of designing gravestones has fallen on me three times: for my father, for my mother, and for a son who died in the womb two months before he was due to be born. It is not a task that I relish, and I was puzzled that my father would take it on so willingly — and so unnecessarily as well, since his mother lived for twenty-three years after he began the book. What had led him to imagine her death and to prepare a monument for her? I found a partial answer to my question in the first paragraphs of the book, which I include here; in this extract, as in other quotations from my father's papers, I retain his distinctive phrasing, spelling, and punctuation, correcting only those nonstandard usages that unduly interfere with the flow or the sense of the passage.

This book will be about our mother.

I feel that she is not understood nor appreciated correctly. And when we do, our selfish motives hold us back from doing good to her. People are very slow in giving up their own to others. For these reasons I want to mark down certain things that she tells us, about her life and remarks that she makes during conversations. She is an intelligent woman and with correct training could have accomplished something, and so her life was run into different channels and her only accomplishments are we, her children and it is up to us, to continue her work and do what she wanted to do, but could not.

The desire to write this down, was long with me, but I never did, for time ago I felt that she would not be with us for very much longer. Now this fear has passed and I hope it was all foolish, momentary fears.

Several nights ago she was very ill. But she did not want to wake anyone. After a while she wanted to wake me, to tell me to write down that no one should blame or accuse each other, for not having been to her what we could have when she would not be with us any longer.

His mother had been seriously, perhaps critically, ill. But that fact did not entirely explain the effort that he put into the book, the money that he spent for the binder at a time when he was unemployed, the care with which he adorned the title page, or gravestone. His "desire to write," as he put it, had begun long before her illness. Why did he feel that she was so poorly understood and appreciated that she needed a biographer, a position that he appointed himself to fill? My mind turned to the stories that my father had told me about her. I thought of a number of anecdotes, and then I recalled how quietly I had listened when he spoke of her. I somehow had known not to interrupt the flow of words, not to fill in with my questions the long pauses when he would sigh and look away. I remembered the silent skepticism with which I heard his assurances that she had seen me a few times when I was a toddler. I completely lacked any direct recollections of her but did not want to challenge him on this or any other point regarding her for fear of provoking an outburst. The sharpest images of her from my child-hood were not his words, half listened to, but objects that she had brought with her across the Atlantic, material proof of her existence which I could examine unencumbered by his voice in my ears. I always knew that she had been the original owner of two of my mother's most valuable, and least frequently worn, pieces of jewelry. I had never paused to reflect on how other people may have viewed them — my grandmoth-er's regret over a scarcity of daughters to whom to bequeath them, or my father's wish to adorn his wife with the jewelry that he had seen on his mother — because they held an immediate and powerful fascination for me. I could gaze for long moments at the round translucent amber beads of the necklace, at the single tiny cylinder of ruddy coral that made up each earring. Their warm colors and curved surfaces bespoke an elegance far gentler and more dignified than the harsh glitter of the sharp-edged diamonds and sapphires that my aunts would sometimes wear. At some point in my childhood, one of my sisters explained to me that the sap of prehistoric trees, when fossilized, turned into amber, and I thought immediately of the necklace. I was fascinated by the image of sticky sap slowly drying into a hard translucent substance. This bit of information made sense to me. The world in which my grandmother lived seemed as far from the one in which I lived as the age of dinosaurs that the word "fossil" brought to mind. When I read that coral was formed by the gradual accumulation of microscopic marine organisms, I had a similar recollection, juxtaposing in my mind the earrings and schools of fish swimming silently past branched corals. Most jewels had simple, precise qualities by which they were valued — hardness, brilliance, scarcity — but they lacked the mystery of the transformation of living matter into gem. I thought it natural that my grandmother was linked to ancient trees, to the bottom of the sea, to distant places and an irretrievable past.

As I reflect back, I realize that I cannot remember seeing any photographs of her when I was a child. I had been curious to see pictures of my older sisters and cousins as small children, so that I could confirm the knowledge that I, too, would someday grow up. The old photographs from Europe — and the debates that they provoked over whether the bearded figure in the corner was Uncle Mottel or some other man — held little interest for me. I wonder, though, why my father did not urge me to look at photographs of his mother: did he want his voice to be the only testimony to her presence, did he himself find the pictures troubling? I recall first seeing a picture of her when I was a teenager. I was struck by her dowdy appearance, by her coarse thick neck, this neck on which I had imagined the precious amber beads. It was hard for me to believe that this was the woman who had inspired such devotion in my father. When I was in college, he showed me a letter she had written to him about me, perhaps because he knew that I could understand it directly, after several semesters of German. I noticed instead that her handwriting was crude, her spelling full of errors, and the sentiments commonplace: "The picture of your dear Benjamin is charming, you should have a lot of *nachas* [pride, satisfaction] from him, Amen!"

My mother was an additional source of information about my grandmother. Few in number, brief, vivid, her stories about her mother-in-law are sharp in my mind. The anecdote that she most often volunteered was a simple scene rather than an entire sequence of events: my mother in her kitchen, scrubbing the floor on her hands and knees, while my father's mother sat on a chair and told her about the difficulties her daughter Elizabeth had with her maid. I heard the story as my mother intended it, as containing the simple cause-and-effect link of my grandmother's arrogance and my mother's anger, and as implying that silence was my mother's only possible response, though I now wonder, as I write, about the conflict between the two women. Did my grandmother frequently drop in unannounced? Was my mother scrubbing the floor when she arrived, or did she begin this chore after she arrived, as a hint to leave? Were they both waiting for my father? Had he spoken to his mother and arranged for her visit without telling his wife? And why did my father, who was sometimes in earshot when my mother described this scene, never come to his mother's defense?

My mother and father contradicted each other more openly about my grandmother on other occasions. When I began to spend my summers traveling, first hitchhiking in Europe, then on my first field trips to Latin America, my father recalled an anecdote that linked me to his mother. When she first saw me as an infant, she noticed that the hair on the back of my head grew in two swirls rather than the more usual single one. She commented that this pattern was a sign that indicated that I would travel a great deal. Nonsense, my mother replied on hearing the story, Ben travels so much because of all the hiking I did that summer while I was pregnant with him, when we were staying at my sister Gert's. I preferred my mother's story because I recalled so fondly the summers at my aunt's vacation house in Connecticut and, I think, because I liked to think of myself as sentient while still inside my mother. Back then, though, I simply heard their disagreement as two rival explanations, though on later reflection I realized that they were entirely compatible. I now think that the rivalry opposed lineages as well as explanations: my mother wanted to keep me from my father's attempts to make me completely an Orlove, without any influence from her side, the Cohens.

As I reviewed these stories, an incident sprung to my mind, after lying unrecalled for decades. It took place when I was about ten. My parents and I were about to go on an outing, a special one, I knew, because my parents were taking more time to get dressed than usual. Impatient to leave, I walked back from the front door — where I had been waiting for them, my coat already on — to my parents' bedroom. I stopped at the door and looked in. My mother was standing still in front of the large round mirror hanging from the wall, her head and shoulders slightly bent, as my father attempted to make the gold wire of the coral earrings penetrate the holes in her earlobes. I, too, stood still as I watched him poke her again and again. I was frozen by the pain that I imagined she felt, far greater than it could have been; by his signs of agitation, the sighing and clacking of his tongue that I knew to indicate extreme frustration; by the fury that I assumed lay beneath her apparent resignation. I watched until my father finally succeeded in his efforts. They quickly pulled their coats on, and we left. I do not recall the event for which their regular clothes would have been inadequate, but only their explanation of the scene that I witnessed. My mother's ears had been pierced, they told me as we hurried off to the subway, but the holes had almost closed up, since she wore earrings infrequently, and so my father was barely able to insert them. Neither of them continued the account, leaving unanswered the obvious question of why it was so important for my mother to wear these earrings, the question that I knew not to ask.

As I reflect back on this scene, a second question comes to my mind: why didn't my mother put the earrings in herself? By looking in a mirror, she would have been as able to find the proper spots in her earlobes as well as he could, and she did not lack the strength to insert the wires. Surely my mother, known for her determination, would not have lacked the resolve to make jabs sharp enough to open up the partly sealed holes. I think that she wished to embarrass him, as a way to gain vengeance for his insistence that she wear his mother's earrings.

As I read my father's book about his mother, I sometimes felt an impatience at his devotion that, I think, was similar to my mother's own exasperation. I was particularly struck by the reverence with which he recorded his mother's proverbs.

Some people think the sun shines, because they exist.

I also know something. What one wants, one has not. What one has one wants not.

A smart man knows what he says, a fool says what he knows.

I became increasingly troubled. How could I square his devotion to his mother's banal statements with my image of him as an intelligent and artistic man? Did he really believe that he was recording extraordinary wisdom when he quoted her:

Before you do a thing, consider well whether it can last.

Do not rue today, what you did not do yesterday, do not think that tomorrow you will do todays work, but do everything today.

I eagerly read the next section of the book, relieved to finish the pages filled with proverbs and curious to read about my grandmother's early life in the small Ukrainian town of Nezhin. Here was a past that I could enjoy imagining, my grandmother's childhood as the third of five sisters, the daughters of a rabbi; here I could indulge the common impulse to uncover one's family picturesque past. A few brief references suggest that my grandmother's parents owned some property and could afford to have servants to carry out some of the domestic work.

I remember her telling us of her sitting in her fathers orchard on a late fall day, watching the leaves and falling shadows.

She told us how pleasant it was for her to sit and watch her mother sleep during an afternoon. The regular breathing, with the face relaxed into its natural self.

Absent from this book are any references to the claim that I often heard as a child, that my grandmother was a descendant of a famous eighteenth-century rabbi, the Vilna Gaon, Eliyahu ben Shlomo Zalman. His exemplary piety, brilliant writings, and dedication to the renewal of the yeshiva as an institution of learning placed him at the head of the Misnagdim, or "Opponents," who opposed the obscurantist Hasidim for their near-idolatrous worship of their rabbis and for their denial of the value of the study of texts, and who also opposed the secularizing excesses of the Enlightenment, which was just beginning to reach Eastern European Jews. As the leader of the Misnagdim, he sought to create a coherent place for traditional Orthodox Jewish life in the modern world. Such lineage would place my grandmother as a member of a Jewish sort of nobility. But this descent from a renowned figure, *yikhes*, as it is called in Yiddish, seems fictitious to me, not only because it is not mentioned in this book or because of my mother's doubts (if all the people who say they are descendants of the Vilna Gaon really are, she said, then he would have been too busy doing other things to have the time to become a famous rabbi) but also because the letters that purported to document this link never materialized. There is not even a reference to which one of her parents linked my grandmother with the Vilna Gaon, whose death in 1797 was not so far from her father's birth in the 1820s and her mother's a decade or so later. It would have mattered whether her father, as a rabbi, was descended directly from the illustrious man or whether he had married into the line of his descendants; either alternative would have been a story too rich simply to be lost in the passage of time. Whether or not he was connected to the Vilna Gaon, though, and in whatever fashion, he does appear as a pious man.

Her father studied a great deal in Hebrew. He had a library of leather bound foliantes. From sitting in a bent position his back hurt him. He used to put the book on the table, rest his elbows on it and so read, standing up, for hours. He used to play chess. A Catholic priest used to visit him and they played sometimes.

This Catholic priest, I later discovered, was also a leader of a minority faith, since the Orthodox Church was the official religion in imperial Russia. The connection that my great-grandfather established with him over the chessboard proved to be important:

> When mother was a small child a pogrom actually took place in her town, but the Catholic priest hid her parents and sisters in his garden and fed them there for four days, until all the violent passions had run out. At times the gangs passed the hedges that hid them.

This last anecdote is one of the few that caught my attention when my father spoke to me of his mother. The version that I heard as a child was more elaborate: my grandmother, bolder than her sisters, peered under the hedge in the priest's garden and saw the hooves of the Cossacks' horses as they galloped by. Did my father have a reason to omit this detail from the book, I wonder, or did he invent it in the decades that intervened between the writing and my childhood?

Most of the stories in the book that he wrote, though, were new to me. I was captivated with their depiction of a remote world, as different from present-day America as the mountain villages where I have lived in Peru.

> There are certain recollections she told me of her childhood. How they used to buy large sheets of paper cut and sew them into note books, how they went swimming and dried their long bodies in the sun. How they used to believe that the Czar drank tea out of a big sugartop [bowl of sugar], so that it should be very sweet. How at one time when she suffered badly from a toothache her father took her to a woman who could disperse pains by certain charms. He did not believe in it but he would do anything to relieve the pain of his children. He always wished that their pain would enter into him so they walked crossed a little brook, and came to a hut in the midst of a rich foliage of bushes and vines. The sight of the house stopped her pains.

> She told me of the time when a neighbor to her father was dying. The man was 98 and in possession of his facilities. He got out of his chair where he had been napping, walked up to the stove to warm his hands.

I am going to die, he said, I have seen the Angel of Death. Walked over to the bed, lied down, and was dead. At that time mother was a little girl.

I read many such stories with delight and then came to one passage that struck me as my grandmother's conscious effort to condense a key element of her childhood into a single image rather than to recount many particular details.

She said: "When I recall any word my father said, it is like a holiday. So correct and true were his remarks, that a splendor came, as when the candles are reflected from the white linen cloth on a holiday."

I, too, felt a glow when I read this section, the kind of peace and fullness that holidays can bring. I think of my grandmother pausing to attempt to convey the greatness of her father and his words. She turned to a religious image of splendor and light, exemplified by a scene from her home. She also had seen him in his synagogue, where she would look through the *mechitzah*, the screen that divides the women from the men in Orthodox congregations, to glimpse him standing by the Torah scrolls and addressing other men. (Did my father tell me about such visits, did I come across them in other notes of his that I cannot recall having read, or did I simply make them up and come to believe them? Why, I ask myself, am I certain that the synagogue was not large enough to have a balcony for the women, that it only had a section on the same floor that was screened off?) But she presented him not as a rabbi in front of his congregation but as a father and a husband, surrounded by females and by the work of female hands. Though my grandmother spoke of her father, she referred to other family members as well, her mother and sisters, also gathered around the table for the holiday meal. Though the table may have been set by the servants, whose existence can be inferred, rather than by my grandmother, her mother, or her sisters, though the tablecloth may have been embroidered by others, even less directly recorded in the book, it was surely her mother who had blessed and lit the candles that stood on the table in a room dark enough for linen threads to gleam in their light. All eyes were turned toward the table, all backs were turned toward the

dimly lit walls and the black night beyond. My father's mother may have felt other presences at the table as well, depending on the time in the weekly and yearly cycles: perhaps the two angels, one good, one evil, who were said to follow Jewish men home from synagogue after the brief Friday evening service to check for the three signs of the Sabbath-observing home (the candles lit, the wine and bread on the table, the

30

beds made); perhaps Elijah, coming for the cup of wine left for him on the seder table at Passover; perhaps the seven men — Abraham, Isaac, Jacob, Joseph, Moses, Aaron, and David — who were believed to visit on each of the seven nights of the festival of Sukkot, each having a different night on which to lead the other six in procession.

A stranger intruded into this happy family, a man who wanted to marry my grandmother.

One must help another person. That's why she married our father. To improve him. Against her fathers advice, who said, If a man at his age can't write better and compose a better letter He is beyond help.

My father alludes to an event that he recounted to me many times while I was a child, that my grandfather needed at one point in his travels to have a business letter written for him because of his poor choice of words and his crude penmanship. He turned for help to the rabbi, who in turn directed him to one of his daughters, my grandmother. This meeting was their first. What aspect of this inability to produce a proper document so troubled my great-grandfather? Perhaps these skills of mind and hand were important accomplishments, worthy of honor in their own right. The word that keeps coming into my mind is one that I heard often as a child but that seems entirely absent from the lexicon of the 1990s: "refinement," that combination of self-possession, decorum, sophistication, and elegance that leads one to speak in modulated tones, that permits one to select and arrange furniture in good taste, and that grants one a familiarity with art, music, and literature. Distributed unequally between the sexes, refinement was more important for women, who displayed this quality in innumerable occasions every day. My grandmother was refined, and the man she married was not.

Her father may also have feared that his daughter would be deprived of comfort as well as of respect, married to a man whose lack of education would prevent him from success in his business, which at the time was buying cattle intestines and selling them to sausagemakers. This prospective son-in-law must have seemed like a bumpkin. He came from the town of Gluchow, about one hundred miles to the northeast of Nezhin, a good bit smaller and more isolated. The main railroad that linked Kiev and Moscow ran right through Nezhin, while Gluchow was on a smaller spur line. But I do not think that her father had the opportunity to select among more appealing alternatives. With five daughters, her father could not afford dowries adequate to lure more prosperous sons-in-law. Nor was he able to draw on his spiritual, rather than his monetary, capital to attract any rabbinical students eager to inherit his congregation from him.

I could imagine that my great-grandfather would feel disappointment that more prosperous or educated suitors did not seek out his daughter. I was surprised, though, to read of his reaction.

> Her father was a gentleman, a scholar and yet when my father proposed marriage he lifted a hatchet with a threat and chased him out of his house. My grandfather was always against this match.

Were a poor handwriting, an unprestigious trade, and a low income enough to provoke such an attack from a pious rabbi, a man whose words had the splendor of holiday candles gleaming on a linen tablecloth? I sense a contradiction between his wisdom and his violent gesture, but I do not think that my father saw them as opposed. My father hated his father, I could write, if the word "hate" were not too short and simple to convey the fear and anger that my father felt, mixed with a great desire for affection as well. He certainly wanted to chase his father out of the house on many occasions and felt violent impulses toward him as well. Too frightened of his father to raise a hatchet against him, my father let his rage out bit by little bit, copying out his mother's stories, approving, perhaps envying, her father's gesture. He wrote his book as much to catalog his father's wrongs as to memorialize his mother's unappreciated greatness. He depicts their married life, both in Europe and in the United States, as a virtually unrelieved misery caused by his father's alternating mistreatment and neglect of his mother.

I have only tantalizing hints of another view of my grandparents' courtship. My cousin Jinny, older than I am, knew my grandmother and had a different story of their meeting. Our grandmother, Jinny told me, thought that her suitor was very handsome and hoped to have many children with him because they would all be good-looking. This story might be true, though it, too, may have passed through many filters. In my father's study I found one source that offers some corroboration, since it suggests that my grandparents had a conventional courtship rather than a strained or hurried one. In 1891 or 1892, my grandmother made a gift for her husband-to-be. It was a velvet bag that served to carry tefillin, the phylacteries that orthodox Jewish men wear during their morning prayers. Each of the two tefillin consists of a small black cubical box with black leather straps attached to it. The boxes contain scrolls with four brief texts from the Torah, written in ink on parchment according to stringent guidelines described in the Talmud. The straps serve to attach the tefillin to the head and arm, the shorter head-strap tied something like a sweatband, the longer arm-strap wound repeatedly around the left arm and hand in such a way that the stripes form the Hebrew letters that spell out one of the names of God. When she gave him this bag, he had been regularly wearing them ("laying tefillin," the Yiddishized phrase that I heard as a child) for a number of years, since around the time of his Bar Mitzvah.

The bag, about six and a half inches by eight, is made of soft velvet, rosy-beige in color. It has an inner sack of brown satin. The two are sewn together twice, at the opening and a bit below, to form a band through which a braided drawstring passes. Flowers and branches are embroidered on the front of the bag in lustrous silk thread. The five cream-colored Hebrew letters that spell the word "tefillin" run across the middle of the bag. It took some skill to make the even stitches that form the thicker and thinner portions of all five letters, and the curved sections of the first three, without pulling or twisting the fabric.

The bag would not have taken very long to make, a week's worth of afternoons at most. It required a good sense of design and considerable patience in the steady stitching. I have tried to imagine my grandmother while she was working, most likely sometimes alone, sometimes in the company of her mother and sisters. She must have felt some relief: twenty-one or twenty-two years old, with two younger sisters at home who were waiting their turns to be led to the wedding canopy, it was high time for her to marry. The rest is a fascinating mystery to me. The tefillin could have turned her thoughts to the religious side of her future life, to the management of a kosher kitchen, in which she would bake challah every week, to her monthly visits to the ritual bath. Perhaps she thought in more material terms, the rich fabric of the bag and well-proportioned embroidered design suggesting a wish for an elegant home. The thought that came to mind may not have been the wedding canopy but the marital bed: did the thought of tefillin lead her to envisage her future husband's bare arm, the leather strap wound around it, did she imagine the unknown texture of a hairy male body as she held the velvet between thumb and forefinger?

As I think of her, my thoughts turn to the Indian peasant women whom I knew during my anthropological field work in the mountains of Peru and Bolivia, those travels that not only formed part of my work as a graduate student and a professor but also gave me a third point from which to triangulate America and Europe. I have often idly and half-consciously visualized a globe with the Western Hemisphere just left of the middle and Europe at the right edge, on which the United States and Russia form two of the corners of a triangle. Peru, down below, is the third. From no place before the Andes had I been able to see in its entirety the line linking me in America with my father and grandparents in Europe; to no other place had I been able to take a journey comparable to my father's in spatial, cultural, and psychological distance. He traveled forward to the New World, while I went back, returning to a place that often astonished me with the immediacy of images from my family's past in Europe. One such image is composed of the Indian peasant women who also weave bags as gifts for the men whom they will marry, and these bags, *ch'uspa,* as they are called in Quechua, also have ritual purposes — they hold the coca leaves that the men will remove in prescribed ways, over which they will mutter blessings, and then slowly chew. How alike these places seem, where older men notice the new bag of the young man who joins them, whether huddled at a mountain pass in the Andes to salute the white-headed grandfathers, as the snow-capped peaks are termed, or whether swaying at the benches of a now-vanished Ukrainian synagogue to worship the Holy One, blessed be He. And how alike the young women, weaving and embroidering in the company of mothers and sisters, recalling stories of other weddings, anticipating the comings and goings of their husbands.

But there is only so much that I can know or even imagine about the fateful meeting between my grandparents, about the beginning of the marriage whose tensions shaped my father. The bag and the single word "tefillin" — the oldest word, if embroidering may be counted as writing, that I found in my father's study — speak only indirectly about my grandparents' courtship. Jinny's story is another source, a brief one that does not fill in very much. If there ever was much affection between my grandparents, it has left few traces, certainly not in my father's book about his mother.

This story, set several years after their wedding, is the first in my father's chronicle of his father's failings, the beginning of the justifications of the raised hatchet.

> At one pesach [Passover], father went to schul, synagogue, it was just the eve of pesach. They lived then in a house about 3 miles from the city. She was all alone with the two children.
>
> Everything was arranged for the holiday, all she could do was to sit and wait for her husband to return. It was very dreary and lonely country. Only the pigs knocked at the door.
>
> A drunkard came up, making noise and threatening. She rid her fears, and invited him in for a drink, and handled the uncouth muishik [peasant] so, that he called her, molodjets [pal].

At this point I must interrupt these stories and list my father's siblings in order. Writing for them as he did, my father simply used their names without any explanation. It is a daunting task to describe the ten children whom my grandmother bore in addition to my father. If I were a novelist, creating a fictional account of his life, I might have chosen to kill off three of his siblings soon after birth, but I would have given him fewer than the seven that survived to adulthood. My task is eased somewhat by the regularity of these eleven births: the first nine came almost precisely every other year, my grandfather proudly comparing himself to a wise farmer who allowed a year of fallow between crops, my grandmother hinting that she was the one who arranged the intervals. The first nine are not only evenly spaced but also ordered into neat groups. The first set was composed of three sons, Henry, Max, and Bernard, with strikingly different personalities, but with some similarities. For a while, at least, they each entered into business with my grandfather but made more money when they struck out on their own. Each had one child, a son (I discount here one daughter, illegitimate, hastily abandoned) but, because of their divorces or the childlessness of their sons, did not come to meet or to have grandchildren themselves. None lived past sixty-five. My grandparents' first three sons were followed by the second group of children, two girls, both of whom died at the age of a few months, one of a fever and one scalded to death, I was told, by a careless servant. After this gap came a set of four: my father was the eldest, then a sister, Elizabeth, the boy-girl alternation then continuing

*My father's family in Malmö, 1918. From left to right: Elizabeth; Robert's father, Benjamin; Robert (my father); Howard; Milton; Robert's mother, Sophie; Gertrude.*

with Howard and Gertrude. Seven years later, when my grandfather was fifty-one and my grandmother forty-six, a pair of twins arrived, not to my knowledge ever announced as the product of any scheme. The older of the two, Milton, became the baby of the family; the younger boy lived at most a few hours.

Nor, as a novelist, if I had wished to convey to my readers the ability of immigrants to reinvent themselves, would I have adopted as a means to this end a device as cumbersome as the changes in names, sometimes made not once but several times, of each of the eight surviving children. I knew the Bernard of this book as Boris, though his name in Russia was Avram. My father is perhaps the most complex case: a few weeks after his birth a Czarist official noted that the rabbi reported his name, which, written in Cyrillic letters, can be transliterated as Schlyoime, the Yiddish equivalent of the Hebrew Shlomo or Solomon. Writing in heavy letters derived from Gothic script, an official rendered it as 37

Schloma soon after the family arrived in Germany, though on still later documents from Germany and Sweden my father appears as Salomon. As a child I learned his German nickname, Salo, when answering telephone calls from his cousin Adolph, the only relative with whom I heard him speak in German. I later saw this name on correspondence, also in that language, between him and his mother. On coming to America he anglicized his name and adopted a new first name, thus becoming Robert Solomon. He was known as Robert or, less frequently, Bob, though Robbie somehow became his most widely used nickname. I also heard him give Solomon as his name when he thought it would impress his listeners, and once, speaking with someone whom he took to be an Arab or a Turk, he offered up Suleiman and smiled, nodding at the rapid flow of syllables that this name elicited, pausing and then continuing to speak in English. But in the book about his mother, the names are stable, Henry, Max, Bernard, Robert, Elizabeth, Howard, Gertrude, Milton. And so I now return to my father's presentation of Russia in the late 1890s.

It seems to me unfair for me to ask her questions and probe into her past and perhaps secrets. To investigate, dissect and analyze any memories that I would get in such a fashion. It is not right. What I should write down is memories that I can remember of her, things that she does and tells us now. But somehow I feel that those things that took place with and within her, before we were or were conscious of them show what a woman she was. The material and the shaping, molding of our mothers personality. She told us of a time when she was pregnant with Bernard, that father was at the slaughter house, his business then was intestines and guts. — Late at night a messenger came running, that father had gotten into an argument with the butchers and threatened to kill. So she rushed over to the slaughter house, her mother tried to hold her back. Where will you go in the darkness my child. The wild dog will only tear you to pieces. But she did not listen, and went out into the dark. With her high abdomen she stumbled through the snow, to save him. When she enter the building, lit with torches, kerosene lamps, upon seeing her, the angry group paid her respects and disappeared, leaving her husband unharmed.

In that incident my grandfather appears as an ill-tempered man, prone to fights and violence. The later anecdotes emphasize a different flaw, his tendency to abandon his wife and children.

At a time the drunkards of the town decided to have a pogrom the rumor had been brewing for several days. My father had hidden in fear somewheres and left the family alone. He was found drunk later. No one would harm a woman and children he claimed later. Bernard made a fist of his little hand. I will hit those bad people with my "kulak" [fist] he said. Late one afternoon the mob had collected, and with vodka and talks fired on their emotions before the act. Hours passed before they started to march, but in the meantime clouds had collected and such a heavy rainstorm came up that the mob was drenched and driven away. Such a rainstorm had not been heard of for years.

The next story shows my father's anger at his father. He was a victim of his father's tendency to abandon the family even before he was born, and his father contrived to occupy his mother so that she could not spend time with him when he was a newborn.

At the outbreak of the Russo-Japanese war [in 1904] my father fled to Germany. He was afraid to be drafted into the war. For weeks he used to hide, until he left. Mother was then pregnant with me. He had left her to go through that all alone and later to wind up all his business and follow him to Germany with 4 children and me weeks old. Her mother wailed he will drag you yet to America.

As my father tells in this account, his parents moved from Russia to Germany in 1905, when he was an infant. In Germany, though, his father continued to be noted chiefly for his absence, leaving his mother to address whatever emergencies might arise.

As at one time Max was run over by a truck, pulled by two horses. He was very badly injured internally. The doctors had no hopes and were ready to pay for the funeral charges, if they were permitted to dissect his corpse. As if anything were to remain after the dissection. He sat in a dark room on a low bench, he sat, "Schiva" the mourning for those dead. But mother fought and argued with the doctors.

It was a long struggle, she won out and saved her second son. At that time she was nursing Howard. The doctors thought Max was her only child, and when they heard that she had four sons and a daughter, they were astonished. She used to be in the hospital two and three times a day. She saved Max, but the doctors said that he never would be worthwhile. Now he has a son. So mother fought and worked all the time, always under handicaps to help her children.

About two years after this last episode came the one moment of relief in her married life. She took her husband and children from Germany to Russia in the summer of 1911, so that her father could officiate at the Bar Mitzvah of her third son, Bernard. Had World War I and the Russian Revolution not intervened later in that decade, they might well have returned for other visits as well, but, as events turned out, this trip provided my father with his only personal memories of the country of his birth. I recall some of the details that he told me: the ride of several days in a train, the family occupying an entire compartment; the warm reception in his mother's parents' house and the visits to her married sisters, living within a few blocks; the visits to more distant relatives on his mother's side. He also made a quick side-trip to meet his father's father, a cobbler who worked and lived in a house that contained only two small rooms. My father described the simple wooden workbench, the dirt floors — had my grandfather become hardened by growing up in poverty, by being unable to remain in school, by needing to work at a very young age? My father mentioned, too, meeting his grandfather's second wife — had my grandfather become embittered by his mother's death, by his father's shifting away from his own children? There is not a single reference to my father's father's parents in this book, though. My father wrote of the trip to Russia to honor his mother, not to comprehend his father. In retelling these stories, he performed a valuable service to his mother. He helped make this trip in 1911 into one of the few enduring triumphs of her life, the consolidation of the bond between her children and all that her father represented.

In 1911 the whole Family went to visit her parents in Russia. The occasion for the trip was Bernards "Bar Mizwo." This is the one thing she is most proud of having done in her whole Life. She often speaks about it, having shown her parents to her children, and so I am acquainted with her parents and her home. When she had decided to hold Bernards Bar Mizvoh in her fathers house, she wrote him a letter telling him of her proposed plan. The very same day, he in Russia, wrote her a letter, please to come to see him.

After this trip, there is a hiatus in the accounts of the life of my father's mother. He does not talk of the first years in Germany, when the family enjoyed relative prosperity, nor of World War I, during the first years of which the family, as Russian citizens in Germany, were enemy aliens. Absent also are the stories of the war years that I heard as a child. I do not know whether my father spoke only of the scarcity of food or whether that was the topic that impressed me the most, but these stories are surely the ones I recall: of my grandfather raising chickens in the attic so that the family could eat eggs, which were unavailable for purchase; of an illness of my grandmother's for which a doctor prescribed an expensive cure, difficult to obtain — an orange, which she slowly ate as all the children watched, the peel left to dry on the stove and later steeped with tea leaves to make a rich and fragrant drink. There is not a single reference to my grandfather's smuggling the family across the Danish border and into Sweden in 1916, where he soon returned to his business in the fur trade. The book picks up my grandmother's life and her marriage again only sometime after their move to New York in 1921. At this point, my father shifts from recounting the distant past to writing a journal of events as they occur. Despite this difference, his parents and their marriage seem very similar on both sides of the Atlantic, even though the stories in Russia must have been seen through my grandmother's eyes, the ones in New York through my father's. He presents his father in New York not as prone to violence or to irresponsible absences but simply as offensive in his manner, repugnant in his character. In New York, at least, my grandmother could count on her sons to accompany her and to diffuse her husband's intolerable manner.

The old man wants to take her to the movies. She invites me to go, even though I have seen it, is it because she will then consider herself in my company. To have my presence put him in the background. Not to be aware of him so much.

The last Sunday the old man took her and Milton for a boat ride up the Hudson. She dragged Bernard out of bed, so that he too should be in the sun. She admired the scenery, but the crowd was repugnant. To top all this, they again realized that the old man is unbearable. His speech — all. And when she knew that she could leave the steamer at 125th St., she was happy to depart and leave.

My father relates the pleasures which his mother missed, the strains that afflicted her.

It is the first beautiful spring day of the year. The wind is cool and gentle yet and she has to stay in the kitchen and fry chicken skins.

I took mother to the doctor. We had to walk a few blocks. I noticed for the first time that she is beginning to stoop. She is bending to the responsibilities and disappointments she carries.

Went with Mother to the grocery store. She was buying what she needed. But because of her present shortage of money she was haggling and complaining so her great spirit and understanding are forced to these inferior actions. But if they were occupied always with greater things they naturally would grow greater too.

Even strangers noted the contrast between the refinement of her character and the harsh conditions of her life.

At one time she had to travel by train and only had money for a cheaper accommodation. When the conductor saw her, he exclaimed. Such a Lady must not ride in a common car and put her in a first class compartment.

However, her own children were unaware of her degradation.

What a pity, almost a crime to mark down here her very bloodbeats, to be recorded. It will show us later how little we did, how little we were willing to give up for her. Her life is an unhappy one. Always has been. How harshly she is being treated. And she has given up everything. Her pride, her independence, given in. All our fault.

Her sacrifices were more than the devotion of an ordinary mother. She recognized her position in a momentous struggle between opposed forces. Refinement and vulgarity wrestled within the family, within each of the children.

> She must feel that she wasted her possibilities and her Life by marrying, as she did. And if she hoped, that at least the children would show improvement away from the paternal side, she has been disappointed. The whole Orlovski family is no good. She said.

If his father's family was uneducated and crude, his mother's family had an almost supernatural quality. The fact that my father's mother in Germany and her father in Russia each wrote letters on the same day proposing the same trip goes beyond mere coincidence. These simultaneous letters demonstrate an extraordinary link between extraordinary individuals, to whom the aura of the Vilna Gaon clung. Exactly what bound them together is unclear and somehow transcendental, a fateful combination of great wisdom and spiritual affinity. Whatever the nature of their connection, it also included my father:

> Elizabeth told me, that mother had told her, that my walk is like her fathers. She can close her eyes, hear my walk, and think that it is her father walking.

> Mother once told me, that the veins on my hands run exactly like the veins on her fathers hands. Often she said, You are of my family, not of your fathers.

Clearly a part of his mother's line, clearly on his mother's side, my father wrote this book to memorialize his mother and to record her struggle with his father. He had an urgent task, then, to bring his siblings to recognize and honor their mother, to raise them so that "the children would show improvement away from the paternal side," to remake or eliminate their father. In the book my father sometimes presents himself to his siblings as an ideal model of sensitivity to filial obligation.

> She had cleaned the stove. Showed it to me, and was very happy about it. I have given myself pleasure. She embraced me. I felt ashamed. So much kind emotion and we take it as of a matter of fact. As if coming to us.

At other times, he shifts into more personal reflections, losing the distinction between entirely private journal entries and accounts written with his siblings in mind. In these passages, he recounts a deep sense of inadequacy.

We all live in a crisis now. Mother said, she takes my word for everything I say. If I tell her, I have been there and done so, it is as if she would be present. And I am not worthy of such a trust.

Several days ago she asked me whether I needed any change. She has hardly anything, and is still willing to share it with me.

I felt guilty lately. I do not do what I could, and did not give her the little attention I can give her. But she showed it to me, she still has it all for me. With the thoughts just wandering, I asked her whether she would like to go to Chicago now for a few months, and I realized immediately that it would be impossible. It is she that holds the last shreds of the family together. And tonight when I came home, she spoke to me. All that I had spoken to her, always was clear and pure. She believed in me, and now even that is shattered. I was near tears and very grave. To hear that. I have a long climb before me to reestablish myself. And no more silly words, but action.

On two occasions my father could not tolerate these feelings.

The constant worrying had made her irritated and she said some harsh words. I played chess, it had been interrupted to eat supper, and during supper I turned back to the game to study the position. "It takes days off my Life" she said. I could eat no food. Everything turned bitter. I saw an open window insane thoughts. She could not eat, and went into the kitchen. I followed her, but we neither spoke. It hurt me that I should have given her pain. It was a break. The first in twelve years I can remember. How much did she carry in silence, before she broke out. I have a bad conscience.

One evening she was displeased at me, she looked at me angrily. A maddening wave swept over me, in that instant I could have thrown myself out of the window, or walked out of this existence. I did neither. I had not moved my chair out of the way quickly enough.

I had to make myself reread these passages several times to believe them. Was my father's guilt for his mother's suffering so strong, was he so filled with despair at being unable to help her, that he really felt the impulse to fling himself out a window? It troubled me greatly to acknowledge the extremes of his humiliation. I could attempt to calm myself by seeking an explanation in the troubled relations between his strong-willed parents; I could turn to an intellectual account, linking the raised hatchet with the open window, my grandmother's father's threat to kill his son-in-law with my father's impulse to kill himself, the crazy gestures of my grandmother's father and of her son to protect her from further pain. These efforts to explore the origins of my father's degradation could not remove my horror at recognizing his anguish.

I found relief only from seeing that these suicidal impulses did not continue. After these two occasions, early on in the book, he did not write of killing himself. By 1929 — at a time when his affair with Katzy (the woman he would marry, my mother) became more serious — he was able to express some doubts about the correctness of his mother's words and actions. He opens one section with her words:

> When I was watching and taking care of you children, while you were young. You were all healthy and in good condition. But now, that you have grown up, and I don't manage anymore you've become thin and fallen off your standards.
>
> She is tired and weak, and yet she got up early this morning to make a cereal for breakfast for us.
>
> Are we really so helpless.

In January 1930, he voiced a second criticism, phrased as a statement rather than a question, though still quite soft in tone. I was pleased to see that my father's obsession with his mother was tempered.

> In her anxiety to do everything possible for her children, she has chained herself down and made them helpless. If they cannot be served, they would rather do without it, than get it themselves.
>
> She went away with Bessie [a cousin who was visiting from Baltimore] for a day. You will excuse me for doing this, she asked. She bought herself a dress, forgive me for doing so. This is carrying her goodness to an extreme.

In May of that year my parents were married and traveled to Europe for their honeymoon. My father became less concerned with his mother. The few entries in the book for the last months of 1930 and all of 1931 show that his feelings of guilt and inadequacy were abating. He did not deliver any injunctions to his siblings, even though they were continuing to leave their mother's home. The three oldest sons, Henry, Max, and Boris, had long been gone, and Elizabeth had married Irving in 1929. Later in 1930 Gertrude and Ted married and set up an apartment, and Howard moved out on his own around that time as well. At some point in this period my grandfather's absences, which at first had purportedly been business trips that took him to Chicago and other cities, became longer and more openly acknowledged. After nearly forty years of marriage, in his midsixties, he took an apartment of his own, leaving his wife alone with their youngest child, Milton, then in his early teens.

Mother was up tonight. I hadnt seen her for quite a few days. The weather had been hot, and in the evenings, I was glad to be home and rest. Mother told us how lonely she felt. She said, "I look at my four walls, are they any different — " Her voice broke. She could not stand it. She is so lonesome, and I disregarded her.

My father mentions my mother only indirectly, in the "us" to whom his mother spoke in his own home, where he now lives with his wife. He records his mother's tears; now, at least, he does not consider throwing himself out a window. Nor did he feel the need to record his mother's life in such detail, since he left long intervals between entries through much of the 1930s. One section, written in 1933, describes the period when she and Milton lived with Elizabeth, Irving, and their daughter Joan, born in April 1932.

Mother was over in our new apartment. The energy she has, to do so much is astounding. She was quite lively. She was telling me about her troubles. She keeps up her work, despite her awkward position as houseworker in the home of her son in law. Burdening them with her youngest son.

She cant stand it much longer. "I cannot tell all, but you understand what I am talking about." she said. The truth is that I really dont know what she meant. So I must have come away from an understanding of her. And that is very sad. And I had believed I could compile many views of her here in this book.

I know and realize that I have drifted away from mother. I am tired of her complaints and sufferings. She does so much for others, they cannot manage to adjust their own lives to their situations and do not appreciate her aid. Myself, I have no patience with mother. The understanding of this condition is a bitter thing.

Her life now is so different. I am sorry for her suffering. All I can do now is to visit her at times and phone her several times a week to inquire into her miseries.

He describes one of these visits, a moment that contained at least a partial resolution of his guilt and her need:

I drove her to her room, she spoke to me after leaving the car. Then said goodby and when I got ready to leave, spoke again. I shut off the motor several times. I was in no hurry to leave, neither could I go away abruptly. It was such a bitter thing, her trying to keep me here a little while longer. And when she had said the final goodbye and I had started under way so slowly she walked alongside of the car, still talking. "Dont think I want to see you just to get money from you." I bitterly, "Do you have to say that to me." She was relieved that I understood. I rode away. Milton was standing in the doorway, a big boy, and so alone and needy.

The final entry occurs after the longest gap of all, over three years without any additions to the book. It speaks of a visit that my father made to his parents, now reunited, in the House of the Daughters of Jacob, a Jewish residence for the elderly. It is written in a handwriting very different from the cursive in the rest of the book, a careful block script with some letters decorated with little curlicues.

Nov. 1938 Towards the end of a day a wanderer entered a house to rest himself. The host was very hospitable and invited the stranger for the evening meal. When the visitor was rested and refreshed, he spoke: "Your neighbor who lives to the right of your house, labors for the world of the present. And he who lives beyond the hills, toils for the world of the future." The host was astonished at such words and wondered for such reasoning. Thus was the answer: "It is to be recognized by the nurture of the neighbor's garden, he who lives toward the right. And again by the appearance of the house of him who lives beyond the hill. Thus we understand, he who beautifies the interior of his home, works for the world of the future, and he who embellishes the external appearance of his garden toils for the present world." Thus he spoke.

After the departure of the stranger, the host realized that his visitor was a wise sage.

Here at the home of the Daughters of Jacob there are magnificent decorations, inside as well as outside. This means whoever participates in the labor for this house shall be blessed in both worlds.

These paragraphs make up the only allegory in the entire book, a shift in form that conveys a change in mood. The anecdote, a version of a story in the Talmud, gives the sense of a remote past. Though my father mentions neither her nor himself directly, he seems to accept both his mother's present life and her eventual death simply and directly. An unusual feature of this page makes me realize that he decided to close the book at this point, even though it still had many blank pages. The paragraphs on this page, the last one with writing in the book, are followed by a long flourish that extends from just below his last words to the bottom of the page, a decoration much more elaborate than the simple horizontal lines that he drew to separate other entries. What a relief for him then, and for me now, that he no longer needed to record her words, her troubles. I imagine my father sweeping the pen across the page and then lifting it, at that moment fulfilling his task of making her life whole through a telling of it.

I might not have even been born, it occurs to me, if he had not finished this book. If he had not begun to question her extreme claims on him, if he had not been able to break away from her, he might not have been able to fall in love, to marry, to have children. I can recognize the overwhelming power of the recollection of witnessed suffering, the despair of ever being able to convey this recollection. What, I find myself wondering, will allow me to close my own story of a parent's pain?

## Chapter 3 FATHER-NOTES

Distributed among the three bookcases in my father's study in California were a dozen or so boxes. He had placed labels on most of them to indicate the names of the relative or friend whose papers he had stored inside: "Max" for his second-oldest brother, "Bonevardi" for an Argentine artist whose studio in Manhattan he often visited in the 1960s and 1970s. The box that made me most curious bore the label:

> Notebook
> & loose notes
> Reminiscences about my father

As soon as I opened the box, I saw that its contents recorded his father in a less organized manner than the memorial book that he had made about his mother. The box held hundreds of scraps of paper, some inserted in a notebook in which he had copied out passages from books that he had read, others set in folders he had improvised from manila envelopes, posters, and odd bits of cardboard. On the cover of one of these folders he had written "about my fate" and then changed the last word to "father" so that it read "about my father." He corrected the slip of his pen, its meaning obvious as such unconscious blurtings usually are. Words had mixed in his mind, and letters as well, sounds, entire languages: in German, his first language, the word for father, *Vater,* is pronounced "Fater."

Although the notes inside did not have dates, I could see that they came from the early 1980s, a few years before my parents' deteriorating health led them to move to California in 1986. A 1981 H&R Block Tax Table, folded down the middle, held many papers. He wrote one note on the inside of an envelope from a Jewish charity bearing the postmark 11 MAR 1983, and another on the blank side of a flyer (from which he must have torn off a strip) that reads:

> HELP US TO AVOID CLOSING *15 BRANCH LIBR*
> The Brooklyn Public Library is slated for a $1,393,00
>
> This comes on top of a mid-1983 cut of $411,000. If our funding is reduced, we will have no choice but those that are least used, borough-wide, and that are We will simply not have enough staff to keep them ope

More than fifty years had passed since his midtwenties, when he wrote the book about his mother. As his eightieth birthday in 1984 was approaching, he began to record fragmentary recollections of his father. Despite the long intervening period, these papers show the immediacy of his feelings. Some notes reveal, often indirectly, the sources of my father's bitterness toward his father. The first note, though, is a commonplace biographical reference to his father's early life: "Bar Mizwah presents 5 roubles calves — head of cattle." These words are sufficient for me to recall the story I had heard several times as a child. Five rubles: the sum of the gifts that my grandfather, the son of a poor cobbler, received at his Bar Mitzvah. He bought a calf for three of these rubles and gave a peasant the other two to fatten it over the summer. Reinvesting the profits that he made from the sale of the calf in more calves and more fodder, he accumulated a small sum of capital and shifted later into buying and selling intestines for sausage casings, eventually moving up to the fur trade. This single anecdote from my grandfather's childhood was sufficient to carry all the themes that my father wished to convey. His father grew up in a Jewish community, in poverty; his father's success in business rested on quintessentially Jewish traits: a sharp eye for recognizing opportunities, a cleverness in making plans, and the perseverance necessary to bring these plans to completion.

In thinking about this story, I recall a similar anecdote about my grandfather's brother, the youngest, the only one of his siblings to cross the Atlantic, Grisha in Russia, George in America, who also began his business career with funds amassed at what I, as an anthropologist, immediately define as a "traditional life-cycle event," a wedding rather than a Bar Mitzvah. He was a handsome man to whom many women were attracted. (Did two of them really commit suicide when he rejected them? Did my father expect me to believe that they did?) He finally proposed marriage to Vera, a woman who, my father often told, brought a large dowry because of the unusual circumstances of her birth. Vera's father was Jewish, wealthy, old, married, the father of grown and near-grown children when he found himself unexpectedly a father once again, of a child born to one of the servants. To keep this bastard half-sister from claiming a share of the sizable inheritance, the man's other children arranged for her to have a large dowry in exchange for relinquishing all other claims to their father's estate. (Once, attempting to introduce order into the story, I checked with my father: yes, the servant had been Jewish, since if she had not been, then neither would have Vera, by customary rules of matrilineal descent; yes, it was unusual to have Jewish servants, and a sign of great wealth, or perhaps Vera's mother was a shop employee of his rather than a servant.) A dowry, invested in a grain mill in the Ukraine; the grain mill sold, the capital serving as the basis for other mills in the United States and then other businesses, raising chickens, who knew how many other ventures as well. I recall a photograph from sometime around World War I, Vera in a long fur coat, George and the children assembled around a long gleaming roadster, a large house in the background. The implausibility of my father's stories carries the envy that my grandfather felt for his more successful brother. Could Vera really have been "feeble-minded," could she really have walked into a drugstore, pulled up her skirt past midthigh, and revealed the contusion for which she sought a remedy, explaining not merely to the pharmacist but to all the other customers who gathered around that she bruised easily because her blood was thin, a result of having been conceived in her father's old age? I recall only fragments of his other stories about this branch of the family. A number of George and Vera's eight children, especially the ones who changed their name a second time (from Orlove to Love, this additional dropping of a syllable an even greater derussification and unjewing than the earlier deletion of -*ski*), who intermarried or who actually converted — all these scandals, it was hinted, the consequence of excessive wealth — did not remain in touch with my father and their other cousins, nor, after the disputes following the settling of their father's estate, with each other.

My memories of stories about Uncle George fill only a few of the blank spots in my father's sketchy notes. Writing as a young man in 1928, he recorded many vignettes of his mother's childhood; as an old man in the early 1980s, he wrote only one story of his father's childhood. Having begun to write about his father, my father shifted his attention elsewhere and began to write about his beloved mother instead. At some points he discusses his maternal relatives rather than his paternal ones. A note reads: "Abraham HaLevi Korb," giving the name of his mother's father and emphasizing in the "HaLevi" his grandfather's putative descent from ancient priests, not as prestigious a title as "HaCohen," but still sufficient to earn him certain privileges, notably the right to be called up to offer prayers over the Torah scrolls on Sabbath morning services in any synagogue he entered. A second note about this man reads:

> Grandpa Korb —
> traveling east in horse & cart.

---

These words refer to his journey, soon after the tumultuous events of 1848, to Russia from his birthplace, a major city and port on the Baltic Sea, then a German city named Stettin, and, since World War II, Polish, Szczecin. The distance is not much more than seven hundred miles, a long day's drive by current standards in California. I would have liked more details to describe this barely imaginable trip across a prerailroad Europe, even to know the simplest facts: how many weeks or months it took, where he ate and slept. In some indirect way, I realize, even these notes may be "reminiscences about my father": this Abraham HaLevi Korb, a man of illustrious Jewish lineage and refined origins in Central rather than Eastern Europe, was superior to his son-in-law, my grandfather.

Even many of the notes that suggest my grandfather's presence more directly are fragmentary in nature. My father spoke to me of walking with his father in Leipzig, the city in Germany in which they lived from 1908 to 1915. They often passed the neoclassical Rathaus, as city halls are called in German, but my father only wrote

> Rathhouse in Leipzig.
> Fascade in the proportion of the Goldene Schnitt.
> sectio aurea
> $AB:AC = AC:BC$

I can only make guesses about these notes: was my father trying to please his father by showing what he had learned at school? This note might record the schoolboy reciting a recently learned lesson to his father, beginning in German, *Goldene Schnitt*, golden section, the Greek formula that determined the proportions of the sides of the ideally harmonious rectangle, and then shifting to the Latin term for the same formula, and finally into mathematics, an equation. Or perhaps my father was recalling a moment when he kept such thoughts to himself, when he had remained silent and gloated in the realization that he was more cultured than his crude father. At any rate, he was still mixing languages when he wrote, blending the German Rathaus with the English house, the English facade with the German Fassade.

In other "reminiscences" in the box, my grandfather is barely a presence. Remaining in the city during the summer, he worked at the business that allowed his wife and children to take summer vacations in the countryside: once again absences, like the ones that my father recorded in his book about his mother.

> I've been thinking about an episode, one of the many that took place when I was a summer visitor on a farm in Germany. For some unexplainable reason I cant find a satisfactory beginning for that ~~tal~~ story. That episode is part of the greater tale, so ~~it~~ the narrative really has not beginning, like everything else in a story ~~its is a see~~ a section is ~~the~~ in the sequence of an earlier beginning. The entrance — door to farmhouse — and the bench next to it, on the right side — where we kids had to wash our bare feet, at the end of the day's outdoor playing, before ~~goin~~ being permitted to go indoors for the evening meal.
>
> I walked back to the house slowly and passed the dog house near

the main gate. There was no watchdog in it. I had been told that, years ago the farmer caught a fox cub and chained it to the dog house. A day or so later the cub was gone. ~~The by its leg~~ Vixen had come and freed her cub, ~~by biting off~~ its front leg. It was a strange story, I thought.

The fox mother's mate is absent, but she is protective of her children, resourceful, ferocious, wounding. I think of my grandmother saving the life of her son Max, run over by a truck, when the doctors had given him up for dead, of her rescuing all her children from being merely Orlowskis. The old man, the wild dog, Benjamin Orlowski does appear in two brief anecdotes, in the first of which he and my father also walk together.

I thought that a number of vignettes, taken from my memory, would lead to an easier flow of description and therefore considered to write of a ~~view~~ flashbacks fluttering and shifting a riffling of ~~the pages in~~ an album ~~leaves~~ of illustrated ~~through an album~~ leaves
  ~~The occa~~ On occasion we ~~children~~ accompanied our father to the R.R. Station when he went on a business trip. The smoke of his cigar mingled with the escaping ~~steam~~ clouds from the ~~railroad~~ steam engine — He wore a derby, a long paletot and carried a Stecken cane — when father walked he firmly pushed the cane to the ground —

The scene at the railroad station fascinates me. I am filled with questions. Who took my father to the station: was it his mother, his older brothers, the servants? Did his father, carrying a cane and smoking a cigar, embrace him before he left? Why did he record his father's departures rather than his returns? I cannot ask him. I have, at least, a more complete mental picture of another scene, described in a second note. It repeats an anecdote that I heard many times as a child:

Father-War map of the Eastern Front, glasheaded pins & paper flags.
Generalstabkarte [German ordnance map]
followed the reports w/ great interest but never gave any signs whom he rooted for.

This was one of my favorite stories as a child, one that my father would often tell me when I asked to hear about the other Benjamin, the one I was named for. This story was a key incident in my father's migrations. He had been taken from Russia to Germany as an infant in 1905 and moved abruptly once again, to Sweden, in the middle of World War I. Had it not been for my grandfather's decision, I knew, my father might still have been in Germany when the Nazis came to power. My grandfather had been right not to reveal his thoughts. The family might have been detained in Germany during World War I if word of their plans had leaked out. They were, after all, subjects of the Czar, enemies of the Germans at the time.

I have a clear image of my grandfather in my mind. He is listening to the radio, a large one in a wooden cabinet. The children stand around, listening too, and watching their father pick up pins from the large map and shift their position. My grandfather would know what to do with the information, just as he knew what to do with the five rubles. The children want to know what he plans, but they must remain silent so that he will not miss a word of the report. He will tell them when the time comes for the family to move, and in the meantime they can only search for clues in his face, in the movement of his arms, in the gesture with which he gets up from the table and sets the map aside when the news broadcast ends. His will is stronger than theirs. He "never gave any signs whom he rooted for."

Sensing that something was not right with the story, I telephoned Bill and Ursula Hagen, a couple of German historians who are colleagues of mine at the university where I teach. As we spoke, I discovered that this image of my grandfather could not have been true. Bill, conferring with Ursula, explained to me that radios did not become common in Germany until the 1920s. In fact, some of Hitler's ability to make such effective use of the radio in broadcasting speeches and rallies came from the newness of the medium. My grandfather, Bill told me, must have obtained the news of the shifting front from newspapers. I felt slightly dizzy as he spoke to me, as if it were not only an image of my past that was beginning to turn blurry but the actual world of visible objects in front of me as well. I do not think that he noticed the pause on the line as I closed my eyes and held my head very still. After regaining my composure, I thanked him and then chatted briefly with both of them about my grandfather.

Later that day, I tried briefly to construct an alternate image of my grandfather reading the newspaper, but I could not become absorbed in the effort of considering whether he read it alone or when the children were around, whether in the morning, afternoon, or evening. I kept wondering instead where the imaginary radio had come from. My father might have put it in, I thought. He certainly embellished his accounts of the past, offering details that he thought his listeners of the moment would like to hear. It is more likely, I decided, that I was the one who added the radio. The story about the map and the pins, for all that it told me, left me with the question of why my father never found out about his father's loyalties. Sensing his reluctance to speak about his father, I did not ask him about this gap in the story. Instead, I simply took another piece of the past, one of the big old wooden radios that I had seen in relatives' houses, and placed it into the story. I think, though, that I was not simply inventing on my own. My father's fear of his own father lay beneath the comfortable surface of the anecdotes about rubles and calves, the visit to the rabbi's daughter, and the chickens in the attic. I knew that my father often remained silent so that he would not provoke that fierce and strong-willed man into anger. In order to put this truth into the brief story of the maps, I had needed to add something, and a radio seemed right, so right that it became real.

My grandfather's secrecy, then, was not a great show in front of the radio but was carried out as he read the newspapers, presumably with less drama. Nonetheless, his secrecy left an impression both on my father and on me. Could my father's and grandfather's mutual silence have been a kind of conversation? Was it a means for the man and boy to work together in protecting the family as a whole? Another slip of paper in this box recounts a later stage in these migrations and suggests a tone of disagreement rather than cooperation between them. It describes a boat ride, the final leg of their journey in 1916 from Germany to the city of Malmö, Sweden. On this trip, my father assumed for one of the first times in his life the position of eldest son. Max had already joined Henry in New York, and Boris, then eighteen years old, had avoided forced conscription into the Kaiser's army by hiding himself on a train that crossed into Holland, reuniting himself with the family in Sweden only later.

> 1st trip Malmo + Copen hagen — chapped lips — Pa took me to the
> bar — Swedish punch — Sweet — thick — Honey — soothed the sore
> tissue, I would ve liked to have some more, for the pleasure of the
> taste of the relief of the pain but Pa said no more. It is a good
> medicine — & is taken only as ~~required~~ necessary

I had heard of this trip before. My grandfather ferried back and forth between Copenhagen and Malmö a number of times before bringing his wife and younger children across, and he took my father along with him on one of these occasions to look for work and housing while the others remained behind. I had not heard about the punch, though. The first glass at the bar must have been memorable not only because it soothed his lips, chapped from the windy crossing of the strait that connected the Baltic and North Seas; it must also have been a luxurious treat to my father, accustomed to the scarcity of food in wartime Germany. The glass of punch could also have accomplished much more. It could have celebrated their escape from Germany or affirmed the opportunities that awaited them in a new country. It could have acknowledged my father's new position as the oldest son living with the family. It could simply have marked the recognition of the newness of this crossing for my father, his first time aboard a boat, his first trip on open water. What my father recorded, though, was his memory of the niggardly denial of the second glass. He does not present his own words, only his father's curt refusal, followed by a brief lecture.

Absent from these notes are the other stories set in Sweden that I heard as a child, also involving, if not drink, food. The family had very little money when they arrived in Sweden and turned to the Jewish merchants in Malmö, who set my grandfather up as a peddler. Among my favorite anecdotes were the stories of my father and his grandfather walking from farmhouse to farmhouse with packs of ribbons, needles, and other goods on their backs. In one anecdote — the only moment that I recall in which my father describes unproblematic cooperation with his father — they walk down a road one summer day, become very thirsty, and steal cucumbers from a field. In another, they stop at a farmhouse and each accepts a bowl of soup with scraps of ham in it, my father (perhaps, I now think as I write, repaying the foregone punch) telling his father to refuse a second serving to avoid eating pork for pleasure, a greater violation of kosher laws, my father claimed, than eating it because of hunger. Here I mingle my father's stories not with my own imagination but with the depictions of Jewish peddlers in novels and films, and with my own experiences as well. *Pekl* in Yiddish, "pack" in English, *q'epi* in Quechua: I am struck by the associations in my own life, with the backpacks I use while hiking in the mountains in California, with the Indian peasants in Peru who carry things, tied up in blankets or large cloths, on their backs. I recall with great pleasure the three days that I spent in a village helping peasant families during the potato harvest. I enjoyed the simple repetitive work of digging potatoes out of the earth with a small wooden-handled hoe. The villagers welcomed my contribution to their efforts and noted with a combination of surprise, amusement, and approval my willingness to shoulder loads, so unlike the disdain with which townspeople regarded heavy labor. The blanketsful of potatoes that I carried on my back, trotting down a narrow dirt path, seemed to be a passport that allowed me to move freely from the public world of the fields into the private realm of the courtyards, to join the peasants in their meals, with abundant bowls of home-brewed beer and ribald joking, that marked the breaks in the days of work and the festivities at their end.

The papers in this box contain only one other anecdote about Sweden, also set in Malmö.

The vestpocket watch —

———————————

The frequent breakage of the crystal —

———————————

Played leapfrog with the Boller [small cannons] on the docks
~~wharfs~~ in the harbor
They were to high
Put the watch in your vestpocket, facing inward —

As I read and reread this short passage, I ask myself why it frightens me so much. The game itself does not seem dangerous (it is unlikely that shards from a broken watch crystal would cause serious lacerations), and these glass fronts of watches would not have been very expensive to replace. Nor does my fear come from the reprimand itself, which is not very severe. The element of alarm comes for me all at once in the unexpectedness of the final line. A voice commands my father, put the watch in your pocket, put it in this certain pocket in this way. Could my grandfather actually have visited the docks one day, perhaps walking from one business appointment to another, and seen my father; would my grandfather then have come upon him from behind, offering no greeting, only a sudden injunction, his voice a sharper blow than if he had struck my father? Perhaps this voice is inside my father's mind, a voice whose existence he sometimes forgot but that could suddenly chastise him, a voice that remained alert during its long silences, watching, ready to speak at any moment. There is no more difference between these two alternatives, it occurs to me, than between the terror of the conscious world and the terror of nightmares. Unannounced, unanticipated, immediately recognized, the voice leaves my father standing silent.

I admired my father's ability to offer such clear images with few words. My grandfather puffs on a cigar and he steps onto a train; he moves pins on a map; he gives a cup of sweet punch and then denies a second cup: how well these incidents convey my father's admiration, yearning, and fear. And yet I sensed that there was something more about my grandfather that my father had not written. My father was also dissatisfied with the brevity of these anecdotes. One slip of paper in the box reads:

Stories about my father —
I ~~was~~ wish to make the story longer —
to have it contain a moral principle, an insight into matters more —
than the matter of daily affairs.

My father had announced his intentions in writing about his mother on the first page of text in the book about her: to record how she had been misunderstood, to preserve her wise sayings, to carry on her work. Although he never stated the moral principle or insight that he wished to illustrate in the reminiscences about his father, he succeeded, at least to some degree, in fulfilling his wish. He wrote three anecdotes whose details "make the story longer," and which contain insights and moral principles — though these lie in the matter of daily affairs rather than beyond them as he had hoped.

The first story is set in Germany sometime before World War I, when my grandfather's business was successful.

> On my way home from Hebrew school, I'd stop at my father's place of business. He employed a number of people, sometimes ~~as many as~~ several dozen of unskilled workers. Many were young men, who worked their way across Europe, on their way from ~~Polan~~ Eastern Europe, Poland, Russia — to America — these young men were if not scholars, at least well versed in the Torah — Father thought it would be well, for me to have a private tutor in hebrew. It really was not a continuous course of study — The young man wanted to impress his employer and was patient with me — when I have the proper pronunciation and translation father would let a few coins fall from his lifted hands. "See, the angels are rewarding you from heaven." I knew this was not the case at all, and ~~ignored~~ spurned the gift. The tutor waited patiently & when he realized I'd have no part of it, he snatched them up. Father ~~made no~~ did not change his expression. I let the worker keep the few coins. I was proud of my learning ability & did not require a reward & was contented.

Here, at last, was a kind of reply that my father could make to his father. He did not speak to him, he did not even move, but his silence and immobility were nonetheless a clear response. Even the worker, recently arrived from Poland or Russia, understood this drama between his employer and his employer's son; the man waited patiently before snatching up the coins. My father's triumph was complete. He embarrassed his father. For once it was not my father who was silent, immobile, but his father instead. He spurned the thing his father most valued: money.

The second story is set at the same time or perhaps a few years later. Here, too, my father emerged the victor, winning something from his father.

*My father in
Leipzig, 1909.*

During the preparation for one Pesach, I am sure it was in 1914. — ~~before~~ in the spring before the beginning of WWI. Father was decanting a keg of sweet Tokay wine, ~~I knew it came~~ it was imported from Hungary and ~~it~~ filled twenty four bottles. It was quite exciting. The bottles & corks lined up, Boris holding the funnel and father carefully tipping the keg, holding it firmly by the ~~containers chymes~~ chimbs — barrel's edges. While waiting for a bottle to be filled I wiped up some of the spilled wine a licked my fingers. "You're not supposed to do that," Boris said angrily & slapped my face. His hand was wet with wine & left the imprint of his palm. Father looked up and exclaimed at Boris, "Look what you've done. You've bloodied his cheeks." The slap had not hurt, but just the same I was gladdened w/ Pa's concern.

This current of violence caught my attention. I recalled the raised hatchet, my father's fantasy of hurling himself out a window. My sister Carol had told me that our father had recounted to her the times that his father beat him and his brothers. I thought, too, of the tensions between my grandfather and his brother George: shouting at Boris, did my grandfather recall times when he had also struck his younger brother, as Boris had slapped my father? No, I decided, this was not a secret. It was much more common for men to hit their sons back in those times, almost a paternal responsibility not to spare the rod. What linked the two stories was not my father's fear of violence but rather his desperate craving for affection, his wish for his father simply to praise him for learning Hebrew rather than carrying out the fatuous charade of angels dropping coins. This story ends on a note that I find sad rather than frightening: my father's willingness to accept such scraps of attention, "I was gladdened w/ Pa's concern."

I notice how rarely my grandfather gave my father any attention at all. In these two longer stories, as in many of the earlier ones, my grandfather is not alone with my father; rather, other people are present as well. My grandfather is in motion, passing from one place to another, one activity to another: leaving on a train trip, attending to his employees, decanting wine; his attention turns to my father and then quickly moves away. Almost without exception, there is some dispute, often minor, usually not violent: will my grandfather reveal to his children

Father-
notes

which side he favors in the war; will my father have a second drink of punch, my grandfather a second plate of soup; how should my father wear his watch; will my father accept the coin.

These elements all appear in the third, and longest, vignette, a story that my father apparently took very seriously. He took the step, quite definitive for this series of documents, of stapling together the different slips of paper on which the story is written. In all the other instances in this box, he bound papers together with paper clips or simply placed them in a folder. These different pieces of paper contain fragments of a story that spreads over many decades, from Germany to the years in New York after 1921, to a move to Chicago in 1944, and to the preparations in 1950 for the return to New York, where my parents remained until they moved to California in 1986.

Library — passed a shelf like my own bookcase. A book with loose cover — surprised to see A my own copy of The Long Journey. 1st vol. What is it doing here? I examine it, and see ~~has several~~ there are a # of decals pasted on the inside cover. Flip the pages of the book and half sheets fall out — ~~Some are there~~ There are typed poems. Some in english and others in german — wherever there was a question of the complete meaning of a sentence, there was a correction, written ~~in~~ with red ink, in the mother tongue or the adopted language, in contrast and furtherance. How can I ~~to~~ bring this volume back home, to its rightfull place? The books in the library are magnetized & a bell rings when ~~th~~ a volume is carried out, unauthorized. = the typed sheets are half size of the regular 8 × 10 examine the sheets closer = Some of them are carbon copies, I saved for myself, having sent the orig. to my correspondants receipients ~~to on~~ in distant places. Well, there is nothing to be done, in this case, when my own book is in the wrong place, I'll have to look for another book, ~~as yet~~ its contents unfamiliar as yet, ~~th~~ to take its place —

When I reviewed this dream, after breakfast, I recognized the origin ~~behind the metaphor~~ transfered into a metaphor.

In a ~~he~~ matters of facts it originated seventy years back, when I was nine years old, ~~or~~ or to pinpoint it more precisely, two years after that memorable visit ~~trip~~ to Russia in 1911, when ~~we~~ the family traveled there to celebrate Boris' Bar Mitzwah.

Returning to pertinent facts. My father's brother & his wife — my uncle Mottel and Aunt ~~reis~~ came for a visit to Leipzig — for the purpose to consult a famous physician for the state of my aunt's state of health. They had a present for me, ahead in time for the intended purpose — my own Bar Mizwah, still three years ~~in th~~ ahead, in the future.

They ~~gave~~ presented me with a fat volume. With black embossed covers and at least six inches thick. It was the Tanach [Bible] — I looked at the pages with much interest.

The ~~text in~~ Hebrew text, was ~~on in~~ on the right hand column, in potent black letters, the left hand column carried the German translation, in ~~German,~~ Gothic type. What impressed me most, was the heading, Caput. followed by roman numerals — at the beginning of a series of paragraphs. Kaputt, ~~in German~~ defines in the German language something being broken, — it was not until many years later, I learned that ~~Kapu~~ Caput. means heading or beginning. = Kapitel, or in English, Chapter — the beginning of another story.

My father said "I'll ~~give~~ reward you with a quarter, if you'll read the book from cover to cover." I never earned the quarter. I carried this book with me, in all ~~the~~ of my migrations, from Leipzig in 1916 to ~~Malmö~~ — Chemnitz — to Malmö, to N.Y — to Chicago — ~~1950~~ ~~and~~ the stress of The handling, ~~the~~ and shipment to other locations ~~had~~ had their effect on the condition of the Book, the cover separated from the binding, the first ~~pages~~ leaves and the last ones became loose and were lost. When we decided to leave Chicago in 1950 — I decided not to ~~take the Book~~ preserve the book, I'd never read it, and it was in tatters — I knew, a sacred book must not be discarded and become a thing of indifferent fate. The law insists on a burial — And that is what I did — Put the volume in a box and buried it in the backlot. — Since then I think ~~often~~ of that enduring Book. I have read many others that manifest a believable ~~truth~~ — doctrine

I was struck with my father's uncertainty over the book: whether to read it, how to treat it, whether to carry it on each move, what to do with it in his dream library. The story also impressed me with its parallels to the story of the Hebrew tutors and the dropped coin: here my father never read the book and did not receive the money that his father offered; there he read the passages easily and rejected the money that his father tried to give him. In neither case was there a balance between the child's accomplishment and the parent's praise or reward, nor was there an affirmation of ability or of worth. Absent, too, was any sense of purpose in learning Hebrew other than as a gesture of submission to a patriarchal will. Between them there was at most a mutual recognition — indirect, clumsy, wounding.

Why, then, did my father not write up this story into a definitive version? I do not think that he was impeded by the complexity of weaving together the elements of the story: the gift from the aunt and uncle, the task his father assigned, the burial of the book, the dream. He often wrote of memory, of incidents that connect past, present, and future, and he welcomed the opportunity to tell his dreams. (I witnessed the same scene on dozens of mornings: my father at the breakfast table, recounting a dream to my mother, who bustled, preparing, serving, and clearing up the meal, readying herself to go to work, not listening to his dream; my father not quite acknowledging her lack of attention, pausing perhaps when she left the room for a few moments, stopping sometimes in frustration, sometimes at the end of the tale.) Was the pain in the story delayed, surfacing only in the dream, still too immediate after seventy years to permit summation, telling? It may have been. Closely linked to whatever the emotional obstacle was that left the tale untold, though, was another obstacle and another uncertainty: the book's name. This jumble of names appears in the story itself — most immediately in his confusion over Caput, but also in his repeated capitalization of *B* in Book, drawing here on other recollected words where *B* was indeed capitalized: the Bible, and Buch, the German word for book.

At three separate points he tries to tell the name of the book. At one point he writes:

TANAKH — OLD TESTAMENT
Torah — Pentateuch
Nevi-im — Prophets Ketuvim — Hagiographia

In this approximation, he links the Jewish Bible — the Tanakh, as he spells it here — with a book known in the wider Western Christian world as the Old Testament, an appropriate name for a book that was nearly forty years old when he buried it, and a testament as well, an inheritance. After the first line, though, my father writes as a Jew: Christ is not God, there is no New Testament, no need to divide the Bible into Testaments; instead the Bible is composed of three sections, which he lists. The Torah, unitary, complete, dictated by God to Moses, for which the English, or Christian, term is derived from the Greek *pentateuch*, five scrolls, whose English names were among the first of the many words that I memorized at Sunday school, as if they were one word, seventeen syllables, Genesis-Exodus-Leviticus-Numbers-Deuteronomy, the Torah divided into sections that are read to the congregation in a yearly cycle every Sabbath morning. Then Nevi-im, Nevi'im, even silences difficult to transcribe, how to render the gap between the *i*'s, how to find an equivalent in English to the meaningful soundless pause denoted by the Hebrew *aleph*: "prophets" is the translation of the Hebrew word, a plural, the speech of people, men mostly but not exclusively, who received signs of one sort or another from God and whose words were filled with divine messages, from whose words are taken the haftorahs, texts also read aloud on the Sabbath. And finally Ketuvim, the writings, writings of kings — David's Psalms, Solomon's three books, Song of Songs, Proverbs, Ecclesiastes — and of others who chronicle the stories of Esther, Job, Ruth, and other tales, less well remembered, these writings all still uniquely holy, some of them read on specific holidays. My father translates Ketuvim as Hagiographia, a slight misrendering of *hagiographa*, a Greek word that means writing about saints, a term that, though widely accepted, is misleading, since it derives from the vaguely idolatrous notion of saints, alien to the Jewish tradition, where people may be wise, righteous, even holy, but never the object of worship, never saints like the icons my father might have seen on his trip to Russia in 1911, like the statues of Mary on Italian lawns in Brooklyn, like the sculpted saints in churches that he visited in Mexico. *T* for Torah, *N* for Nevi'im, *Kh* for Ketuvim (some quirky linguistic rules at work in this last minor shift): an acronym, telling the movement from the unity of God's voice to the plurality of human voices, from the Torah and the immediacy of God's conversations with Moses in the clouds of glory on Mount Sinai to God's withdrawal, to prophetic speech, and then to holy writings, greater and then lesser forms of divine inspiration. It says, *T*, God spoke; *N*, people spoke; *Kh*, people wrote. If a title of a book could make up a narrative, it is this one: this word "Tanakh" alone contains a book, is a book. And my father knew this division of the Bible well. Most religious scholars would approve, I believe, of his separation of Torah on one line, Nevi-im Ketuvim on the next.

The second note gives a more standard, less exotic spelling for the Tanakh, using *ch* to render the guttural throat-clearing sound found in Hebrew, German, Yiddish, Russian, but not in English:

Pyramids. Palmtrees. Pendulum. | Tanach — Prophets —

Biblical images, surely, images from the Torah, the pyramids built, as some believe, by Jewish slaves under Pharaoh, the palm trees perhaps the date palms, one of the seven goodly plants of the Promised Land: but what pendulum?

The third note turns to the final section of the Tanach, translating Ketuvim once again as Hagiographa, spelling it correctly this time:

Hagiographa —
Psalms, Proverbs
Job
           Canticles, Ruth
Lamentations,
                   Ecclesiates
~~Erteh~~ Esther, Daniel.
Ezra, Nehemiah —
Chronicles —
Sacred Writings
Wisdom of Sirach

The 3rd ~~division~~ of the 3 Jewish divisions of the ~~Hebrew~~ Old Testam

Here he lists the books of Nevi'im in their standard order, though lining them up unevenly on the page, uncertain how to spell Esther, and using for one book a Latin-derived term, Canticles, rather than the name better known to English-speakers, Song of Songs. And then he adds, obscurely, the title of another book, Wisdom of Sirach, accepted, like Proverbs and Ecclesiastes, as a "wisdom text." Like the two books of the Maccabees that contain the story, told each Chanukah, of the Syrian and Greek desecration of the holy temple, Jewish resistance, and the miracle of the lights, it forms part of the Apocrypha, a Greek term again for books that are read, revered, but considered non-canonical, not part of a bible.

And finally my father breaks off partway through the word "testament." Some sudden impulse led him to interrupt the movement of pen across paper, the brief, almost automatic, barely intentional transformation of the word in his mind into the word on the page. Instead he records two intentions in sequence, to write the word and to stop writing it. The conflict between the two was so acute, so unresolved, that he did not take his usual next step of neatly drawing a line through the uncompleted word. Nowhere else, in all his papers that I have read, does he leave a note so abruptly, in midword. Drawing on English, Hebrew, German, Latin, Greek, he could not name the parts of this book, could not name the book itself, the unread buried book still losing its pages in his dreams.

Chapter 4  BROTHER-MAIL

As a child, I was the youngest member of the family, surrounded by people older than me: my parents, a grandmother, a number of aunts and uncles, the thirteen of my sixteen first cousins who, like my two sisters, were born before me. I often heard these relatives tell each other stories about individuals they knew but whom I had never met. As I became conscious of how uninformed I was, I developed an interest in genealogy that began early — I prepared a detailed family tree when I was twelve — and extended beyond the usual limits of kinship. I listened attentively while my mother and sisters, talking about the family ties among our cats, discussed the white paws or kinked tail or friendly disposition that had been passed from one generation to another. The names of my parents' siblings were among the lists I early committed to memory. Like the nine planets from Mercury to Pluto and the seventeen stations on the local subway line from Brighton Beach to DeKalb Avenue, these ordered sets of Orloves and Cohens were crucial facts for me to learn in order to locate myself in a universe that included many unvisited places and unseen people.

The box labeled "MAX ORLOVE" awakened my curiosity as soon as I saw it in my father's study. Of all my father's siblings, Max was the one about whom I knew the least, little more than the humorous juxtaposition of his name with that of his wife, Minnie. This pairing always reminded me not of hemlines (the miniskirt did not appear until after my childhood) but of the paired thermometers that record maximum and minimum temperatures. I knew only the most basic facts about Max's son: his name was Seymour, he lived in Chicago, he had married, he had some children.

My curiosity, though, went beyond the simple desire to explore the unknown. The box reminded me that Max was the only one of the Orlove aunts and uncles about whom I did not know a great deal. I suspected that something had been concealed from me. Had Max violated some basic principle of conduct, offending his siblings so much that they refused to mention him? Surely the fact of his early death in the 1940s could not account for this near-silence. My parents had no reluctance to speak of the dead, or even of death. I could distinguish the living from the dead in the family's stock of anecdotes not from the habits of many other Jewish families — the marking of the names of the deceased with "may they rest in peace," the memorial candles lit on the anniversaries of deaths — but from hearing directly of the deaths of relatives in stories that clearly revealed their characters and their destinies. I often heard of my father's sister Gertrude and her pneumonia in her late twenties, brought on, it was intimated, by the burden of nursing her aging mother-in-law while she also cared for her two young daughters; too devoted to these responsibilities to take care of herself, her health deteriorated, and her daughters were suddenly left motherless.

My lack of knowledge about Max sprang to my mind when I saw his name written on the top of the box. In my first hurried glances through the letters that it contained, I thought that I had found the secret: Max, like my father, had nurtured a private vision of himself as an inventor of a machine that would bring him fame. But no, I soon realized, Max's invention simply proved once more his already-established oddness, and in any case my father's machine, a device that cast shifting colored images on a plastic screen, was more a work of art than of science. Later, more patient readings offered at best a partial solution to the mystery whose existence I had imagined — the letters written after 1930 point to a series of economic failures and to strained relations with his wife, but other uncles experienced these difficulties without being carried, as Max was, outside the orbit of the family's visits and conversations. Nonetheless, I was not disappointed in the letters but was pleased instead with the richness of detail that they gave on topics with which I was already acquainted: Sam Orloff's death, and, more important, the fur business in which the Orlove men worked for several decades. Max, living in Chicago during the years he wrote to my father, worked in this trade, sometimes alone, occasionally for a larger firm, but most often in partnership with the oldest brother Henry. They would buy cheap furs and then cut them and sew them into collars and other goods. Sometimes Max and Henry hired workers, sometimes they worked by themselves. They would fight, dissolve their partnership, and then establish it again. The stationery itself on which Max wrote told the story: they would have new letterhead made up each time they formed a new partnership or moved their shop to a new location.

When I was a child, I had heard many stories from my father about the fur trade, the business in which he had worked for most of his life. I knew that his father, after trading in intestines that he sold to sausage-makers, had shifted to buying and selling furs, or "skins," as I heard them called, sometime before the turn of the century, while all the family was still living in Russia. There were a few humorous tales — my father and grandfather traveled, when they lived in Sweden, to a small town north of Stockholm where the trappers would come to the market in the square, and where, one particularly cold winter morning, they awoke to find the floor of their room covered with ice, my father having knocked over a full chamber pot in the night — and one moment of unmitigated success, when my grandfather sent the first shipment of furs after World War I from Sweden to New York, where prices had been driven high by postwar prosperity and by the scarcity of furs because of wartime interruptions in trade.

Most of my father's stories, though, presented errors in judgment, missed opportunities, and angry recriminations. From his pauses and sighs, from the intense look on his face, I grasped the urgency of his task of keeping these stories alive. I believed that I needed to remember the events in each story and to reconstruct the long sequence of shifting relations among my grandfather, his sons, and the series of shadowy partners that marked the family fur business, whose eventual decline ended my grandfather's vision that the Orloves would be to furs what the Rothschilds were to banking. Despite my genuine fascination with the epic struggles of the Orlove men — much more appealing to me than my grandmother's proverbs — and my wish to please my father by learning the stories, I felt that I was a failure as a listener, unable to register all the details that he told me with such passion. Nor could I remedy my deficiencies, since he would give me an angry look when I asked him questions about some particular aspect of a story, a fierce glare that lasted a brief but painful moment before he returned to his telling. After several occasions on which I felt that my questions did nothing other than prove my inadequacy as the recipient of family history, I would simply listen, taking in the stories as best I could. I cannot now recall, for example, whether it was my uncle Henry or Boris who had been sent, at age sixteen, by my grandfather to sell furs in Brussels — or was it Amsterdam? — where a cousin of my grandmother's — or had it been a business acquaintance of my grandfather's? — found him, staying in an expensive hotel and spending the profits wildly; had the empty bottles on the floor contained champagne or cognac, and did my father agree with his father, who blamed his son for wasting the earnings, or with his mother, who faulted her husband for sending so young a child off on so important an errand?

Unlike my position as a passive listener to my father's tales, I could read the letters from Max at my own pace, returning to those that interested me and skimming others. I began to fill in the gaps in my knowledge. I learned not only particular individuals and events but also the whole set of ties that had stirred my father so deeply, the bonds with the other men in the family that had impelled him to speak to me in such a way that I could neither listen as he wished nor stop listening.

To the letters themselves, then. I include portions of twelve of the thirty letters that I found, cutting material mostly to eliminate repetition. My editing has been very minor, as it has been with quotations from my father's papers. I have retained Max's abbreviations, which often crop up when he wrote in haste. Only two of these, I think, require clarification, "pcs." for "pieces" and "sq." for "squirrel." Aside from Wagreich, a business associate, the proper names refer to relatives. I will list the siblings once again in their order of birth: Henry (married to Jane), Max, Bernard (whom I knew as Boris), my father Robert, Elizabeth, Howard, Gertrude, and Milton. George was the youngest brother of my grandfather, and Sam and Ben Orloff were more distant relatives of his, probably cousins. It is possible that Ben Orloff and my grandfather Benjamin were named, more or less around the same time, for some recently deceased Benjamin of an earlier generation, possibly a great-uncle. The one genealogical link of which I am certain is that Sam's one son was Edgar, a close friend of my father's. I do not know whether Ben and Sam were brothers or cousins. Their alternate spelling of the last name suggests some of the history of the people who carried it westward, shifting Orlowski from Cyrillic to Roman characters as they moved from Russia to Germany and Sweden, dropping the final syllable in America, and not coordinating its spelling. I have seen another variant, Orlow, written on postcards that George's wife, Vera, had received from relatives still in Russia.

Max also includes a number of terms from the fur trade. Many of these are self-explanatory or unimportant. I will define only two. "Fitch" appears in the 1953 edition of *The American College Dictionary* (the volume to which my parents often turned when they were playing Scrabble and one challenged a word that the other had made) as: "1. the European polecat, Mustela putorius. 2. its fur. Yellow fitch is often dyed to imitate other furs." For "plate," I had to turn to a more complete source, *Webster's Third New International Dictionary*. This work includes sixty distinct senses in which plate can be used as a noun, of which the sixteenth is "a square or oblong piece of fur composed usu. of waste fur and small inferior pieces that are matched and sewn together and used for inexpensive garments or linings."

The first item is the only postcard in the box. The "holidays" to which it refers are Rosh Hashanah and Yom Kippur.

> Sept 25, '24
>
> Dear Brother,
> Am getting married to-day — Why have I got no mail from you.
>
> > Happy holidays
> > Regards to all
> > Max

I wondered about this card: could Max really not have told the family earlier about his plans to marry? I do not think that his wedding to a woman of an Eastern European Jewish background similar to his own would have been an unannounced, impulsive trip to City Hall. The resentment at a lack of recognition from other members of the family, though, keeps cropping up in Max's letters, as does his tendency, apparent in the next letter, to write openly of his hopes and disappointments to my father.

Oct. 3rd '25

Dear Robert:

It is late now and I read your letter, which tuched my own philosophical string to answer you your last part first. Philosophy means (Philos — the friend — sophia wisdom) The Friend of Wisdom. Schoppenhauer went farther than you — he said: The world will end the sun wil shrivvel into a cold black star — all life will have been in vain and why do people built Citys & Empires and struggle with all the knowledge of such end. Nitzsche said: Each man is an individual superman he must be free to do what he pleases and none to stop his desires. Plato wrote the Utopia (nowhere it means — no place) and explains the cooperation of mans work would make the life a joyful time. All were right in there sense and explanation but none advocated utter idleness, as such a thing is abhorrable for any thinking being even if a man would decide to do nought he would have to force himself to do nothing and this would be a strain on his energys anyways so he better get busy and work. Then arises the question when is enough work done — when shall a man start and when finish — this is a riddle too and each mans capacity is different in many degrees — but one thing is certain he must work for this, what he needs immediately. His intellectual and or manual labor are the scale how long and what kind of work he must do or can do. But then again comes the future and for that most deeds are done. A man wants little, ask anybody what he expects in this world — though it is little it is much very much and the nerarer he gets to it the happier he becomes and all in all it is for freedom and freedom is the fulfillment of the free will desire no matter how different each mans idea of his freedom may be — he must work to attain it!

You see I could spinn this letter into a very long discussion I do not know if my letter is interesting in the style I'm writing now — but I'm tired and like to close the epistle.

I'm really glad that mother moved into a more convenient flat and neighborhood.

About business I'm awfully busy — I might make a lot of money — But believe me it is not easy a man must be on the alert to keep apace with the competition and dishonesty of this world.

I had a greek working it took me 4 months to find out that he stole each working day enough bellies to make one plate. Think how I had to figure, weigh and count the bellies, etc. etc. untill I noticed it untill I was sure — untill there was no mistake — and then the final wind up with that man I kicked him out of my place, and am doing his work now as I cannot find a suitable person to do it as my operator is a very fast worker and I have my shop working in a system like a clock I have about $200 payroll every week, naturally I sell what the men work up and turn the money around before they get their pay as I'm watching that too! 2 days work pay the labor for week 2 days work pay the material for week 1½ days work and finished material are my profits which goes right back into business.

I received Henrys telegram but am unable to send the martens before Monday or Thuesday as I have them out on memo. I have ready for shipment 400 gray fox tails 100 russ. Foxpaws 10# beaver 15# of white Bellies how much are white Bellies in N.Y. now?

Thats all so far

With best regards for Mother as always.

Max

Its exactly one o'clock now. Naturally I'll keep on shipping for Henry — but his prices seem far below.

The next letter shows Max in another moment of elation, not about philosophical matters but about the possibility of a new business partnership and, even more, about the birth of his son (who was, aside from Henry's illegitimate daughter born in Germany in 1911, the first of the generation of Orlove cousins to which I belong):

May 19. — '26

Dear Brother: —

Oh, do I have a boy a grand fine fellow and I like him, I'm wild about him, I'm going nuts for him. Its a swell kid and I surely will try my best for him. Oh, gosh, I never knew that such a happy feeling could overcome me as it did now that I know I have a son, a kid, my own, my flesh, my blood and he looks like me and he also has the famous Orlove curl in front of his head, Mother knows what I mean I'm sure.

Naturally all my spare time is taken up with my sonny and even when he sleeps I am fond of watching him and watching him without getting tired.

I have now decided to make the circumcision [ordinarily held on the eighth day after birth] on June the 4th at the same time with the "Pidion ha ben" [the ceremony held when a woman's first child is a boy, usually held on the thirtieth day] you see the little one was born under condition where this delay is necessary. I took him and the Mother, which is feeling excellently home on last Saturday. If his Grandfather wants to come to the "brith" [circumcision] he will have the honer of being "sandikeh" [the man who holds the infant boy on his lap during the circumcision] and I myself invite him to come.

About business I have very little to write as I'm busy making plates for the need of a living, but when I'm around buying bellies for my own use and I pick up something I buy it along and so I have one bag ready with very good stuff which Ill ship out before Saturday.

The Greek with the 300 paws is bosh as I told father at that time, if a man has no goods but expects to get it, then its week to place hopes of buying it.

The furrier in the Sq. paws has one bag ready I offered him $4 but he asked $10.00 although I'm going to buy it tomorrow morning with some compromise from him.

Bellies are here high. I think if you can pick up beige, rose marten and coco for me up to $4.50 a lb. I could use 20–30 lbs. but only these collers only.

What is most on my mind and I intend to write to you is, that you should come down here and work with me in Chicago, I do not want to write much about as it is your own will and chance to make real money with almost no start at all.

You can average at least $60 weekly very, very easy buying pieces and in the hight of the 2–3 month season $100.00 *everyday*.

I will keep on making the plates and you on the outside buying the stuff and if we will work in partners here on both no want nor worry will grind us down and the profit on the bellie plates is enough to compensate for the easiest living here — and the profit on the pcs. is all gravy.

Write me about it. Father could take Howard in your stead.

If Mother depends on part of your earning capacity it can be arranged that she shall have at least that what you are offering here now.

Now I'm meaning all this for your benefit as you must get out of the rut you will remain otherwise in N.Y.

I surely see some help for me too, as this affair is not a one man affair here. One buys, one picks and makes stuff ready. You have seen sposmadic possibility here in Chi. but when you'll be here we can work it in a way which will surprise you yet.

Give my kindest and best regards for all especially dear Mother.

As always

Max.

Also the very best regards from my wife, and she tells me to write and say that she will write personally to Mother as soon as she feels a little stronger.

Write soon.

Did Milton get the Book I send him.

I became absorbed in reading these letters of Max's about the fur business not only because they told me a great deal about my father but also because they fascinated me as an anthropologist. Of all the papers that I found in my father's study, they are the ones about which I could most easily write an article for a professional journal. I was particularly intrigued because Max's partnerships with Henry could be seen in two different ways: as family relations (a part of the society) or as business relations (a part of the economy). At times my thoughts centered on the business side. In my imaginary anthropological article, I could present the partnerships as family businesses. The outline of this argument is clear: the market for cheap fur items like the plates made of squirrel bellies could best be filled by small firms without a heavy investment in machinery and without large expenses for permanent workers. It would be efficient to have at least two people working together, so that one could sew while the other bought and sold. It made more sense to take on a partner, who would have more incentive to work diligently (and less incentive to cheat or steal), than to hire someone on an hourly basis or even on a piece rate, and what partner could be better trusted than a relative; hence the family business, even though it ran the risk of collapsing because of its small size and the massive competition from other firms. The twist in the analysis comes because the family relationship between the partners that supported the business also weakened it. The partners were tied together as brothers but separated as husbands and fathers in different households. Each partner could accuse the other of fudging expenses, of taking money from the business for personal ends, and, above all, of caring about his wife more than his brothers. The instability in family businesses, then, came not only from the competition in the fur trade but from their family basis as well.

Alternatively, my imaginary article could emphasize the family side, examining not just the ties between the partners but the links among all the relatives, the other brothers and the father as well. They were all involved with one another, making deals, extending credit, whether or not they had legally incorporated as partnerships. It was advantageous for them to be spread over different cities, for buying and selling from one another, and for passing on information about prices in different places. In short, they were a business family rather than a family business. If the goals of a family business are to avoid bankruptcy and show a profit, the goals of a business family are less well defined. The brothers worked hard, impelled not only by the need to earn money but by other desires as well: for approval from their father, for affection from their mother, for recognition of the family's name by other Jewish families in the fur trade. In this alternative view, the risks of failure were greater. After a bankruptcy, the members of a family business could cease being partners and could then move on to make arrangements for their debts and to look for other kinds of work. The members of a business family, though, would remain relatives and could never leave one another, could never end the accusations and counteraccusations of blame for their failure.

To appear in an anthropological journal, an article about the Orlove fur business would need to resolve the differences between these two approaches — the family business and the business family — by discussing more general theoretical and methodological concerns. However, I wanted to take my understanding of the tensions within the family businesses — or business families — in a different and more personal direction. These letters helped me recognize why my father fled that world, and why he was so drawn to art. As I read about the disputes among my uncles and my grandfather, I could sense how he despised the petty connivings of the fur business, and how noble painting and drawing seemed to him. The calm solitude of his study, I realized, was a refuge from the tense intimacy of the fur shops, with their bickering, conspiracies, and outbursts of rage.

In writing this book, I am returning to these matters of family and business. In some sense my father and I are partners, as his brothers were: I am simply assembling pieces (of paper rather than of fur) that he collected, adding some of my own to them, and finding a buyer. Had we attempted this book while he still had been living, would we have fought as Max and Henry did? It would have been impossible, I think, for us to advance very far on such a project. I can imagine us in long discussions of single sentences or even words, much as Max and Henry debated the purchase of lots of squirrel bellies. Would I have just written chapters on my own, and then asked for his consent for their publication? Our discussions would have rambled on, I think, never reaching any definitive resolution. At any rate, my father certainly hoped that his words would reach other readers, as a passage from his diaries in 1931 shows:

> I save every piece of scrap paper, I ever scribble a note on. I don't want to lose any thought I have. As if I were afraid to lose part of myself. Someday I would like to put them into a book, that of course would take a lot of time. And I waste away enough time as it is.

I believe that he thought that I could help him in this project. He had told me on several occasions that he would leave his diaries to me after he died. I recall less dramatic moments as well: his appreciation for the manila folders that I brought him when he sorted through his papers, his interest in my comments on the collages that he made of newspaper clippings and pictures from magazines. I can imagine at least one sort of book of his work that he would have liked — a slim volume, perhaps less than one hundred pages, printed on an off-white paper of thick stock, with rough untrimmed edges rather than smooth ones. This book would have contained a series of loosely connected paragraphs, some short, some long, all reflections on abstract themes of Art, Life, and Time. I cannot know how he would have reacted to this longer book, though I suspect he would have liked at least some parts of it. I have sometimes wondered which sections would have most gratified him, and which revelations of family turmoil would have distressed him. I have wondered, too, whether my inability to resolve these questions about his views has allowed me to have an active dialogue with him in my mind, a dialogue that impels me to keep writing.

Early one morning, after a night when I had stayed up late to proof-read a draft of a chapter of this book, I found myself lying awake in bed, still groggy from not enough sleep. I heard my father's voice outside the bedroom door, asking in a solicitous tone, "Ben, can I get you a cup of coffee?" I was touched that he knew how much I would like one. My awareness of his concern and my gratitude for his offer remained with me when I awoke and realized that I had been dreaming of lying in bed, when I took a shower and dressed, when I sat at the kitchen table and slowly drank a cup of coffee.

I have had only one dream in which my father mentioned the book specifically. It was a short dream, in which we walked down a street together. In the middle of a conversation, he commented to me, "Don't forget to mention my naturalization papers." I take this injunction to be a correction of what was a minor error of omission in his view, and thus to be a suggestion as well that he felt that there were no errors of commission at all. And so I refer to the papers here, in the one section of the book that is literally ghost-written. About this document that made him an American citizen, issued on January 20, 1928, I can only note that, despite the important position that the swearing-in of the new citizens often occupies in films and novels about immigrants, this event (which was held, in his case, in the Bronx County Court House) did not attract much notice in his family. My father did not mention these naturalization papers in the book that he wrote about his mother at the time, nor did Max make any reference to them in the following letters to my father, written late in 1927 and early in 1928.

Dec. 25 1927

Dear Robert:

I owe a letter to Mother first, but as I think that a letter to you, also satisfies her desire to hear from me and if this letter is not going to be long, I will write to her to-night too — otherwise I again must postpone it.

First of all I am greatly worried about the conditions at home in general and individually. I have given to Elizabeth a fountain pen, while she was her, and not one regard did she write to me, well I'll swallow that.

Bernard [in New York] asked my adress from Henry [in Chicago], what, can he not get same from you or mother [both in New York]?

The old man and his actions are an unanswerable riddle. Above all I worry about Mother, she needs happiness and during all these years I have not felt that she was happy. On the 9th — I awaited the day for many days — I sent her a telegram to congratulate her [her birthday was December 9], but saw, that all that, was so insignificant with what I owe her that tears came in my eyes and when I reminded Henry of the 9th he rushed out to send a telegram too, but I'm still waiting for the conformation whether my telegram reached Mother — if not — please write me — as I have called a messenger and paid him the money and I want to be sure whether he dispatched same or pocketed the money. Please do not fail to write me about the telegram.

Business is quite, but as my moneys keep me quite too in business I cannot kick. I'm making Sq. Bellie plates and knock out about $100.00 a week and am contendet.

In one of your letters you wrote to Henry you wanted a proposition in business, I do not know what your aim is but know I can give you one, and you can discard it as soon as you feel like.

Max then describes his scheme: my father will buy squirrel bellies in New York and ship them to Chicago, where Max will make them up

*Brother-mail*

into plates. He will then sell them to a relative of his wife's who works in the coat business. Max then closes the letter with an exhortation:

> I am not giving you the proposition that you shall long deliberate about, no but knowing that you are idle now, and that buying bellies is clean and quick, and above all I think it will pay you handsomely. I am asking you for your own sake try it, you must, you will and you can; because there is money in for you, happiness for Mother and the time where I have to run for bellies will be devoted to work and if necessary I will work late and Sundays; now is the time, the oppertunity is tested and your risk is none, just try it, Plates can be sold!!

> Write me immediately do not forget about the Telegram with very best regards to Mother

As always your Brother

Max

> P.S. The most import: the baby is swell, smarter every day he boxes with me already, he tells me stories in baby kauderwelsch [gibberish]. He listens dilligently what he is told to do, and does it. He does not wet the diapers anymore (Hurray) it was some job sometimes!! He likes cod liver oil like an Eskimo. Sings a song like Caruso (to me at least!) Plays with mothers soldiers like a General, names all cats & dogs in Elisabeths book and laugh at some and yells at some. Talks (screams) to me in the telephone. He can dance, oh boy does he dance.

> Ben Orloff comes up sometimes, and boy can Ben eat a combined Sailor & Soldier and the Baby imitaties his actions a Ben sayd "a Bandit." I am going to take some pictures of him soon, before the year ends.

> He already wears the Grand pas silk suit from Paris and looks very beautiful in them.

Max.

> P.S. The letter to Mother I must postpone, to my regret.

M.

Squirrel bellies, it occurs to me, must be very small, smaller than the paragraphs on this page. I think of the effort involved in cutting the bellies from the rest of the hide. It must be difficult to sew them together, too; wasting a quarter-inch all around would make a proportionally greater difference than on larger skins. I think, too, how far removed the 1990s are from the era in which fur coats were common. They now seem a luxury as dated as the sorts of women commonly imagined to have worn them, heiresses, debutantes, starlets, an item associated in the present with such contexts as the opera and country clubs. My firmest proof that furs were once quite ordinary comes from a series of candid photographs taken on the New York subway between 1938 and 1941 by Walker Evans, best known for his pictures of southern sharecroppers, especially the illustrations that accompanied the text in James Agee's *Let Us Now Praise Famous Men.* The subway photographs were taken during the winter—Walker used his coat to conceal his camera. Over eighty of them were published several decades later in a book entitled *Many Are Called.* Most of these candid shots show one or two people, sitting across the subway car from him. Many of the women in his pictures, chatting with each other or sitting silently, are wearing fur coats or cloth coats with fur collars, though they do not otherwise appear to be rich. Some men also have fur collars on their coats. The last photograph, taken down the length of the car, shows a larger number of passengers—a more representative sample, in social science terms. A number of women with fur collars appear in this photograph, which centers on a blind musician, a chipped enamel cup suspended from his accordion.

When I was a child, my father had advanced beyond Max and Henry's level, up from squirrels to rabbit skins, which, if not as luxurious as mink or even fox, were more valuable than squirrel bellies. His job then was as a patternmaker, one of the most highly skilled of the positions within the needle trades generally. He designed fur toys in the 1950s and early 1960s, much as he had designed fur hats in Chicago in the mid-1940s. In a technical and economic sense, it was a bit like figuring out jigsaw puzzles, trying to make efficient use of the irregularly shaped furs with as little waste as possible. Artistic skills were also crucial, since my father had to understand the visual and tactile properties of the furs and the final product. The patterns themselves were like patterns for making clothes, pieces of cardboard (the paper used in dress patterns would have been too soft for fur, which is much heavier than cloth) that were used to guide the cutter's knife.

*My father at work in the fur district in New York, c. 1960. Note the pattern pieces hanging on the wall.*

I recall the heavy brown cardboard pieces of old patterns hanging over his worktable in the house on East 17th Street in Brooklyn. I saw furs less often, on my trips with him to the fur district in lower Manhattan: a subway ride, a walk of a few blocks past old brick buildings, then entering the door of one of the deep, narrow shops, the owner striding rapidly over to us, to shake my father's hand, to look carefully at me and to address a few questions to me (it mattered to both men that my replies should be clever enough to show my intelligence, yet still sufficiently respectful to demonstrate my good manners). I could walk around the shop a bit, not drifting far out of sight behind the stacks of furs and enormous rolls of brown wrapping paper, not intruding on the Italian and Puerto Rican workers at the tables far in the back, but able nonetheless to touch the soft fur of a sample left out on a counter, to run my fingers along the firm white underside of a rabbit skin tacked out on a tanning frame. My father would suddenly summon me back, and I would accompany him and his associate to a nearby restaurant. The beginnings of the meals stick especially in my mind: absorbed in their conversation, the two men ignored the menus in front of them, and I nibbled leisurely from the great variety of rolls in the basket on the table, from bowls of pickles that always contained the hard green tomatoes whose firm texture and vinegary odor are still clear in my memory.

"He blew us to lunch," my father would announce to my mother after our return home, suggesting also that the business exchange went well. My parents would discuss the encounter in great detail, and then my mother would ask me how the food was, but I could not fully convey how exotic the restaurant and the whole fur district seemed, and also how privileged and comfortable I felt in the presence of my father and the other man. I could at best suggest how content I was with the meal, with the entire outing, by telling her about the cheese blintz or the kasha, none of us seeing anything unusual in the fact I had eaten in a dairy restaurant. In the heavily Jewish fur district, many restaurants assured their more observant clients that they scrupulously followed the prohibitions on mixing milk and meat by omitting one or the other entirely from their menus. How distant that time seems to me now, in this era of environmentalism, vegetarianism, and animal rights, that furriers might select a meatless lunch, innocent of the thought that people decades in the future might claim a connection between eating animals and selling their hides.

When I read Max's letters in 1990 and 1991, I found echoes of these memories from the 1950s and early 1960s, and of my first lengthy visit to Peru as well. I spent the summer there in 1971, traveling throughout the highland region near Cusco in order to choose a town or village to which I hoped to return for a stay of a year or two to do the research for my doctorate. The place that most attracted me was the town of Sicuani, located at an elevation of 11,500 feet in a narrow river valley surrounded by mountains that rose several thousand feet higher. In addition to the beauty of the town, I also had professional reasons for selecting it: few anthropologists had worked there before; a half-day train ride from Cusco, it was far enough from a city for me to feel as if I were living in a remote place, but not so far that it was difficult to get to; I found the economic themes that interested me — a sizable market and branch offices of the export firms that purchased wool from the local Indian peasants. But something else struck me much more immediately and powerfully: the dozens of small shops run by furriers. They made rugs, hats, slippers, and even some stuffed toy animals from the skins of young alpacas. I visited several of these shops during my brief visit that summer, drawn by the familiarity of the worktables, the cardboard patterns, the tanning frames, the piles of skins. I did not speak of these shops to anyone when I returned to the United States. They were an irrelevant coincidence, I thought, separate from my principal goal of examining the great themes in Latin American studies: poverty, exploitation, peasant rebellions. Nonetheless, these shops often came to mind when I prepared grant proposals to fund my field research. I got to know a number of the furriers during my seventeen-month stay in Sicuani in the early 1970s. When I returned to Berkeley, lonely, frightened at the prospect of finding a job, I had difficulty in imagining how I might begin writing my dissertation. My professors demanded a first chapter. Desperate for something that I could begin to write about, I turned to my field notes on the furriers and to my memories of them, and prepared a short section that grew quickly into the first chapter. The rest followed within a year. In 1977, the dissertation was published as a book, a copy of which my father kept in his study. A photograph on page 105 shows a young woman with two thick braids and a trace of a smile. She is posed behind a worktable. The caption reads:

> This woman is the wife of the owner of a medium-sized furrier shop in Sicuani. Note the partially sewn rug on the table and the pieces of patterns hanging on the wall.

From another furrier shop in Chicago, Max wrote to his brother:

> Dear Robert: —
> This will be a wheighty, interresting and long letter and therefore when boring things will occure, please excuse then, as I do owe you a letter.
> Naturally the first and most important question arriving with this letter will be how is Max getting along with Henry.
> You probably will remember how the business was all conducted

*Furrier shop in Peru, photographed during my field work in Sicuani, 1972. Reproduced with permission of Academic Press, Inc.*

and it went on the same way untill I noticed that Henry was about $300.00 overdrawn on me — Now there was also an item of $288.00 which Henry took when he moved from New York the Furniture but he told me at that time that this money he wants to take care of his investment; Then there were the $25.00 which Mother got monthly and knowing Henry I told him that this money should go as a business expence but if he'd try any monkey business and burst up the business I'd want it as his drawing as Mother applied this money on a $1000.00 loan he made from here.

Well so were the situations and I kept quite in spite that Henry would nag me and nag me right along — so many little things and big things came up it was excruciating to stand them.

It came a time where I needed a lot of money to take care of my Canadian holdings [Max had spent some time in Montreal, where he served in the army during World War I; he had been in partnership with Henry, who was living in Chicago then] and I sold 200 acres of woods, with this money I cleared all my incumberance on all holdings and had $400 left. I took $200.00 and put it into the business with the understanding to withdraw it any time I want to — or better as I needed it. As I thought if I'd need it quickly I should have it — but I never needed it — I figured to use it when I'll move into my new house and buy furniture with it.

Henry knew it — and surely he should have never objected to all that — how could he — I never objected when he needed money for assistance, When he moved, or when he bought Jane a 180.00 cloth coat — but when I made Minnie a Fur collar out of pieces he harped on me for picking the best pieces and devoting my time in making the piece of Fur and not attending to business — but he sat around reading or playing bridge or going to a show or going to look at stamps. I said nothing — but kept quite.

I spoke to him about all this with an understanding heart, and I never wanted to hurt him — I could never object of his taking money when he needed some, but I told him that I will not take less than he — but I'll draw as much as he does after he took his sum not before; I thought that would curb him — once he had to pay Sam Strissik $185.00 he took the money and later he had Wagreich send some dyed white fox tails to him which he entered as a purchase of $50.00 to try to reduce the $185.00.

Than I spoke to him about the leisure time there was and we should turn it into profits so we ordered some Furriers Suppleys — but Henry never went out to sell anything — so I took 2 special days tried hard and disposed of all stuff naturally with a profit.

And so it went on — and Henrys drawings increased with the excuse I need the money. Jane helped him plenty to spend and regard me as a nuisance to Henrys business. And when Elizabeth was here she prejudiced her so much against the Familie I married into that it was no wonder to me the way she acted towards them — I'm very sorry that much things happened Elizabeth will not admitt that she was influenced but let it go the way it is — only I want to show you how Jane influences Henry — anytime anywhere with or without company if any one of the Orloves are mentioned she sayd, the beast the dog (Sam Orloff) etc. and all that works little by little — when Henry was here and Jane in N.Y. yet I happened to read several letters of Janes to Henry and they were horrible — but if Elizabeth wants to defend her against Minnie or anyone — tell here to read this line — Henry once received a letter from Jane wherein she wrote: "*Elizabeth acts or acted like a mad woman*" it worked on him no matter how little.

And so I had to contend with that too. Many a times when Jane saw me she would not ask how is Minnie how is the baby not even during a time while sonny was ill.

I seemed to have made a detour here but it was necessary to see the scenery.

In Fathers letter Henry writes that I bet on Dempsey and that I gambled — that is all bust! — I did bet on Dempsey all right and lost not more than $30.00 with about a dozen people — as you know the fight was in Chicago and people spoke weeks and weeks ahead of it and as I came into contact with many Furriers I was tempted to bet — but I did not bet for gain — but only for sportsmanship — to be a great fellow amongst them so that I was more able to aproach them as a friend to buy the pieces you know what I mean with it.

But the first of October came near and that was the trouble — I bought for over $800.00 I had to pay over $100.00 insurance and one month rent in advance. So I wanted to draw an amount to equalize Henrys drawing — mind you *drawings* only and also my $200.00 which I had put in after selling the bonds. (I received bonds in payment for my 200 acres.)

Naturally there was a hulla balloo — but what could I do — all my hopes — of starting a new home seemed in vain, and I was contented and kept quite and went around to sell some more acres — but time flew — and Henry came around and told me that Elizabeth visit had cost him $200.00 and he must have the money — he too must pay his insurance and he had not paid his September rent and it was past the 15 September.

Well here I was in doubt, and to make things worse Minnie ordered the Furniture from the Factory they wanted a $250 deposit, I had to sign the lease and pay the October rent in advance. And I had given my insurance man $100.00 already. Well I made out the checks for the Furniture $225.00 paid the rent in advance. Then I told Henry about it but I said I'll make the $225.00 for the furniture good as I asked the Furniture man to hold it a few days. I had the other two bonds yet but a little tied up with something — so that was all — and Henry said all right if you'll make the check, good o.k. and I'll see about it, naturally he said all that after long arguments and deeply insulting me. (Well, even the first week he was in Chicago, he said to me you god damn fool and Minnie was present and she can't forget that.)

So at that time we stood at equal drawings even balance.

And here it was aking in Henry he needed over $100.00 for pay his insurance than rent Jane had ordered a Fitch collar and cuffs for over $50.00 and then he had incindary expenses which had to be met — and he felt irritated.

Now the Dempsey fight was over and some told Henry that I had lost on Dempsey — some called up you know it was only a matter of fun and a little money no one man exceeded $5.00 — Henry bet on Tunny well — he could have lost as well as I — but that did not stop him denouncing me.

Our bank balance was low, naturally I knew nothing what Henry had in mind I went on my business as usual. Somebody spoke to me that he needet some beige tails (Ermine) I told Henry who the man was — he took the package sold it for $75.00 when I asked him for the check to be deposited, he jumped around and said I am through with the business — I don't want to stay with you you are using up all moneys, etc. etc.

I heard that often from him but this time it soundet different it soundet not Henry but Henry & Jane.

Well, we'll divide and go apart it suits me I said and I left, but than the same day a check came in for $500.00 and Henry needet money so he did not deposit it in the Bank either but cashed the check for his own use and there I got to talking and I figured up with Henry.

Now the new argument came in he claimes that he investet $1044.26 but out of this investment he once took the above mentioned $288.00 and than as he was the cause of the breaking up of the business I want him to charge himself with the $300.00 Mother received he does not want to do either and I said all-right have it your way and I kept quite.

And so it was a week, Henry got in over $900.00 cash and kept it all, he paid his debt and then he went to buy pieces — from houses I already had the goods and good as bought only waiting for money.

I did not have a cent and I asked Henry on Saturday to give me $10.00 as I had nothing in my pocket — he sneered at me and said no — that worked me up.

Then came a standstill I immediately went raised money sold the bonds deposited the $225.00 I drew for the Furniture in the Bank and went around buying pieces for myself.

But Henry had his energy exhausted, now he sits around and mops around the place he does not go out to buy he runs in to Cohen and asks them to tell me to go back with him and forget all that what happened.

Now I ask you how can I do it or how shall I do it — It is bitter hard — you cannot fully understand how it hurts me to turn him down because I know he will eat up the money in a short while. And than I know how it hurts to be turned down because I was many a time turned down and I know how the blood simmers when the fateful no is said. But I cannot help it for Mothers sake I have not tried to break but Henry did — and now he is sorry — because he is helpless.

And the devision of the business I will let him do the figuring and devical and I'll keep quite, if I'll get something out of it allright — if not — than not. I'm quite and calm. *Henrys* figure show that my assets are about $1000.00 in the business and his I figure are $3500.00. Well let it be so. I do not want to make any more hollaballoos.

One things I know and every concerned knows we both made a nice living when we were together — and why should we not make a living when we are apart.

He made over $15000.00 during the time and lived away out of this summ $10000.00.

Thats that.

Now you surely want to know how my family is getting along. I can write you everything is o.k. Minnie laughed when Henry called her up that we were apart, because he called her often and nothing came out, we stayed together. But when I told here we are going apart she cried. Otherwise she is happy in her new home, I let her pick the furniture and did not mix in and so much more she enjoys it and is happy, we have a beautiful bedroom set, Parlor set, etc. we have 3 rooms in a new and modern Building not far from the Park and good transportation.

And little Seymour — no description can fully justify his escapades, his cleverness and adaptability to ape grown ups.

He'll show you how an old man walks with his hands on his back. He likes to see water run and at any chance he opens all the faucets or continually turns the flush in the toilet.

He liked Herring and pickle and even yells for it. Or he'll go and take all the keys out of the locks takes all things out of the ice box — or builds with the blocks intelligent turrets.

He gets cod liver oil. He has 12 teeth a new large bed for himself a new stroller and a smile to be kissed.

He goes to bed in a happy mood and awakens with a clear healthy jovial voice. Sometimes he bites and it really hurts but you ask him to do it again so much he is liked.

And than no one can show him a bad thing the other day I rocked him on a kitchen chair and for two days we had to watch him not to turn over the chairs on himself. He understands everything you tell him but he does not talk yet.

Or he lays down near me and reads the newspapers with me; but he does not care if it's up side down.

Well I could write much more about all but its late and I convey

at the end here the sincerest regards and wishes from Minnie to all
as always with best wishes to Mother

Max.

How confining this world seems to me. The male relatives were
locked in close ties and yet were unable to trust each other fully. The
women faced even stronger limitations. The anthropological voice returns to suggest the way that the business and the family fit together.
Business was men's work, family was women's work, and the two were
always in tension. My grandmother was the eye of the hurricane, the
still point around which her husband and sons rushed, eager to remember her birthday, troubled that they could not provide her with adequate
comfort and honor. There were specific roles for sisters as well: Elizabeth traveled to Chicago as my grandfather's emissary, since he could
not find anyone else who could check so thoroughly on his sons and on
his daughters-in-law as well. No wonder, then, that my father's other
sister, Gertrude, refused to play such a part and became a bohemian,
involved with art and with scandalous lovers.

The trickiest position fell to the women who had married into the
family. At best, they could be of help to the family business as prudent
shoppers, spending money carefully to buy the furniture and clothing
that would win the Orlove men respect. The wives also brought their
own relatives with whom business partnerships might be arranged. But
there was always something dangerous about these sisters-in-law. They
could convince their husbands to take the best furs to make collars for
them, or to tap into the partnership's account for household expenses,
and, even more seriously, they could set the brothers against one another, as Max accused Henry's wife, Jane, of doing.

And yet wives, essential to families, also had a fundamental role in
business, as the next letter shows.

Jan. 10. 1928

Dear Robert. —

This letter is to you, but also to the whole family. Since I am
away from Henry, I have not straightened out the old affairs with
him, and daily he told me the same, he can not spare any money.
Henry took in a partner about 10 weeks ago, and it did not go,
theire expenses were eating them up. The man knew nothing about

the business and on top of all he was lazy as a sloth. And so Henry had to let him go on the first of the year — it actually hurted me too, I saw everything was slipping from him, during periods where I was tied up and knew of any merchandise to be bought, I told Henry to go and get it, but somehow, he could not buy it, there is something lacking in Henry. I saw it more than even during the last 3–4 month. He was slipping and slipping naturally he worries a lot and feels very bad about many things, especially where now many things turn out the way I predicted as Bellies vs. Skunkstripes. He sold many pounds of Bellies and worked up the Skunkstripes, instead of doing it the reversed, and now Strip plates are dead to the market and Bellie plates are a rariety.

During all the time I worked bellie plates myself, worked them untill it hurts.

To-day I got in alot of orders from one house over $100.00 alone on Sq. Bellie plates etc. I decided to work late so that I can make a quick delivery. The Cohens and all were gone, Henry came in and asked me why can't work to-gether and the wind up came to talk.

Henry looked so haggard to me, pale and scared. Elizabeth saw him when he was a picture of health and now he looks pale and on the second look paler, his mouth drawn and I am sure quite a difference from last summer.

We kept on talking and explaining each other but I was determined not to go in with him anymore.

Then all at once Henry said: "Max, you know, Jane is pregnant." "What," I cried. "We go in to-gether." And I said nothing more, dropped my work and to-morrow — I mean to-day Thuesday we start in again. I figure, the lesson Henry has had and the additional responsibility will make him more reasonable to get along with. And so I'm sure Mother will be twice happy; to hear, first, that we are together again, and second that she'll become a Grandmother for Henry and Janes future Baby, Henry told me she is in the 3rd months and Jane admonished him *not* to *tell anybody*. But I can not keep the secret to you, but ask you to help me out now, and keep mumm whatever to Janes Mother. Thats that. Please keep a secret for me.

Under no circumstances write to Henry or Jane about it, let

they tell you the glad tidings and I hope we'll all be happy and lucky now —

Otherwise little new news, excepting my baby is the king of boys even if I must say it; he is cute, smart, happy and playfull.

With best regards to Mother<br>
as always<br>
Max.

Regards from Minnie to all.

P.S. After this season we will open a good sized matching place too —

P.S. Who hopes that some day the Orloves will amount to something.

Why did Max write this letter to my father, I wondered. Was he concerned to record another episode in the endless business negotiations among the brothers and their father, or was he keeping open the possibility that he and my father might someday go into partnership? Was he prodding my father, then in his early twenties, to follow the older brothers' path to marriage, fatherhood, and respectability? Was Max trying to present himself as a dutiful son who, despite the great distance that separated him from his mother, sought to make her happy? I turned over these possibilities and then finally settled on a simpler one: he just felt the urge to tell someone the news. Rather than speaking to his wife, who had argued with Henry, Max wrote to his brother. There was nobody whom he could trust with this bit of information better than my father, nobody who would understand better what this information meant to Max.

And once again I was surprised. In the next letter, Max disclosed his secret, a project that he had been working on for years. He felt that my father was sufficiently intelligent and educated to understand the complex themes that he discussed, and, more important, Max trusted my father with his deepest hopes.

Feb. 27.　1928

Dear Brother Robert: —

This is a purely personal letter to you and owing, not to be able to have a heart to heart talk with you, I must write this letter just to get off some steam! there will be nothing of business here.

To the point: I have read in the newspapers, and no doubt you too have taken notice of the report that Lindbergh was shown a working model of a motor that seems to revolutionize the whole motive power of this era.

It is *very* sad for me to say that they have found the nucleus idea of my cherished life work. I do not know how near they come to my theory, but all said, they have struck the vital point, and so much more bad for me that I was just emerging from the heap of obstacles that kept me from building a model myself. I always was under the fear that I must have plenty money to start on this gigantic work, as in the beginning I believed that a model or small motor will not work, but only a big and real big machine would give cause to prove me right. (The cause of this believe laid in the manipulation of certain physical laws, which I adherred too).

After going with this idea around I have seen that it was impossible to attack the problem in the stage I had it formulated — as I needet hunderts of thousands of dollars and most probably 3–4 years time and the requirements of very scilled mechanics and engeniers and the rework and rework of any flaws in this struckture.

And so I turned around and tried hard — real hard mental work (I learned everything by heart and know now all laws on magnetism, electricity etc. relating to this invention so that at any given moment I could think and figure at it — in any place without any book help.)

I turned around and worked on the thing downwards that means I found means and ideas and calculations wher by I could make the machine into a small model, which could be made quick cheap and positively prove me correct. And so I worked all my thinking life on this thing. All other work and all other thoughts have not given me so much heartache with pleasure and exilleration. So you can immagine how dearly I hung on this.

The first time I knew that I was right I was experiencing the happiest moment in my life. When I wrote you that I took up the study of higher mathematics I was just giving my invention the suprem acid test and it withstood I was there right, right and I rested to await the opportunity to show this great discovery to the world.

It does not mean that I have all the time neglected to interrest people with it but no I have tried several times to turn the inneterest on it with several people the most outstanding are: The very first time to a private ingeneer but as more interrested he got the more I left him, as he only asked questions, and questions, but never, encouraged me as to its possible profits for me, and the only profits I wanted was the name that I made it, that was my ambition and it still is and if there is a God who has given me this thoughts and has let me develop them, he surely will not pass it out of me into other peoples hands!)

The second party were the Simond Shukkert works in N. York City. (I am mentioning only all the most important ones)

The "head macher" [*makher*, literally "maker"; big shot] told me we were alone and I should proceed — but for goddness sake, a man sneezed in a closet, naturaly he came out and had a pad and pencil in his hands — and I walked out — they wishing me good luck after fruitless asking to remain and explain further: —

Then I was in Bridgeport and I boldly wrote to the U.S. Government, I do not quite remember if it was the same day or next day that the Bridgeport papers came out with extras telling about an invention which was offerred to the Government pointing out, which I interpreted as caused by my letter but nothing came out of this either. I even had no direct reply — but am sure that several times, when I was drawn into conversation pertaining in that line, they were contact men of the Government and they must have given an unfavorable report concerning this whole affair. —

Then while I was in Detroit I wrote to Henry Ford about this matter and it fizzled out the same way as with the Government.

Than while I was in the Army I was approached several times in Canada yet, concerning my invention. But not untill I was in England I was called out of the ranks and asked if I would not want to work on it and the english government would give me all things I need; and I was free and easy, to do what I pleased. But through some fate some desire overcame me not to divulge my secret as I was only in the Army and by holding it of, I might be spared to go to France and so it happened. I was several times asked about its completion on paper and so I only made the explanation so that they would get more interested in it — (and on that, what I mostly insisted was not at all to be concidered in the working machine); and further more, complained of not having things I needed to take reference from and so the drawings and papers etc. Went to the war ministry in the meantime the war endet, and I demandet my immediate discharge. I was told that 10 years after the war is over the papers would be free to public access in the British archives — but the 10 years are not up yet — I figure then earliest August 1928 or latest Nov.11. — '28.

And so I came back to the States.

The last great shark I tried to interest in that was "Goldberg" — Bernstein, but nothing came out of this either. —

And so I'm back where I started the letter someone has discovered the fundamental law by accident, the way the papers write I gather from it, that it was not his intention to make such and such a machine but a certain "true north pointing magnet" and he struck this, well many ideas have come at the same time to different people at different places.

All I have got to say is, that my model is very simple and very easy to construct after explaining it to anyone it is easier to make than an electric Bell. (But this seems to be too clumsy yet).

What am I going to do about? nothing, merely wait a few days and than see what I got to do.

Naturally I would very much like to do it now, this moment, but by golly, I've got no mesumen [money] for this small thing either. But waiting and my hopes are more on the stress than yours.

Please excuse me to Mother for not having written her, but assure her that we received her letter and are priding ourself with the invitation she send to Minnie and Seymour, but by golly, we have no mesummen now to come.

With best regards to her as always

Max.

P.S. If you are not inclined to answer this letter do not do it — as it was only written, because I felt I had to write it to you, but personally I do not expect a comment on it.

The baby is fine and happy, and rascally cute in pranks — He really likes me more than Minnie and how — wait and see, come to Chi. Max.

As I read this letter, I kept turning my head away from it, to look at the ceiling, out the window, anywhere but at these pages in which Max recorded his anguish. I could not bear to see how utterly isolated he was, how intensely he craved recognition. I was troubled for myself as well by the thought that I had uncovered a history of insanity in the family. Was it delusions of grandeur about his discovery from which Max suffered, or was he having a manic episode? Paranoia was a more certain diagnosis. It seemed impossible to believe that there really could have been a spy hidden in a closet who revealed himself by sneezing and who then emerged, notebook and pencil still in hand. As I reread the letter, this impression sunk in. It was simply crazy for him to write to Henry Ford and expect a reply.

My concerns were allayed by the next letter, which Max wrote the day after this revelation about his invention. Apparently he sensed that his first letter required some explanation, in words and in pictures.

Feb. 28 1928

Dear Robert: —

Again I am writing you. Instead I should write to Mother about my private life and the happy times I have with my Seymour.

But I must write you in justification of my last letter, so that you will know more what I am talking about. This letter I want you to consider as the most important one I ever wrote you; because I am going to explain you my whole invention.

Max then went on to explain how he would take pairs of magnets and attach them, so that their positive poles would point inward and their negative poles outward. He thus hoped to have a magnet with two negative poles. If this magnet were placed inside a circle of other magnets whose negative poles faced inward, the bar magnet would spin endlessly, propelled by repulsion between its two negative poles and the negative poles of the magnets in the circle. This spinning magnet would generate electricity. Even though none of these models worked, my uncle believed that, contrary to the laws of physics, he had invented a perpetual motion machine. His letter continued:

I hope you will understand what I tried to explain in this letter. Please do not show this letter to anyone -no one!! and also do not consult anyone about any phase of it better ignore it all and burn the letter before asking any stranger no matter what good friend is to its merits. Please, Robert, no matter how you feel towards it be mum about to all others, except mother.

With best regards to Mother as always

Max

Please answer this letter.

I would very much like to know what my father wrote in his reply to Max's letters. How much encouragement did my father offer? Did my father reveal his own hopes for success to Max? My father also spent long periods alone, engaged in the efforts to perfect his creations. My father hoped that his drawings and prints would express his unique spirit and would bring him recognition, very much like Max's hopes for his invention. From Max's next letter, I can glean some hints about my father's response. Max seems pleased with my father's reply, and I can tell that my father asked specific questions about the machine which Max was glad to answer.

March 12. — '28.

Dear Robert.

I expected an earlier reply, but it's o.k. just the same. I am glad that you take an interrest in this affair, but now to answer your questions.

Go ahead and ask all you want and I'll explain them. The first on is easy. The phenomena of attraction and repulsion are equal but in opposite direction. This law is very far reaching and one of the main principles of my invention. When unequal poles attract you get, you can draw from each pole electricity from the positive pole, negative electricity, from the negative pole positive electricity, and only so long as you move each pole towards the other, but than when you pull it away, the electricity flow is reversed.

Now the second question: it gave me a shudder, I was so dumb-founded at first that I laid down in bed for about 10 minutes hard concentration, and I could not find the reason how this question popped up within you. But it's all-right. You must have misunder-stood me, or I did not go into great details at this point of the thing. I want you first to consider the effect of an action, and secondary the reason of the action. The two equal poles will and must repell, even if one is immouvable and the other rests on a mouvable rotating socket, the force acting on both will turn the desired on. You seem to be here under the impression of straight line force, but you do not consider that to maintain the straight line the thing in the way will be pushed away. It acts something like on a windmill the wind goes straight towards the wheel, and the wheel turns to let the wind pass on in a straight line (but weaker). A horse pulls the wagon, still the wheel does not drag but turns.

Yes the magnet will try to receed in a straight line but will have no alternative but to turn. If you take a Furriers beating stick and press both ends to-gether the stick will bend. I thought I'd explain your first question with one sentence, but I want you fully to comprehend it and so I have your letter next to me and see on your drawing that you think that the equal poles out of theire merrit are trying to run away from each other, but its not so, it is like a parody.

To simplify manners I want you to think that each end of the magnet gives out a stream of water, and therefore if two *equal* poles meet they meet headon like this ≫→ ←≪ and not like your drawing ←≪ ≫→, so, if two water tanks spout water with great force and the two waters meet than a repulsion exists and than again, if one is immouvable and the other only in a circle, the mouvable one will be repelled in a circle. Is this all clear to you now? It does not act like two hating men running away from each other, but no, they run against each other forcefully and the impact causes the repulsion. Do not worry how the attraction works I'll explain that too.

Max took five more pages to answer my father's other questions about motors, wires, electricity, and magnetism, and then closed with "Best regards to Mother as always." His subsequent letters continued to describe technical aspects of his invention. He offered complex accounts of the wiring of armatures and of the advantages of hollow magnets over solid ones. At a few points he speculated more broadly. He commented that if the earth could move in perpetual motion around the sun, then so could the magnets in his machine. And once he proposed what his next invention would be: an electron-extracting machine that could convert lead into gold.

A letter from March 21, 1929, closed with some reflections:

> Only a few experiments remain which must lead to the unlock-ing of this invention. And funny it can be done so cheaply and still I am holding back and back—because the time not the money is lacking I must work in the business and I cannot rip out 3–4 month and seclude myself into a worryless sphere where I can work and save work for all coming generations this is my ambition and I cannot conceive the idea why I shall be rong—when all my knowl-edge and all Science points to the on point. And it is so simple, that it makes more staggering—more anxious to get throu with it—and still there is the hold where I must pay first:
>
> And well, if I am rong—I am right; in having tried, having thought and figured on a possibility which next generation will surely have.
>
> As always with kind regards for Mother and all
>
> > > > Max

Once again Max had confided in my father, this time about his aban-donment of his invention. He mentioned magnets briefly in another letter and then made no more reference to them, to his machine, to his grand dreams. He returned instead to his earlier themes of the fur busi-ness. While Max had been on his own, Henry had entered into a part-nership with their cousin Sam Orloff. That partnership had also come to an end. The next letter, coming after the ones about the invention, let me see the fur business not just as a means of earning a livelihood or respect but as a way for Max to release the same energies that he put into his perpetual motion machine—his restlessness, his pride in his intelligence, his hopes to create a marvel.

Jan. 4.—30.

Dear Robert:

To-day I have written to Wagreich to release 29½. lb. of Bellies (Sq.) to you, which I have in stock with him. During this coming week I will slip the other Sq. Bellies I have here in Chicago for your own disposal.

I have put one restraind to this affair for your own benefit. I do not think it advisable that you should get all the 100 lbs. at once for various reasons which some of them are

1.) In the case you will be pressed for money you will dispose of the lot or some of it.

2.) I do not know the man you go in with — but in spite that you will have picked the best you could, there are precautions to be taken (you shall not be suspicious with the man, nevertheless, he might cause a lot of trouble by having all the lot in his possession — which are too numerous here to mention.

3.) It will give the partner no rest to work the lot up faster with the knowledge that all the plates will be ready for sale in one large lot.

4.) I also want if possible for you to cut the plates into collars for the trade and you surely will get more by doing so.

5.) That this is the best time to work them and preserve the lot under this condition.

6.) 100 lbs at once will cause you maybe to work the best bellies and the rest will not come under the knife at all.

7.) You can always see better how you get along and also have a better look in the mechanics of manufacturing and production cost etc. by small lots with the knowledge more to come.

8.) It will give you more prestige with Wagreich by holding the plates until ready with them.

9.) It will keep your partner more bound to his promise or contract as he would be anxious to see the end and give you the best thats in him.

10.) which is the main reason, you will have at the end a sum of money to work with and make a nice living as long as you want to work, buying pieces — and maybe if you will like it, manufacture also.

Max then warns my father never to forget that many workers are lazy or dishonest. He also gives him detailed advice on techniques for dyeing furs and for nailing them on frames. He closes:

get started and good luck to you

as always with best regards to Mother

Max.

P.S. And now an other story.

Sam Orloff left Henry. And even before, Henry hinted and hinted to me I should go back with him. But I cant — not for the money sake — I cannot make money with Henry — but for my health sake and piece of my mind I must not. The aggrevation and fears I go through with him do not let me do it.

Besides when Henry made the last blow up — I begged him almost cried not to do it. When he grabbed the goods and did not want to pay me out and I felt so bad he thought I was done for and he was master of the situation and I a nothing — But I predicted and knew this would come as the final end. I told so to Sam & Henry — but I was crazy *and I did not get paid to day yet and do not expect anything.*

I got nothing out of the old business and I started with borrowed money and I made more than he. Besides I got the goods for — the *plenty* Spring Ermine bellies and about 500 different good Foxtails and paws. Over 300 Sable tails 1200 Sable paws 200 german Fitch skins and other things besides the goods with Wag.

Henry lost more than he gained by doing that to me — his yearly summer blow up of the business,

Max.

Later that month, Max and Henry did go back into business together. They bought and sold furs but did not work them into plates or collars. A subsequent letter told the story of Henry's cousin and former partner:

March 6. — '30.

Dear Robert:

The case of Sam Orloff — is an iota in the breath of life, of this generation, still you feel it is an immense immensity casting a shadow on many a happy remembrance.

Where ever you thoughts will begin to search they cannot penetrate the cause of such an end, yet you will not dwell with a superflues explanation — and therefore you try and analyse the causation

— like a chemist a compound or an element. Step by step you build up with your limited reasoning power the finaly of a life, which, otherwise might have been grand and famous.

One thought creats an other; one action an other thought or action and so it weaves itself into one thought and only one action.

An acorn can only become an oak provided that all circumstances help it step by step to develop, nourishing ground — moisture — sunshine and devoid of all destiny live germanation.

The human race developed through evolution and so did human thought and human desires develop step by step — sometimes, somewhere segragated and than strongly overwheelming all tradition, sometimes retarding — but always striving to better itself for the sake of others to come.

Now Sam Orloff — alone in this world had to rely alone on himself — he hardly remembered parental love and parental teaching as well as parental punishment — Life was in his eyes harsh to him, these were his first realized thoughts. Naturally he tried the best to be what is right — and right here let me tell you — no one complained about him in a way where the blame should only lay upon his shoulders.

He had no one to thank for any favour as he asked none — whatever he had, he knew it was his honestly earned — and with hard work and sweat.

You cannot blame him that his thoughts and desires cut towards the ocean of Bolshevism, Socialism or any other names for Heaven on earth.

And he read books — books and books dealing first and last with the nirvana among the living.

Again and again the big names were mentioned and he read them too — but to drink this is to drink deeply or not to drink at all.

Whatever thoughts were left with him he could not adjust himself with the ideal and material things. So when he came to the ultra ideal works they seemed out of focous and a fear was manassing his horison of desires.

The words — 'all must end ultimately' — were written on all things as a trademark and advertisement. Here his none resistance was piling up hindering his progress. Friends seemed to be no friends arguments useless — he never would argue — your idea all-right —

Than all this fight in this world — what was it for, for gain — for gain — but see the loss — the loss to gain that gain. The loss was more valuable than the hoarded gain.

There again he drew in — and let things whirl as they may.

This life saw a future, a happiness, he got married he saw his own babe — He also saw Russia — Russia — the land of the most miserable — giving the hope of all desires a concrete form — a possibility of rest of fullfilled dreams — happy Russia — Russia.

But look — how its bought — whatfore — all with dead — for the dying — Ideals shattered — but still the future will gain what the past has contributed. Here the matter rested — he worked — saved — read correspondet. Yes, but oh — he was not free — a wife a baby — his own thoughts could not be the undisputed thoughts — yes he had an argument, he gave in — maybe he had many more — married life is not the breath of spring all the time.

Well, he let that go too. But Russia — his first hate his hope — was changeing — it was his love now and every thread of thought was woven after the new Russia and he was happy and desireless.

Oh the pain — how long will it last untill all is well — not in my days — maybe not in my boys days but Russia — will be "Russia" Not in my boys days? Oh calamity — I must provide for him — he took out insurance — saved again — But when he had no work he migrated to Chicago.

Sam Orloff had also Ben Orloff — the farce of capitalistic system — Ben knew what Sams A.B.C. was — and that was Bens education. But Ben had trouble — well, and all trouble are self made — and he cannot tie himself up with Ben — oh the pain — that is against the ideal of the happy life. Sam and Ben were inseparable.

A chance in Business — against Sams will — Business is a crime; oh the aching mind and heart but maybe through business I might get independent devout more time for my ideals — maybe I can hasten them for all concerned.

And Sam Orloff said to me: "I can see that Communism is a long way off, and I got to go with to-days system," "That's right" I said but now I see it was a confession under duress — he did not mean it.

He met all kinds of men — Businessmen — smart, witty — mean and good men — He spoke to them they were nice — promising — but all were lying lying thieving — for money — cursed money — but all admitted money was not every thing — money money all the time — it's nothing they admit — but how they love to get it — how they cheat — how they dissapoint, liars — liars — cheaters. Oh my mind can not grasp it — I am sick — sick — I wish I could go to — to Russia — oh I cannot go there yet.

Look at Max & Henry a couple nuts — what fore? what fore? oh I am sick from all that — I wish I would never have started for business I'll go I'll go back to work.

Work — hard work — I am getting older — Ben is better off dead — dead — yes Ben is better off dead — Oh I'm sick — I'm older — I'm poor I was once sick — yes — was I cured — am I healthy — I better find out — whats the use, I'll get worse, — worse, — sicker — my wife my child — what with them — what will be.

Oh the "Doctors" they say I'm well only to have me slave for capital and my wife and child slave — slave — sick slave — cripple, Ha — how much money — money — geld — can I make for them — how much have I got — If I get worse — worse — my savings will be gone gone — my son — will be slaving, slaving for capitals sake. Oh poor wretch — how can I get out of it — I want to get out of it — away — away — no I'm not crazy not that — not that. But I must get out of this mess I'm in.

Sam said last time I saw him "Good bye Max — I might not see you again." "Sam, what's the matter are you going away — aren't you going to stay with Henry." "No, Max, I have something in mind to-do." "Good by" and here I shook hands, the last time, with Sam Orloff.

Sam Orloff went his way. Dissapointed — as never before, Russia — is taken the smallest children away from theire parents — they are breaking up the home — are they really doing — that — . No, Russia cannot do wrong — the children — the Parents — Oh Parents do not know how to raise children rich people give them away to nurses — colleges send them to travels — Hurray Russia is right I'm right — I know — but oh — I'm sick — oh my pain — terrible pain — where — why — yes I was sick I'm still sick — and I got to work — my wife will get sick — my boy will get sick — from me I can't help that — what, I must help it now — soon to-morrow.

Oh I'm only a slave — even if I'm not sick the Doctor experimented on me he inocculated me with germs, germs — the capital Doctor — oh the pain — I am helpless I'll make my Family helpless — lets see — when I'm gone — the boy will get the insurance $2000.00 it will be $4000.00 when he'll be 21 years. He will learn a trade and than go into business — if no Communism will come. My wife — she is young yet, she can raise him — all my money is not gone yet, but it will if I do not go.

I'll die — I'll be dead — I'll be better of dead than alife — If I don't kill myself — I'll end in a crazy house — I'll be dead anyways and a burden to them.

Poison, Iodine — It gives life it takes life — Sam Orloff drank Iodine.

He was saved — he went to work for a week — Oh shame you crazy fool — they all laugh at you but they dont show it, they seem sympathetic, I must slave — work for them, capital first — than my wife and baby — oh what for its no use.

They all will know it — I cannot face it — I am a shame.

But I must have rest — rest — Nirvana — I want to forget — So many have died — for the noble cause. My cause is noble — I die for my son to save him — to save him from being a low slave — a poor slave — It will be over quickly

I am sorry — but I am sick — I am better dead than a live burden to him —

I owe no one a living — I cannot save as much as I can leave now — maybe less. Whats the use I am sick — I ought to be dead last week already why do I live — to hang papers — papers

I am a slave — I want to be free.

My wife wants company here — she wants to go and visit — what for it's no use — I'm sick I'll never get well — only in death, my spirit will be free — all will be over — over — death is my future — I'm going to die — to-day.

And Sam Orloff send Wife & Baby to a show — and he died with his shoes off, (jewish costum for suicides) by turning all six gas stoppers open.

I felt bad to hear it — and went with Minnie to see Ruth — it was on a Sunday — and little Seymour had to stay home with someone he said "Daddy today is sunday and why do you go on Sunday away from me." But my heart was full with grief — I met Henry there — it was pitifull. Henry went home Minnie went home too — I went to the Undertaker and had a last silent solitary look at Sam Orloff.

He laid there quite — a stiff — Who knows what his reall reason was to do — what he did.

But his life was done — it was the first dead relation I saw.

I liked Sam Orloff — He never was "falling zur last" anyone [being a burden to anyone] — he was quite and may he rest in peace — and find the peace he so much desired.

I have not seen Ruth yet since that awfull Sunday.

Ben Orloff was not at the funeral — I did not go there either.

As always

Max.

p.s. Be very carefull telling it to Mother — Write me how George Orlove takes it and the old man —

I reread the letter many times. Even after I returned it to the box, the images stuck with me: Sam filled with hope, with desperation; Sam's careful plan to send his wife and son to the movies, to remove his shoes, and then to turn on the gas. Max's words remained with me as well: the way that he switched from homilies about acorns and oak trees to reflections on human progress to a recounting of Sam's life and finally to a series of brief phrases. Days later, after another long session of reading and rereading the letter, I noticed that I could not always tell whether Max was quoting things that Sam had said to him, or whether he was imagining what Sam might have felt. Nor did I know whether this distinction mattered to Max. I recognized the reason that Max wrote to my father all along: my father would understand, as Max did, the intensity of Sam's vision. They were all dreamers: Sam with his politics, Max with his invention, my father with his art. They all rejected the pettiness of such relatives as Henry and my grandfather, whose visions reached only to success in business, whose ambitions did not transcend the acquisition of houses, of fancy coats for their wives. Max knew that my father would recognize what they had in common with Sam, a deep faith in the powers of the imagination to create a utopia on earth. Neither Max nor my father were Communists, as Sam was, but they could understand his sense of exaltation when he believed his hopes would be realized, his despair when they collapsed.

As I reflected on the letter, it occurred to me that other relatives would have had a very different reaction to the news. A suicide in the family would have been a great scandal that needed to be handled carefully. The furriers in Chicago and New York would have quickly spread the news. What if my grandfather had not been told, and if he had been greeted by someone in the fur district in New York who offered him condolences about the sad death of his cousin Sam in Chicago? Henry, the oldest son in Chicago, had an obligation to pass the news on as soon as possible to his father, who then would have told his brother George. They would then have planned how to contain the shameful news, how to take care of the widowed Ruth and the orphaned Edgar. But Henry did not send a letter or telegram. Most likely he would have scorned Sam as an idealistic fool, not tough enough to make it in this world. Henry did not bother to tell their father the news. When Max wrote to my father, though, it was not out of obligation to the extended family but from something more urgent, the need to relieve his pain.

Only a few letters followed this one. The Depression that followed the stock market crash of 1929 had a severe impact on the fur business. Several small fur businesses in Chicago hired Max, never for a period longer than a few months. Max once again tried a partnership with Henry.

Feb. 9. — 31 —

Dear Robert=
Well, Henry left — and left me with all the zores! [more usually rendered *tsuris*, troubles] At first he argued and implored all; that he must take over the business to safeguard the liabilities — now he collected all the outstanding over $500.00 sold the best merchandise and took away the rest. He left me here with over $1400 debts. He paid no rents. He left the moth-eaten junk. — I'm talling you he was so lazy that he did not even keep the moth's out the place and

when he made a package to show the trade a sample — he threw it in a corner after he came back and the moths had a swell party from numerous packages in all corners.

Whatever his contention, his argument or his point of view — he lived up to the moment until he got the gutts out of this mess and blew. I can mention the numerous details how he juggled the accounts to his advantage — but that what he did in the end is horrible. The people here are threatening me of taking even my furniture and put me out as bankrupt and faker. And how I worked for him and how he miss used me and not even to close up the Inc. But let this all pass up I think I might pull out — but only than when I get Henry's cooperation and that is — . So — let me alone! and the main thing — he knows my correspondence adress, etc. — I want him to keep his dirty fingers of this affair — and leave his selfish and dull mind alone to any proposition with them — All in all I want him not to write to them or try to communicate in any manner with the party and parties.

I had a letter today from them which is very sanguine and if all turns out with a *little* luck I will make a lot of money.

But I do not want any interferrence.

I will send you theire letter too in a few days.

As always

Brother

Max

And then the letters from Max end suddenly. Max's last letters contain no suggestion that he was angry at my father, that there was some dispute that caused them to end their correspondence. Nor is there any clue that Max was about to become obsessed once again with an invention or some other such project. Some of my older cousins have vague memories of a story of a lawsuit: had some other partner threatened to sue Max, whom Henry and my grandfather rescued by settling out of court? Or had Max been the one who threatened to sue, creating a scandal by challenging some other furrier until relatives intervened? Even under such circumstances, I find it hard to believe that Max, who had revealed his deepest secrets to my father, would suddenly cut him off. Perhaps he really had had some kind of mental illness, a nervous breakdown, or a paranoid episode. The last letter in the box, written by Minnie, offers a few ambiguous clues about his money problems and his troubles with his family:

March 13 1932

Dear Robert:

Received your letter, and Max got his, but I don't know what sort of effect it had upon him.

You know I suppose that I am living with my sister and he is staying elsewhere. I don't know where. I very seldom see him.

Last week he brought $5.00 for the baby's shoes. I appreciate that. His not doing anything, and I don't know what the result will be.

I spoke very seriously with him and told him I'd be content with almost nothing if he would only make up his mind to do something, but to no avail. I can't move him, he's very stubborn. He says he can't do anything until he has at least $150.00. My family is broke. They signed for him, you know, and are still paying for him.

It's very bad not to have a home, for the baby, myself and Max. At least I've got a good bed to sleep in. As for him, I don't know where he spends the time. It's very difficult to live with my sister as she has her own family, and Seymour is very wild, and uncontrollable.

How is mother? Why don't I hear from her?

Well that's how things stand now.

Regards to all

Minna

P.S. Seymour attends the first grade in grammar school.

Several months after I wrote the first draft of this chapter, I found a pamphlet in my father's desk. It was entitled "Memorial Booklet," and the title page stated: "Presented through the courtesy of Gratch-Mandel Funeral Directors." Max's name and the date of his death had been neatly written, in English and Hebrew, in the appropriate blanks; the booklet also contained various prayers, dates of ritual importance, photographs of the interior and exterior of the chapel, and a statement of the funeral director's responsibilities, entitled "Science Tempered with Sympathy." The pamphlet also contained a yellowed newspaper clipping, which, though not bearing a date, can be assigned from its reference to Seymour's age either to 1945 or to 1946, the year in which Max died.

### THREE ARRESTS HALT 'SLICK' CHECK FRAUD

The arrest of three men, one of whom claimed to be a wounded ex-Marine, yesterday cleared up what Detective Timothy O'Connell said was "the slickest check fraud I've ever seen."

O'Connell said he was holding without formal charge Arthur Cerullo, 18, of 1262 Taylor St., Tony Zaccagnini, 23, of 1542 S. Spaulding Av., operator of a veteran's taxicab, and Zaccagnini's driver, Seymour Orlove, 19, of 3518 W. Congress St., the alleged Marine.

Police said that the men had admitted cashing 10 payroll checks issued by St. Luke's Hospital. Cerullo, a page boy there, obtained the checks through his access to outgoing mail, police stated. His confederates then bought currency exchange money orders which they cashed at a bank.

*Brother-mail*

## Chapter 5   COUSIN-PICTURES

O f all the books in my father's study, his diaries were the ones that I expected to offer the greatest insights into his life. Even as a child, I had occasionally glimpsed the row of volumes that he kept on the second shelf of the right half of the large freestanding cabinet in the living room. I saw the left side more frequently, since that was where my mother kept her good silverware and jewelry. My father unlocked the right side less often, only when he wanted to consult one of the documents that he placed there for safekeeping. At those times I noticed the books, since the crimson of their cloth bindings stood out sharply among the dull-colored boxes and envelopes in which other items were stored. I examined them more closely when I looked at them in his study after his death. He had a complete series of books, labeled Daily Reminders, from 1928 to 1946, the years stamped in gold leaf on the bindings. He made brief entries in them, almost every day at the beginning, tapering off later on.

Among his papers, I found other sorts of diaries as well. My father jotted some reflections in small notebooks from 1921 to 1927, but his serious diary-keeping began in 1928, both in the Daily Reminders and in a second set of journals that complemented them. The Big Diaries, as he termed the large leather-bound volumes, contained dated entries, more extensive than those in the Daily Reminders and separated by longer intervals — a week or two or even a month. In the Big Diaries, which ran from 1928 to 1933, he reflected in greater detail on major incidents of his life and also discussed more abstract themes—the essence of true love, the proper aspirations for modern youth, the nature of life in a great metropolis.

I began to leaf through these books, hoping to read about my father's life before he married my mother. I think that it is common to be curious about one's parents and to wonder about the—how should I say it—romances, love life, sexual activity that one's parents had as separate individuals before they met. This curiosity is particularly acute in my case because of the tension between two unstated axioms of my childhood. The first held that my father was the more attractive of my parents, the one who more often aroused the interest of members of the opposite sex. I recall visits with him to art galleries in midtown Manhattan. Though he was already past sixty years old and dressed in out-of-fashion ties and jackets, he nonetheless succeeded in charming the elegant young women who worked there. I can see their tilted heads, the long glances, the smiles, and I still have the copies of expensive catalogs that he convinced them to give him without charge. The second axiom claimed that my father had been awkward and diffident with women, and if it had not been for my mother's initiative in starting their romance, he might never have married at all. The first suggested that he had had lovers, or at least many admirers (if that word can be used in the case of a man) before her; the second, that he had not.

My readings of the diaries supported the second view. His involvements with different young women were infatuations that moved slowly, if at all. I was initially surprised to see that he had been drawn to his cousins, but this pattern began to make sense to me: his emotional life was already bound up with relatives, and his female cousins might have been the only women whom he saw regularly enough to overcome his great timidity and reserve. These were safe crushes, too, since he could not intend to sleep with a cousin or to marry one.

The diaries trace, for example, his unfolding interest in his cousin Betty, one of the daughters of his Uncle George. My father hoped to arrange a walk in a park with her, but she did not consent at first. When it finally took place, the walk was unsatisfactory, he could not find words to express himself, they chatted about trivial matters. He spent a week trying to decide whether to call her again, and then he saw her talking with another man at a party. Several weeks later he invited her to the movies, but she brought a girlfriend with her, and he wondered whether he would spend time alone with her. My sympathy for his shyness turned into pity, and then exasperation. I skimmed through the diaries, hoping to find that he acted toward Betty in more definitive fashion. But no: they went downtown to a museum, and on the subway ride back, she nestled up to my father while he worried whether he should put his arm around her or take her hand. He could not figure out what to talk about as they walked back from the station. When they reached her house, she stood close to him outside her door. He finally gave her a brief peck and then turned and ran down the hall so quickly that he stumbled, fell, and bruised his hand. As I read this account, I grunted involuntarily. It was as if my vocal cords were acting on their own, trying to get me to speak, to shout to my father that he must act more firmly, that he must embrace and kiss this woman whose affection he craved.

My frustration turned into puzzlement. Other men of his generation, even his own brothers, pursued women more actively. When Henry was only seventeen years old, he had a brief affair — possibly his first, certainly not his last — with a neighbor's maid. Boris and Howard had certainly had many lovers before they married. My father was as handsome as they were. Had he been the one most affected by his parents, incapacitated by the fear and hatred that he felt toward his father, by his devotion and guilt to his mother? He did not avoid women altogether but was attracted to them instead, caught up in some conflict that I did not understand, even though I could sense the pain that it caused him.

I went back and forth between the two sets of diaries, but neither gave the thorough picture of his love life that I sought. The notes in the Daily Reminders were too brief to tell me much, while the longer entries in the Big Diaries were too melancholy and, I discovered, too self-conscious. Had he written the diaries in German, the language that he spoke most easily, they would have been more personal and more immediate. By writing them in English, he spared me the effort of struggling through them on my own or of locating a translator, but he bequeathed to me books that were as much the result of his efforts to teach himself English as they were a record of his innermost feelings.

Having failed in my search for an authentic diary, I was very pleased to come across a set of twelve photographs, ten of which date from

June 21, 1925, a little less than a month before my father's twenty-first birthday and well into his fourth year in America. These pictures tell a story that is simple enough. My father traveled to Baltimore (almost undoubtedly by taking the subway from the Bronx to Penn Station and the train from there) to visit another cousin, Irene Blechman. Unlike Betty, a first cousin, Irene was a more distant relative, the daughter of a cousin of my father's mother's, and hence a woman with whom there was more possibility of genuine romance. He spent the day with Irene in the company of some friends and other relatives. A number of pictures were taken by several different individuals. The camera passed from hand to hand, often when someone who had snapped one picture wanted to be included in the next. There are no individual pictures that my father and Irene took of each other, though there are a few that show the two of them together. She later wrote flirtatious inscriptions on the photographs and sent them to him.

I found these photographs, ten of which form a single group, and the other two of which are clearly related to the group, divided between two boxes (each containing about a hundred photographs) in the closet in my father's study several months after his death. The twelve photographs were probably separated long before my parents moved to Davis, the town in California where I live, since my father's rather hurried packing for the move from Brooklyn consisted not so much of reordering the contents of small boxes as of placing them in larger ones suitable for shipping. The division into two groups most likely had taken place when some relatives had visited my parents in Brooklyn. In the course of conversations with such visitors, my mother or father would sometimes bring out the photographs that they stored in boxes, in manila envelopes, and, in the case of some of my mother's more treasured pictures, in round metal cans that had formerly held fancy chocolates. Some of the recent photographs were their joint property, but many of them, especially those that dated from before their marriage, belonged to one or the other. It was these that they were most eager to display and that visitors were most curious to see. Sometimes, when one of them produced these old photographs, it stimulated the other to do the same, so that two sets of portraits and anecdotes would contend for the guest's eyes and ears. More often the competition was among the visitors, especially if there were more than one or two of them. The visitors might begin by passing the photographs in an orderly manner among themselves and by calmly exchanging stories, but they soon shifted to a more disorganized grabbing of photographs and to interrupting my parents and each other with alternative versions of the lives of the portrayed individuals. Small piles of photographs would accumulate on laps, on footstools, on the arms of sofas, as attention shifted to more intriguing photographs or to the few major heirloom pictures that were presented at every visit. And so the session would continue, with different stories recalled and related, until it was interrupted by the announcement that a meal was ready or by a reminder that it was time to catch a subway back to the Bronx, and the piles of photographs were hurriedly placed, not quite in their original order, back into the boxes, envelopes, and cans.

Even more than the diaries, the twelve photographs served as a welcome complement to the stories that my father told me. By editing his diaries, I had the opportunity to satisfy the impulses that I had often felt during his lengthy monologues: to interrupt him, to insist that he acknowledge my presence. With the photographs, the shift from his stories was even greater. I could silence my father. I could dispense with his words altogether and replace them with other sources — visual images, in the case of the photographs, and words as well, in the brief, teasing inscriptions that Irene wrote, a delightful counterpoint to my father's ponderous accounts of events.

The backgrounds against which the people posed allow the ten photographs to be grouped into two sets of three and a third set of four. I have given each set a name on the basis of a principal feature — a stoop, a bench, a store — present in all, or most, of the pictures in it. These three groups can be arranged in chronological order, as if they were stills from three scenes in a movie, on the basis of the angle of the reflection of the sun in the stoop pictures and the changing of the shadows from the stoop pictures to the bench pictures to the store pictures. To arrange the pictures in order within the sets, I have found some clues in Irene's inscriptions and in the positions of the individuals in the pictures in relation to one another and to the background.

I call the other two pictures, which precede these ten, the studio portrait and the beach snapshot. The studio portrait differs from the others in a number of ways. It is the only one posed in profile (it shows

Irene with a fresh face and open smile, her face turned just enough toward the camera that the lashes of the eye on the far side of her face can be seen, outlined against the brim of her hat). It is the smallest, the only one taken in a studio (the remaining eleven are all informal snapshots) and the only one that has been hand-tinted, with the fur collar of her coat painted a soft brown and the flowers on the hat in greens, blues, and pinks whose delicate pastel tones are enhanced rather than diminished by the contrast with the twelve cherries among them, which, though very small, are bright red. It is also the only one with an inscription on the front: the back gives the name and address of the studio in Baltimore, and has FEB7406 stamped on it, suggesting, as does the fur collar, that the picture was taken in the winter. Written on the front are the words "Cousin Irene."

In the beach snapshot, Irene's face is almost entirely in shadow, but there is enough light to see her querying expression. What question does her expression ask, I wonder. Here I am, on a nice vacation, the picture says, suggesting that her branch of the family has enough money to afford some trips. It also seems to say that she is interested in my father, though the proper tone of the inscription, with its use of his last name and its referral to their cousinly tie, suggests that she is a little shy, or perhaps merely concerned to avoid drawing the attention of other relatives who might reproach her for a less seemly message. Though I have looked at this picture many times, I think that my father looked at it even more. I find myself thinking that her expression as well as her inscription encouraged him to make the trip to Baltimore.

I was pleased to discover that the beach snapshot has physical evidence of its later history. This evidence, located on the upper edge of the photograph, consists of two yellow smudges, the traces of Scotch tape that held the photograph in an album or on a wall, possibly my father's. Had this photograph been taken on a Memorial Day weekend late in May, my father traveling a few weeks later to visit her? Knowing him and seeing the tape, I imagine that he had delayed nearly a year between receiving the photograph in the summer or fall and going to Baltimore the following June. As I reflected on this possibility, an idea popped into my head: she sensed his uncertainty, she sent him the studio portrait in the winter as a sort of invitation. Since I found no correspondence between them in my father's papers, I cannot be certain.

(Irene's inscription): *Taken while on vacation at Ocean City, Beach, Maryland. To Robert Orlove, From Your Little Cousin, "Just Irene."*

The events of June 21, 1925, though, are better documented in the three sets of photographs.

The record of my father's visit to Baltimore begins with the stoop photographs, taken late in the morning. They all show individuals who are sitting on the stoop of a brick building or standing near it. Irene and Robert (as I, following Irene, call him here) are both present in only one of these three photographs, and even in that one they are not next to each other.

The first stoop picture—with "The Tall [and] the short taken in Baltimore Sunday, June 21st 1925" written on the back—shows Robert and the Short Girl, as I, combining pieces of Irene's inscriptions, call the fashionably dressed young woman next to him. The Short Girl is sitting comfortably on the stoop, Robert's hat placed at her side on a step. Her knees are crossed, her hands rest on her lap, her mouth is opened in a calm smile. Robert stands next to her. He seems comfortable in her presence. His posture is relaxed: his knees are slightly bent, and he has placed one foot in front of the other. He keeps his balance by resting one hand on the corner of the stoop, the other on a brick ledge above a basement window. He looks directly at the camera with a firm, assured gaze. I find him to be stiffly dressed for his visit to Irene, in a suit with the top two jacket buttons closed and a striped tie, but, I realize, fashions were much more formal at that time.

Like the beach snapshot, the first stoop picture has a square smudge on the center of the upper edge; it is the only one of the ten to bear such a mark. My guess is that Irene put this photograph up somewhere before sending it to Robert. She may have placed it where other family members could see it, possibly on a mirror. Of all the pictures of him that are at all flattering, it is the only one that does not include her, so she may have chosen it to avoid criticism from her parents or teasing from her siblings.

The second stoop picture (inscribed "The boy & girl themselves — sweethearts    Ain't love gr'r'r'and 6/21/25") contains the Short Girl and her boyfriend, or, following Irene once again, sweetheart. The photographer, perhaps Irene, has stepped a few feet further from the building and to the left of the spot in which the previous picture was taken. This shift in position brings into this photograph a window with the glaring reflection of the sun, the first of the intrusive elements in this set that a

more skilled photographer would have taken care to avoid. The Short
Girl remains on the same step, though, I suddenly notice, Robert's hat
is gone. She has uncrossed her legs and now sits more stiffly, her left leg
bent at an awkward angle. She has turned her face slightly away from
the camera. Her closed mouth makes her look less animated than she
was in the preceding picture. A different man stands next to her, also in
suit and tie. I see confidence in his open jacket, in his arm around her
neck, but I also sense a hint of discomfort: he has placed only the outer
edge of his hand on her shoulder, so that his palm is suspended above
her shoulder rather than resting on it. I wonder what had taken place to
account for this positioning. My imagination rushes in to fill this gap. I
find myself thinking that Short Girl enjoyed meeting Robert and talking with him. Perhaps she picked up Robert's hat — it would have been
awkward for anyone else to reach for it — and made a little joke as she
handed it to him. Her sweetheart, sensing that she liked Robert, became
jealous. They had, not an argument, but a moment of annoyance with
each other that they almost entirely suppressed because of the presence
of the friends and relatives, the camera, and the passers-by on the street,
but which I believe I can detect nonetheless in his proprietary stance
and the slight withdrawal of his hand, in the detached reserve of her
posture.

In the third stoop picture, Robert and the Short Girl are once again
next to each other, though in the decorous context of a group picture
that also includes Irene and two other women. The Short Girl is smiling
contentedly, but Robert looks uncomfortable, woodenly holding his hat
in left hand. Irene's inscription suggests that she takes his closed eyes to
be an expression of flirtation, but they do not give me that impression.
He may be squinting in the sun, or he may happen to be blinking, but
I think that he has cast his glance downward in embarrassment at the
presence of so many women and at the contretemps that he caused between the Short Girl and her sweetheart.

I feel some sympathy for Robert's discomfort, but Irene seems entirely unaware of it. Here, in her first appearance in the ten photographs, she is absorbed in posing for the camera. Crouching close to the
ground, one arm is draped across a leg, the other pressing her broad-
brimmed straw hat to her head, her whole body leaning slightly to the
right. The shadow that the hat casts across her eyes may be uninten-

(Irene's inscription): *Who are you flirting with? O! what a bunch — What could be worse 6/21/25.*

tional, but the slight opening of her mouth, the tilt of her head are not. She seems to be amusing herself by posing as a vamp. The woman next to her is hamming it up, too, looking tough rather than sultry. She is also crouching, one forearm resting on her knee and her hand dangling loosely. The other hand is placed firmly on her hip, thumb behind, fingers forward in what now is a masculine gesture and probably was back then as well. Her left eye squints in the bright sun, her right eye peers out from the shadow cast by her wavy bangs. Could Robert tell how Irene and the other woman were playing and posturing? I do not think so. The people in the top row are looking over the heads of the two in the bottom row, who are more involved with each other and their game than with the others.

The angle of the sun is very similar in the second set of pictures, the bench photographs, so they must have been taken soon after the stoop photographs, and nearby as well. Houses and windows similar to those in the first set appear on the far side of the street that is in the background of the first bench picture. Robert, Irene, and some of her relatives, including her father, most likely walked across the street, where they pose on a bench made of a metal frame to which six long wooden slats are attached, three forming the seat and three the backrest. Behind them is a cast-iron fence. Irene is present in all three pictures, with some younger female relatives in some but not in others, and each picture contains just one man, her father in the first two, Robert in the third. Here, too, I imagine a rivalry between Robert and the other man.

The first bench picture (inscribed "The Blechman trio  Father daughter & niece—Ain't we just lovely—No we ain't. 6/21/25") is unusual in that it is the only one of the ten photographs whose shape is different from the rest, nearly square rather than rectangular. Its height is the same as the others in this set, but it is not as wide. The left third of the picture is cropped. The photographer may not have advanced the film correctly, or the studio technician may have had some problem in developing the film. In this picture Irene, still wearing her hat, still with her mouth slightly opened, slouches a bit on the bench. She drapes her arm around a girl, roughly six years old, who sits next to her, with white knee socks and a giggly smile. An inscription on a later photograph reveals this girl's name to be Dorothy. In a dark suit and bow tie, Mr. Blechman hovers over his daughter and niece with some possessiveness. He stands behind the bench and leans on it, grasping it just behind Irene with his left hand and resting his right elbow on it near Dorothy's shoulder. The lower part of his face has a rather sinister shadow across it. The bright reflection of the sun off his forehead (he is partially bald) makes this shadow, through which he glowers at the camera, appear darker and his expression more hostile.

The second bench picture ("Part of the family & me") shows a milder Mr. Blechman, sitting in the middle of the bench, legs crossed, one hand resting on his knee. This softening is in part accidental. The photographer is positioned so that a bush is directly behind Mr. Blechman, giving him the appearance of wearing a feather headdress like a cigar-store Indian. There is also more light on his face and on his shirt, revealing him to be quite stout. He is taller than Irene, the difference in height emphasized by her pose. She sits right next to him and stretches up to reach his shoulder, on which she rests her arm. She is smiling widely. On the other side of her father sit two young girls: Dorothy is squirming on the edge of the bench, looking with annoyance at the other, who has not appeared in any previous photographs. This object of Dorothy's irritated glance is a few years older and much more civil. She has her ankles crossed, her hands folded properly in her lap, her eyes turned slightly downward. The photographer, evidently returning the direct gaze of Irene and her father, has not noticed someone walking down the street and, somewhat blurred by motion, into the left edge of the photograph.

I have put considerable effort into reconstructing the actions and emotions of the photographer and the four individuals during the moments just before the photograph was taken. It took me a while to convince myself that Robert was this photographer. Of the hundreds of his other photographs that I have seen, none have errors as striking as Mr. Blechman's headdress or the inclusion of the individual whose walking renders her fuzzy. This photograph, though, was taken several years before any of the other photographs of his, so his skills could have improved in the intervening period. Moreover, he was probably more intimidated by Mr. Blechman and Irene than by his later subjects, and hence more prone to error.

Having resolved that the camera was in Robert's hand, I then turn my thoughts to the individuals in the photograph itself. Mr. Blechman, the paterfamilias, must have stationed himself first in the middle of the bench, Irene joining him from one side, the other girl and Dorothy from the other. My imagination is captured by Irene's posture and by Robert's lack of attention to Dorothy's wriggling and to the passer-by's intrusion. I find myself thinking of her as a flirt: suddenly nestling up to her father, she stretches her arm up to his shoulder and smiles, assuaging his stern temper and startling Robert into depressing the shutter.

The third bench picture has a dark blurry band across the top, an intruding finger of the photographer, probably Mr. Blechman. The photographer is certainly shorter than Robert, as can be seen by the apparent position of the top of the bench in relation to the background. The photographer is also closer to the bench than in the two preceding pictures. (Does Mr. Blechman want to protect his daughter from this distant cousin, this handsome man who seems interested in her?) Robert and Irene are back together within the photograph's frame for a second time. On this occasion, they are next to one another. She is sitting on the bench, her head tilted up from under the brim of her hat with a smile even more open-mouthed and confident than in the earlier picture. Despite her father's proximity, she has cuddled up next to Robert. She leans on him and even seems to be resting her elbow on his thigh. His arm is draped over her, his thumb and fingertips touching her shoulder, but his slightly curled hand resting about an inch above it. Is it the presence of her father that prevents him from touching her, or his innate shyness? With his other hand he holds his hat in a vertical position on his lap, thus covering his lower abdomen, and possibly an erection as well.

I do not sense a moment of action in this picture, as I did in the previous one. If anything, Mr. Blechman, disapproving of his daughter's pose, may have waited a while before snapping this photograph. Such delay would explain why Irene and Robert look as if they have been holding themselves still. Her smile looks frozen, and Robert's posture is stiff, with his shoulders slightly hunched, his knees awkwardly bent. The strains that this delay would have caused could also account for Robert's wrinkled forehead and tensed eyebrows.

A long interval separates the bench pictures from the next set. The shadows are much longer, suggesting that the photographs were taken

(Irene's inscription): *This is how we looked — isn't the scenery beautiful — that's the only thing that is beautiful — because we spoil the effect — I decided to send this one so you wouldn't get swell head about the other — 6/21/25.*

late in the afternoon. Moreover, Robert and Irene have left their hats somewhere. These details all suggest that they had lunch at Irene's house and then went for a walk. Mr. Blechman, who had chaperoned them on their shorter morning stroll, did not join them this time. They were accompanied instead by several women of varying ages, who might have been relatives or friends. They seem to have ventured further in the afternoon than they had on their morning walk across the street to the bench, since this walk took them to a street large enough to have businesses and billboards. It is the shoemaker's shop on this large street that I had in mind when I named this set "the store pictures."

The first store picture is probably the one that she mentioned in the inscription on the third bench picture ("I decided to send this one so you wouldn't get swell head about the other"). It is also the picture that Irene liked the best ("The Ideal"), and the one that she used most overtly as a flirtatious invitation ("Your idea please") to develop a cor-    127 respondence. She may have preferred it to the others simply because it is the picture in which she looks best. I suspect, though, that she liked it for the same reason that I do: I find its open expression of affection and enjoyment to be very appealing.

Robert has put his left arm around Irene, grasped her firmly (his fingers are curled around her elbow), and drawn her to him. She welcomes his attention. She leans on him, her upper torso against him, her arm and hand dangling in a carefree gesture. They gaze directly into each other's eyes. He inclines his head toward her, while she tilts hers up toward him, as if in an effort to bring themselves as close to each other as possible. Their warm smiles are spontaneous and relaxed, not like the frozen grins of the bench picture. He has raised the front of his right foot an inch or so off the ground, a gesture of delight, I think, rather than embarrassment.

I have looked at this photograph again and again. I, too, find myself smiling, caught up in their moment of complete happiness. I am relieved to see that Robert was able, at last, to express his attraction to a woman directly. This photograph satisfies me, and yet I return to it to search for additional clues about Robert and Irene. I speculate that she may have been holding him around the waist, too, since her right arm disappears under his shoulder. But he has his right arm bent behind his back. Perhaps they are holding hands behind his back, unseen both by the photographer and by me.

I realize, too, that the mood of affection is increased by one feature of the composition. Robert's dark suit offers an appealing visual contrast to Irene's light dress. The choice of background, though, could hardly have been more distracting. I have wondered about the photographer, most likely one of the other women who appear in the other photographs in this set. She may have been so caught up in the attraction that Robert and Irene felt for each other as to ignore every other detail in the frame, she may have been inexperienced, or she may have been following the conventions of the 1920s for snapshots, different from and less sophisticated than the ones of the present. Whatever the explanation, I find some elements jarring: the arrow that shoots out from Robert's forehead all the way to the right edge of the photograph, part of an advertisement for Wrigley's spearmint gum; the three words to the right of Irene, a slogan that strikes me as old-fashioned: AFTER EVERY MEAL.

(Irene's inscription): *The ideal. Your idea please 6/21/25.*

Her body covers the initial *e* of the second word, and the right edge crops the final *-al* from the third word, so that the text reads AFTER VERY ME. My eye is caught as well by the shadow that Irene's hand, suspended in space, casts on Robert's crotch.

Irene's teasing inscription to the second picture in this set ("What an awful daddy you'd make you're scared to hold adorable Dorothy — Baltimore 6/21/25") could only have recreated for Robert the misery that his expression and posture suggest he felt at the moment it was taken. Robert glances downward, his eyes closed, his face suggesting reluctance. He holds Dorothy in a clumsy position. Resting his left hand in the crook of his right arm, he has made a kind of seat for Dorothy in his left elbow and supports her with his right hand. She sits frowning, her upper body pulled away from him. Once again, I imagine him as the passive victim, unable to object as others thrust the little girl into his arms and tell him to pose. The poor technical quality of the photograph adds to the mood of Robert's and Dorothy's unhappiness. In addition to having dark blurs in the lower right corner, this photograph is the only one that is badly out of focus and the only one in which the principal subjects are significantly off-center.

I have wondered why Irene sent this picture to Robert. She may not have wanted to end with "The Ideal," a picture of a moment in which she yields to him. She may also have enjoyed the teasing inscription in which she challenges Robert's adequacy as a man. The next two pictures, the last of the store pictures and of the entire set of ten, are a greater puzzle to me. I find it even more difficult to imagine Irene's motives in sending them. She had shown good judgment in selecting single photographs to send on earlier occasions: first the studio portrait, then the beach snapshot. The stoop pictures and the bench pictures form coherent sets. They all display Irene, Robert, or both, except for the second stoop picture, which contains only the Short Girl and her sweetheart, and which demonstrates that the Short Girl could not be a rival to Irene for Robert's affection. The first store picture is, simply "The Ideal," and the second one is amusing, a pretext for Irene's teasing. Only by sheer speculation can I invent a reason for Irene's wish to include Rose or one of the other individuals who first appear in the last two store pictures: had Irene wished to send to all the relatives in New York the image of some cousin who had recently arrived from Europe?

The third store picture ("Rose as she is 6/21/25") is the only one in the set of ten in which an individual appears unaccompanied. The photographer stands at a greater distance from the subject than in the other pictures, heightening the appearance of Rose's isolation, since much of the picture is a blank brick wall. Making an effort to smile, Rose stands with her body half turned away from the camera, her feet pressed together. The very edge of the billboard appears in this picture, and a portion of the shoemaker's shop, with the words PUT ON IN MINUTES appearing in the window.

The last photograph ("Another bunch — still as bad — if not worse — Still got Dorothy. 6/21/25") is another group shot, showing, as the third stoop picture does, that these people were accustomed to having their pictures taken. Some stand, some squat, and they all arrange themselves neatly in rows. Since both pictures appear at the end of sets, the possibility occurs to me that people who had been left out of the other pictures prodded the photographer into taking group shots before they all moved on to another spot.

In the middle row of this picture stand a middle-aged woman at one end, another previously unseen woman wearing a wristwatch at the other, and the sallow woman of the previous group shot (now also without her hat) in the middle, with her arms around the other two. A third new woman in this picture crouches in front with her arm around Rose, who now has a more genuine smile. Robert stands in the narrow space between the row of standing women and the building, his eyes again appearing to be closed. He holds Dorothy somewhat closer to him. Her face is cut off by the middle-aged woman. The words in the window are now clearer: RUBBER HEELS PUT ON IN 10 MINUTES. The group is standing in front of a shoemaker's shop.

I can only speculate about the events after this last photograph. Robert returned to Irene's house, picked up his hat, and went to the station, accompanied, I imagine, by Irene and several other people, who saw him off on the train to New York. I have found myself wondering about his thoughts during his ride back to New York. I think that he reviewed the news of the Blechmans, since his mother would have expected him to deliver a full report about her cousins in Baltimore: their health, their finances, the state of their houses, the meal that they served him. His thoughts would have kept returning from this future conversation back to Irene, to the rapturous near-kiss of "The Ideal," when he drew Irene close to him and they gazed deeply into each other's eyes. He would not have sustained the excitement and pleasure of that moment, though. He would have been thrown back to the frightening protectiveness of Mr. Blechman's stare, to the humiliation of being forced to pose with Dorothy and groups of Irene's girlfriends. My eyes wander across the photographs, loosely arranged on my desk, in the same way that I imagine his thoughts wandered across the images of the preceding hours. I enter a kind of reverie as I shift between the moments of my father's attraction to this pretty woman, clear-eyed, smiling, vivacious, and his other moments of shyness and awkwardness in her presence. I feel his exhilaration at her easy joking manner, and then his concern that she may have been too superficial, too forward. Suddenly I am gripped by a panic. I realize that he will never find love. This pattern will repeat itself again and again: he will meet a woman, he will be drawn to her, but she will just toy with him. She will never take him seriously, he will never overcome his reticence, he will always slip into fear and doubt. This will be his fate, always to travel alone on a train at night. Scenes in my own life spring up: fifteen, twenty years ago, I am also returning from seeing a woman, I walk down a street at night, alone, I also fear that I will never find a woman who will love me, who will remain with me. My heart races. Only after several deep breaths am I able to calm myself, to remember: no, he did find a woman, he did marry, I was born; I, too, met a woman, Judy Dresher, we fell in love, we married, here is our home, our family.

I return to my image of my father in the train. I see him getting off in Penn Station, taking the subway back to the Bronx, walking the few blocks to his family's apartment late at night through empty streets, coming home very late at night, falling on his bed. Finally relaxing, as I am now myself, he sleeps very soundly.

He and Irene must have corresponded. At a minimum, she would have enclosed a note with the photographs. I do not know whether, or how long, they continued to write to each other. If he ever traveled to Baltimore again to visit Irene, his trip went unrecorded. At some point, the connection between them faded. Irene must have found other men to be more interested in her, or more expressive of this interest, than my father. His diaries in 1926 and 1927 record some further inconclusive wooing of his cousin Betty. He met a woman named Freda; they strolled through parks, visited museums, ate out in restaurants. In the summer of 1927 he found himself increasingly attracted to a neighbor and a friend of his sister Elizabeth's, Frances Cohen, known to everyone as Katzy, the woman with whom he would have a passionate affair and whom he would marry.

*Cousin-pictures*

## Chapter 6   W I F E - S O N G S

My father's study, filled with his diaries, letters, and notes, contained few pages that recorded my mother's words. I would have been pleased to find any papers that would have started to fill this gap; I was delighted to come across some of her sheet music. Their very presence led me to recall many occasions when my mother sang, incidents that would come to mind in odd moments in the months while I was working on this chapter. It was my childhood summer vacations at my Aunt Gert's house in Connecticut that I first thought of—or, more precisely, the flurry of activity when some car-owning uncle would stop by our house in Brooklyn and pick us up for the trip to Carmen Hill, right on the border of Fairfield and Litchfield Counties. I was thrilled by the drive itself, streets and avenues in New York leading to highways and then to unpaved country roads. It was one of the few occasions in the year when I would enter an automobile rather than take the subway or a bus. Caught up in the excitement, my mother would lead my sisters and me in "She'll Be Comin' Round the Mountain" and other campfire standards of that sort, and then switch to old popular songs, ones I knew only from hearing her. I can only recall fragments of one, which she sang with particular animation on these drives:

> In the land of San Domingo
> Lived a girl called Oh-by-jingo . . .

From the fields and from the marshes
Came the young, and, oh by goshes . . .

The principal occasion for singing at Gert's house was the long walk along a dirt road to the lake where we swam. We repeated over and over the one verse of a song that somebody had started but that had never been completed:

When the road goes bumpety-bump,
It's Carmen Hill.
When you stub your toe on a lump,
It's Carmen Hill.

This brief stanza insufficient to satisfy our wish to sing, we would go on to other humorous songs: some well known, like "Down by the Old Mill Stream"; others less so, like the "Frozen Logger"; and even more obscure ones, including my favorite, whose first lines introduce one of the two main figures:

From six weeks of hunting
In the woods of Maine
Comes the Harvard student
On the Pullman train.

It took a few more verses to have a young woman also board the train and sit next to him ("Blushingly she asks him / 'Is this seat engaged?' "). In the next several verses, the protagonists gradually become acquainted. A cinder flies into his eye, and she offers to use her handkerchief to remove it ("'Oh, kind sir,' she asks him, / 'Will you please allow me / To take the durn thing out?' "). As we sang, I eagerly awaited my favorite verse, which followed the one describing the entrance of the train into a long dark tunnel. We smacked our lips to make kissing noises as we hummed this wordless final verse.

My mother would also sing on holidays, joining in with equal enthusiasm in "Dayenu" or "Adir Hu" at Passover seders and in "Good King Wenceslaus" around Christmas (we had a tree and sang carols for several years in the 1950s, celebrating an occasion that, like Halloween and Thanksgiving, seemed entirely American and devoid of religious meaning). She picked up left-wing folk songs, including some on the odd thick records with dark blue labels which we had in the house:

I saw the weary miner
Washing coal dust off his back
And I heard his children crying
Ain't got no coal to heat the shack.

But the banks are made of marble
With a guard at every door
And the vaults are stuffed with silver
That the people sweated for.

Most of our records, though, were more recent and more mainstream folk music: "If I Had a Hammer," "Buffalo Boy"; The Weavers, Tom Lehrer, and Theodore Bikel, the Austrian-born Labor Zionist actor and folksinger. My mother liked equally well his records of Yiddish and Israeli music and his international ones, from one of which I had my first exposure to music from the Andes, "Viva Jujuy," from northwestern Argentina, and the Bolivian "Pollerita." The melodies and lively rhythms of these songs caught my attention, and they somehow engraved themselves, syllable by syllable, in my memory, unlike the Greek and Russian songs Bikel also sang, whose melodies I could hum but whose words I did not know. Singing the Andean songs to myself years later, after I had learned Spanish, I realized that I understood most of the lyrics of the two songs, and I was particularly struck with the echoing plaint, "*no me olvides*," don't forget me. I had thought that the few remaining bits were nonsense syllables until I learned Quechua and noticed all of a sudden that I understood the refrains that I had learned over a decade earlier: "*sara mana pelaku*," unhusked ears of corn. I was pleased by the discovery that my exposure to Quechua had begun not in a university classroom, where I took an intensive language course one summer while I was in graduate school, but much earlier, when I was a child, sitting in my living room in Brooklyn, my attention caught by the voice of a Jewish folksinger.

Here in Davis, in her early eighties, weakened by her progressing emphysema, my mother would entertain friends of mine with stories of her childhood in New York, trick-or-treating not on Halloween but on Purim, going in costume from door to door and greeting the neighbors with a Yiddish song, "*Haint iz purim / Morgen iz roys / Git mir a penny / Un varf mir aroys*" (Today it's Purim, tomorrow it's over, give me a penny and throw me out). She startled my children Jacob and Hannah once, when they brought her a book in which the words to the song "Erie Canal" were illustrated with watercolors. Rather than reading this book to them, as they expected, she summoned up the breath to sing it, and here was Grandma, not half-collapsed on the sofa, but sitting up and belting out:

> Got a mule and her name is Sal,
> Fifteen miles on the Erie Canal
> She's a good old worker and a good old pal.
> Fifteen miles on the Erie Canal.

In their apartment in Davis, she and my father maintained the same musical division of space that I remembered from Brooklyn. She might sing to visitors in the living room, but he listened to his own music in his study, the radio tuned to KXPR, a local public radio station, virtually identical to the only station he ever played in Brooklyn, WQXR, "the radio station of the *New York Times*," nothing but classical music and the news. It was not merely his repeated childhood moves across national, linguistic, and musical boundaries that cut him off from popular songs, I think, not merely their mutual efforts to keep private realms within their joint lives, but also his longstanding aspirations to high culture and refinement, as well as his disdain for what he saw as my mother's commonness.

I found twenty-five pages of sheet music in my father's study, or rather, twenty-five photocopied pages of sheet music, held between heavy covers by a shiny black plastic spiral binding. My nephew Daniel Meyerowitz, who lives in the Bay Area, not far from Davis, made up the book for her. On one of his visits to her, fairly soon after my father died, he asked if there was anything that he could do for her. Yes, she replied, my sister Toots (using the nickname by which her sister Pearl was known not only to relatives but to virtually all her friends as well) has been looking for her copy of a songbook she used to have but hasn't been able to find ever since she moved to Florida. Toots misses the book, my mother continued, and it's been bothering her, I'd like to send it to her as a present. My mother gave Daniel a detailed description of the book, a collection of songs that were popular when she was young, and he agreed to look for it in used-book stores. After a long search, in which he was unable to find a copy available for purchase, he borrowed a similar book from the library and brought it up to Davis on a subsequent trip. They looked through it in great detail, and she chose her favorite songs. He had her selections photocopied and bound up to make the book that he gave her on a third visit to Davis.

I carried this book of songs on a few of the walks that I took with my mother when I visited her. We would go out the front door and down a slightly sloping walk to reach the path between the rows of attached one-story bungalows for the elderly, each with a little patio and garden area in front. This path was just wide enough for my mother and me to walk side by side, she holding on to my arm, one or the other of us wheeling her portable oxygen tank. On some days she would feel strong enough to walk the two hundred feet or so to our regular destination, a bench near a large lawn with a few trees. We would sit on the bench for a while, and she would nod or wave to neighbors as they passed by, engaging some of them briefly in conversation, and then we would undertake the walk back. On occasion my mother and I took a different route and walked another few hundred feet past the bench to the place she called "the center," which contained the mailboxes, a small laundromat, and a recreation room with a piano. Here she did play once or twice the songs that Daniel photocopied, along with some of the sheet music someone had left in the piano bench, mostly cowboy songs ("From this valley they say you are going / We will miss your bright eyes and sweet smile / But remember the Red River valley / And the cowboy who loved you so true"). More often, though, she opposed my suggestion of a walk to the center: it was far away, she didn't play as well as she used to, the piano was out of tune, the bathroom in the center was far away from the piano and what if she had to go all of a sudden. I found it easier to leave the book in her apartment than to carry it as a sign of my intention to propose a further walk once we reached the bench.

My mother did look at the book a number of times, though, usually while sitting on the sofa where she spent most of her waking hours. She knew the lyrics well enough that she did not have to read them. Instead, she would open the book to a specific song and sing snatches of it to me and to whomever else was present. She might reminisce about music, principally about playing the piano while she and her sisters would sing, a scene clear in my mind as well. Late on a Thanksgiving afternoon at Toots's apartment, my mother and her sisters — usually four women altogether, sometimes five or even all six of them when May had been invited and Bebe, the one sister who had left New York, was in from Louisville — would assemble at the piano, their mother Gussie watching, smiling, their husbands on sofas and in armchairs in a collective state of overfed stupor, one or two of them, Seymour or Abe, actually snoring. The sisters sang, laughed, and, when the mood was right, improvised a chorus line, arms over shoulders, three or four or five, or, if my mother left the piano and joined in the singing, six stockinged legs in the air.

During one of my many readings of the songs, I was excited to notice that they contained copyright dates, four from the 1920s and two from the 1930s. These years include the ones I often heard my mother speak of, "when all six of us girls were at home," after the birth of the youngest sister, Bebe, in 1917, and before my parents' marriage in 1930. At home as well were her parents. Her mother was known to all by her nickname, Gussie, rather than by her given name, which I have been unable to track down despite considerable effort. She appeared as Gussie on all the documents that I could locate, though she listed herself sometimes as born in New York, sometimes in Russia; I have settled on Kamenetz in Byelorussia as her most likely birthplace. My mother's father, whom her cousins recall as Uncle Hymie, was Chaim Lazer, though this was not the name given to him when he was born in 1883 in a village in the Polish province of Lomze. He had not learned to walk or talk by the time he reached the age of three or four, so it was decided, with apparent success, to attempt to turn him into a normal boy by giving him new names, Chaim, meaning life, a common choice for an auspicious name, and Lazer, which may be a variant of Eliezer. His two older sisters certainly knew his original name but never revealed it to anyone and probably did not speak it, even between themselves, either while he was alive or after he died. They were, however, the source for a fuller account of his metamorphosis: he was taken to the bank of a river, he was buried up to his neck in sand, he was unburied at dusk, at which time he was first addressed by his new name. I am still unable to decide whether I believe this story. It is almost too exotic to be plausible, but the specificity of the details suggests that it is not an invention.

Chaim's parents were innkeepers in Poland, garment workers in New York, and pious Jews in both places. They wanted their only son to dedicate his life to study in the yeshiva, the kind of place from which his eldest sister found her black-coated husband, but he chose Americanization instead in the form of secularism and socialist politics. (My mother always described him as an "ardent socialist"; it was not until I was well into my teens that I discovered that the adjective "ardent" could modify other nouns as well.) He owned and operated first one newsstand in a hotel lobby, then two newsstands at an intersection near a busy subway stop. During the period of the songs in my mother's book, the family moved from neighborhood to neighborhood as my grandfather's business achieved modest success. My mother was the only sister born on the Lower East Side. By the time Ruth arrived in 1908, little more than a year later, they had moved to the more genteel Harlem, part of the growing Jewish population in an area then inhabited primarily by Germans, Irish, and Italians. At some point in the early 1920s they took up their northward journey once more and moved to the Grand Concourse in the Bronx, one of the several broad avenues in the outlying boroughs that urban planners had hoped would replicate, in the crowded city of immigrants, the elegance and solidity of the Parisian boulevards.

My mother's stories, though, did not trace this steady ascent to comfort and respectability. She emphasized instead the continuity of this period, "when all six of us girls were at home." The sisters were inseparable. When they walked to school, the policeman on the corner of Lenox Avenue would stop traffic with a blast of his whistle and a "Here come the Cohen girls!" When their parents would take them to visit their Tante Sarah, they would form a single mass, burst through the door to her apartment, and check the tables, knowing that they would be covered with food. In the most frequently repeated detail, my mother spoke of how the six of them shared two double beds in one room, warm together on cold winter nights. One or another of them, awakened by the need to urinate, would inevitably be joined by her sleepy bedmates, whose bladders found this urgency contagious — three sisters scurrying down the hall, clutching a big blanket over their shoulders, rushing first to the bathroom for quick turns on the toilet and then back to the bedroom to settle themselves back into their triple warmth.

I thought that the copied music would give me some insight into my mother's life during the years she was at home and the later period of her marriage. In particular, I thought I might find some sign of her father's death from influenza in 1923. This event, sudden and entirely unanticipated, changed my mother's life in a number of ways, of which the loss of economic security was one of the most important. Her father had managed the family's money. He saw no incompatibility between his socialism and his willingness to invest his profits from his news-stands on Wall Street. An avid follower of the stock market (my mother recalled him at the breakfast table, his temples flexing as he clenched his jaws while he read the financial news), he had accumulated a fair amount of money. After his death, my grandmother — bewildered at the prospect of handling her inheritance, certain that money should be in-vested cleverly — entrusted her half of his estate to a friend of the fami-ly's, whose assurances that he would continue her husband's careful in-vestments proved to be lies. My grandmother saw little of the money. She supported her six daughters on the other half of his estate, held in their names. My mother, fearing the family to be on the brink of penury, dropped out of high school, took some courses at a secretarial school, and was hired to work in the office of Lucius N. Littauer, an elderly German Jewish industrialist who ran the small philanthropic foundation that he established when he retired. She gave the bulk of her earnings to her mother. The family was able to remain in the same apartment, and my mother's younger sisters finished high school and went on to college.

In the songs, though, I cannot detect a break marked by her father's death. I was puzzled that this event did not leave clearer traces, since she missed him greatly. She spoke of him fondly and valued her memories of the few occasions when her mother and younger sisters stayed home and he took her somewhere alone, to Socialist Party rallies mostly. Her grief was evident, too, in her efforts (of which she spoke openly) to find a replacement for him in her employer, "my Lucius," a kind man who gave her affectionate greetings and paternal advice as well as occasional gifts and small loans. At times I have wondered whether her father's death was the first of many disappointments that she faced with silent stoicism. I am more certain of my belief that her sisters sustained her. In her phrase "when all six of us girls were at home," she suggests with great conciseness that the unity of the home depended more on the presence of all the sisters than on that of both parents.

Unable to divide the songs into those that fall before some key event and those that fall after it, I have at least been able to place several of them into the simple category of "love song." The other songs have something in common as well, since they speak of some form of exploration — travel, adventure, or contact with different kinds of people. Travel is certainly the theme of the song that Daniel placed first, "California Here I Come." The song always reminds me of a song from my late teen years, the Mamas and the Papas' "California Dreamin'." For my mother, it must have evoked her recent decision to move from Brooklyn to a place with a better climate:

> Where bowers of flowers bloom in the sun.

This song probably reminded my mother of the dread with which she anticipated the winters in Brooklyn, the effort that it took to go outside once that season arrived, to step over slush-filled gutters, to negotiate icy patches on sidewalks.

> When the wintry winds are blowing,
> And the snow is starting in to fall,
> Then my eyes turn westward, knowing
> That's the place I love best of all.

My mother was certainly impatient to leave New York once she had made up her mind to move, a note echoed in the song:

> That's why I can hardly wait
> Open up that Golden Gate
> California, here I come.

As I listen to this song in my mind's ear, I do not imagine my mother as a seventeen-year-old, when the song was published in 1924. This is the song that I knew best before seeing the book, and I cannot free it in my mind from the associations with my parents' move here. However, other songs make me think of my mother as a young woman, eager to seek out the heady excitement that New York offered during the economic prosperity and cultural ferment of the 1920s. My mother was part of the first generation in her family to grow up speaking English rather than Yiddish at home, the first to contemplate finishing high school and even going on, as her sisters did, to college. What a new world was at her disposal: Modern Library editions of classic and recent literature, public concerts, and, as the song "The Birth of the Blues" portrays, even the arrival of what then would have been called Negro music:

Oh!
They say some people long ago
Were searching for a diff'rent tune,
One that they could croon
As only they can.
They only had the rhythm
So they started swaying to and fro
They didn't know just what to use.
That is how the blues
really began:

They heard the breeze in the trees
Singing weird melodies
And they made that
The start of the blues.
And from a jail came the wail
Of a downhearted frail,
And they played that
As part of the blues.
From a whippoorwill
Out on a hill.
They took a new note,
Pushed it through a horn
'Til it was worn
Into a blue note!
And then they nursed it, rehearsed it,
And gave out the news
That the Southland gave birth to the blues!

Ever the anthropologist, I feel a desire to address the political content of the song: on the one hand to apologize for its racism (the "they only had rhythm / so they started swaying to and fro" and even its unwilling-

ness to name the "they," the "some people," located in "the South-land"), and on the other to be glad for its antiracism (its acceptance of black music, and the possible flicker of protest against southern jails and their wailing prisoners). But that is my reading: my mother, twenty years old when the song came out, certainly did not analyze it but simply enjoyed it, sang it, danced to it, open to the syncopated rhythms, to the clever rhymes, to the exploration of life beyond her neighborhood. This enjoyment stayed with her. "Jazz it up" was one of her standard phrases. I recall her using it to describe what a bay leaf and some garlic powder could do to an otherwise unappealingly bland pot roast. Her other term for this effect, "give it some oomph," was also derived from this musical era, or at least related to it. She would accompany the last word of this alternative phrase with a firm swing of her hand and a nod of her head, as if she were a bandleader marking the downbeat.

I was not aware of the rhythms and melody of the song at first, since I focused on the lyrics when I read through the book. I heard the song only later, when I asked Jane Keller, a neighbor of mine, a piano teacher, and a member of a local chamber music group, to play through the songs in the book for me. When I heard, rather than read, the song, it became more complex and more engaging to me. I was surprised that my neighbor, who was accustomed to sight-reading, had difficulty with the shifts in rhythm and the occasional substitutions of naturals for sharps and flats in "The Birth of the Blues." My mother had always brushed off compliments about her musical abilities, so I always assumed that these popular songs were easy to play. There's really nothing to it, my mother would say, it's not that different from typing on a typewriter, the work I do at the office. Thinking back to this comment, it occurs to me that her equation works both ways, since she also took pride in her skills as an office worker. To type memoranda, documents, letters, to cut mimeograph stencils (these tasks were also forms of sight-reading, it occurs to me), my mother needed dexterity, rhythm, and, granted the sheer weight of the mechanical typewriters of her era, some physical strength as well. Once again I realize how I grew up with contradictory voices. In this case my father's is the dominant one. I am ready to assume, as he did, that any piece of classical music is more challenging than popular music, that artistic activity (in this case, music) is invariably more demanding than office work.

The earliest song in the book, though, is not about the distant West or South; it is a simple love song, sung by a woman:

There's just one fellow for me in this world
Harry's his name

That's what I claim
Why for ev'ry fellow there must be a girl
I've found my mate
By kindness of fate.

I'm just wild about Harry
And Harry's wild about me.
The heav'nly blisses of his kisses
Fill me with ecstasy.
He's sweet just like choc'late candy
And just like honey from the bee.
Oh, I'm just wild about Harry
And he's just wild about, cannot do without,
He's just wild about me.

Hardly the song of a shrinking violet, of a passive woman: I try to think of my mother singing this song as a fourteen-year-old, as she was when it came out in 1921. Did it appeal to her in its depiction of an equal relation, both people "wild about" the other? I like this slangy phrase, suggesting animals and sexuality. I keep listening to the song, hoping to glimpse her as a young teenager. A phrase in the song brings to my mind her forthrightness, the initiative that she displayed in pushing my hesitant father along at key points in their relationship. "I've found my mate," the singer declares, as my mother might have declared in 1927 after she met my father or in 1930 after they married. In 1921, though, she must have been thinking more simply about pleasure. I try to peel off from the song's "ecstasy" the current usage of this word as a simple code-term for orgasm, and I find that the song describes simple kisses, enjoyable ones ("just like honey from the bee") that take the singer to another plane ("heav'nly blisses"). The pleasure in the song, at any rate, is not only the remembered pleasure of the kisses, but the current pleasure of the singing, the cheery rhythms, "And he's just wild about, cannot do without, / He's just wild about me." As I hum these lines, my mother's face comes into view, singing while she plays the piano at Toots's apartment.

When I went over these songs with my mother, both of us sitting on the worn sofa in her apartment in Davis, the one she discussed at greatest length was the second of the love songs, Rodgers and Hart's 1926 classic "Mountain Greenery." As she explained, she had chosen this song for inclusion in the book not merely because she enjoyed it so much but also because it was a particular favorite of my father's sister Gertrude, the sibling Robbie was closest to and in many ways the one my mother liked the most as well. Gertrude was the youngest of the siblings born in the two-year intervals (Milton, born seven years after her, was the baby of the family, still a child when Gertrude was a young woman). Dark-skinned and dark-eyed, full-mouthed, with Slavic cheekbones, she was a more striking figure than her one sister, Elizabeth, who was taller, a more classic beauty with regular features, a trim waist, and long legs. My father and Gertrude were linked by a powerful sense of being different from their other siblings. They were the artistic ones. In their visits to galleries, in their trips to wild spots in the country, in their parties with mutual friends who were painters and poets, they sought something grander than the materialist ambitions of the other Orloves. Young Milton aside, their brothers were caught up in the rivalries and excitement of my grandfather's business, while Elizabeth prepared herself to become a wife of a prosperous Jewish man. Gertrude's fearlessness in opposing their parents as well as their siblings inspired awe and respect in my father. She withstood her parents' frequent criticism, which turned especially sharp on several occasions — when she developed a strong friendship with a somewhat older woman whom relatives thought to be a lesbian, at whose country house in the Hudson Valley she spent weekends; when she took a job they deemed beneath her as a clerk in a large Manhattan store that sold paintings and sculpture; when she entered into a romance with, and later married, a man she met at that store, Ted Crofut, a gentile, of old New England Yankee stock, a poised, charming, and elegant man. My parents accepted Gertrude and Ted much more readily and warmly than the rest of the family did. And my parents spoke of them often when I was a child, Gertrude's passion all the more poignant because she died young, a victim of pneumonia when she was twenty-seven, and her daughters, Sheila and Jinny, four and two — the girls raised by Ted and the woman he married a few years later. "Mountain Greenery" was Gertrude and Ted's song.

On the first of May
It is moving day;
Spring is here, so blow your job,
Throw your job away;
Now's the time to trust
To your wanderlust.
In the city's dust you wait,
Must you wait?
Just you wait:

In a mountain greenery,
Where God paints the scenery,
Just two crazy people together;
While you love your lover, let
Blue skies be your coverlet,
When it rains we'll laugh at the weather
And if you're good
I'll search for wood,
So you can cook
While I stand looking.
Beans could get no keener re-
Ception in a beanery
Bless our mountain greenery home!

(He:)
When the world was young,
Old Father Adam with sin would grapple,
So we're entitled to just one apple,
I mean to make apple sauce.

(She:)
Underneath the bough
We'll learn a lesson from Mister Omar;
Beneath the eyes of no Pa and no Ma
Old Lady Nature is boss.

For weeks after we went over the songs, my mother would sing the first of the chorus:

In a mountain greenery,
Where God paints the scenery,
Just two crazy people together;
While you love your lover, let
Blue skies be your coverlet. . . .

and then continue to hum verses of the song. Widowed, infirm, my
mother recalled the passion and rebelliousness of her youth, of the decade of the 1920s. And these are the images that most appealed to me as
well: wildness once again, uncivilized nature, and open sexuality. The
couple in the song makes love, out of doors, right in the open, under
the blue skies rather than in some hidden wood. The city of dust and
jobs is far away. The rhythms of their voices show the equality and balance between them. Sometimes they sing together, sometimes one
sings, then the other, a teasing conversation in song.

And yet this song was not my mother's. The "two crazy people together" were not her and my father but rather Ted and Gertrude. How
was this song specifically theirs, I wondered. As I thought the song over,
I realized that I could visualize them in an imaginary picture, or, to be
more precise, in a shot from an imaginary movie. The song is in fact
somewhat cinematic; Rodgers and Hart wrote it for a film, "The Gar-
rick Gaieties," and gave it a stagey quality by setting parts of it as a duet.
And, a few visits of Ted's aside, I knew the two of them from photographs and from some prints and a carving of Gertrude's head that my
father made. In my mental movie, Ted is slim, tall, dressed in a elegant
jacket and loose trousers; Gertrude, short, dark, is in a belted dress, and
her eyes flash. The sun is on their faces, light breezes move their hair,
and they are singing the duet:

(He:)
When the world was young,
Old Father Adam with sin would grapple,
So we're entitled to just one apple,
I mean to make apple sauce.

(She:)
Underneath the bough

We'll learn a lesson from Mister Omar;
Beneath the eyes of no Pa and no Ma
Old Lady Nature is boss.

A Christian, a man, he speaks for both Christians and Jews, proposing rebellion against the rules, and against the rule, of the Christian and Jewish God. Adam tasted the fruit, let's taste it too, he says, recalling the brief time in paradise before the expulsion. She's got a different tree in mind, the Rubaiyat's bough, and she's staying under it, right there with a jug of wine, a loaf of bread, and thou. She's a Jew, a woman, she can lead both Christians and Jews outside God's authority, outside parental authority, outside the West, taking them to somewhere beyond both Christianity and Judaism, to the Orient, to where a woman rules, Old Lady Nature, oh wilderness were paradise enow. Her paradise is better than Adam's, and they will not be driven from it. "Dusky Jewess" was a phrase that was current in the 1920s, and Ted may have thought of Gertrude as one, as a woman who could lead him underneath the bough. She saw in him the handsome stranger from the new land whom she would take to her own paradise, someplace beneath the eyes of no Pa and no Ma.

These first four songs of my mother's all date from a brief period, 1921 to 1927, that coincides almost perfectly with my mother's years as a teenager. (Born in 1907, she was fourteen in 1921, twenty in 1927.) In the last year of this period my father moved with his parents and siblings into the apartment house in the Bronx where my mother was living. At first she struck up a friendship not with him but with Elizabeth. They were both working as secretaries. They sometimes went to the movies or museums together and would stop by each other's apartments, Elizabeth walking up to visit the Cohen girls on the fifth floor, my mother coming down to the Orloves on the second. My father, still shy with women, was at least able to move beyond the circuit of his own cousins. He developed an interest in this spirited friend of his sister's, who in turn was attracted to him. My mother was eager to explore, or at least to imagine, new places, California, blues bars; she chose a man who had lived in several countries, a cultured European who knew many languages. She found, if not a Harry, a Robert whom she was wild about and who was wild about her. In walks through the large wooded parks in the Bronx, in ferry trips up the Hudson, in excursions into the Catskills, they escaped, if only briefly, to mountain greeneries. They were married on May 17, 1930.

Here was another event, like her father's death, that might have created a break in the songs, and here, too, I have been unable to divide the songs into two periods, her single and her married years. The only change is one of rate: the intervals between songs suddenly increased at the end of this first period. The average interval in the first set of songs is only two years, but five years passed before the next song in 1932, then six years until the last one.

After scrutinizing these two songs, I have found only indirect clues about my mother's feelings toward my father. It is from my father's diaries, from the stories told to me by my parents and by the numerous other relatives who witnessed their early years together, that I know of the tensions of that period. My mother certainly was drawn to my father, a tender, exciting, and worldly man, as he was drawn to her and to the strength of her passion for him. She had doubts about herself, though. However strong her ties to her sisters, however competent she was at work, however vivacious at parties, she questioned her attractiveness, her sophistication, her ability to care for her widowed mother and five younger sisters. And she also questioned her impulses, the attraction that she felt for him. Was he the right man for her, was he right as a man? His periods of unemployment and depression concerned her — the more extreme manifestations of his emotionality and his need for protection, qualities that drew her to him but that seemed unmanly, feminine. His ambivalence was even more troubling. Ted and Gertrude threw themselves into their affair, but my father was often tentative and indecisive.

Uncertain of my father's commitment, perhaps seeking to push him into a decision, my mother planned to take a trip in Europe with her sister Ruth, using their scarce savings for round-trip passage on an ocean liner, and then impulsively invited him along. Passion led them to travel together, as did other reasons: my father's curiosity to see Europe again after nine years in New York, my mother's wish for an escort and a guide. They married suddenly, almost on the spur of the moment — a quick civil ceremony and then dinner in a restaurant with only a few friends rather than a larger wedding under the traditional canopy. My mother gave my father his ticket as a wedding present. When I was a child, my mother spoke of their honeymoon with great fondness: the amusing passengers on the ocean liner as it crossed the Atlantic, the beauty of Sacre Coeur in Paris and the mountain scenery in the Alps, the interest in seeing cities in Germany where my father lived as a boy, the thrill of visiting his artist friends. She told me how they complemented each other, since in virtually every city they could get by either with his German or with her French, the product of her studies before she quit school.

Only later did I hear of another side to their honeymoon. The ticket that my mother gave him was the source of the first major argument of their married life and, I believe, the most serious one as well. Before they left New York, he sold the return half of his ticket and gave the money to his mother, who was caught up in the bitter disputes with his father that culminated in their separation a year or two later. I think that this moment was not only one of great conflict for my father, caught between his old ties to his needy mother and his new ones to his generous wife; it was also one of satisfaction that he had finally found a gesture dramatic enough to show the depth of his devotion to his mother, a gesture nearly as self-destructive as flinging himself out a window would have been. He must have recognized how asinine his act was, since he claimed that he would obtain the money for his return passage once he arrived in Europe by borrowing it from friends or relatives in Europe — or, in different versions of the story, by reclaiming some funds that someone owed him or his father.

Did my mother believe his assurances that he would buy his return ticket once they arrived in Europe? I think that he would have at least been able to persuade her to wait and see whether his plans succeeded. As I think back to this period, I wince at the despair that he must have felt when he realized that he would have to tell my mother that the expected money had not arrived. Later failures of his spring to mind, ones that occurred when I was a child. I would look into the kitchen as he told my mother about the boss who dismissed his request for a raise, about the art dealer who rejected his drawing from a show. I recall him sitting at the table, his abject posture as he sat motionless, his heavy sighs, the defeated tone of his voice; I recall myself walking to my room rather than adding to his misery and mine by remaining. Now, too, I set his diaries from 1930 down on my desk and close them before I remind myself that I cannot erase their contents. Even after I open the diaries, I find myself looking out the window, thinking rather than reading, as I recall moments when my mother would become irritated with minor transgressions of his. "Robbie, how could you?" she would begin, going on to express her sudden anger at his neglecting to call from New York to tell her that he would be home late for dinner, or at his forgetting to stop by the bank to pick up the cash that she needed for errands the next morning. She would barely listen to his excuses. Her silence, I felt, was a sign not that she had forgiven him but rather that she had resigned herself once again to his inadequacies.

My father's diaries offer hints of her reactions. They had returned to Paris from Germany:

> Riding all night was bad, but the morning was worse. It got very chilly, a cold sickly light came up, everyone was cramped and broken up. We reached Paris. Slept for two hours, then mail. Did not get what we wanted.

I try to imagine my father in Paris when he told my mother that the money that he had expected had not arrived. She must have been furious not only at him but at herself as well for having married such a weak man. I do not know whether she upbraided him for placing his mother before her, or whether she received his words with cold silent scorn. I am certain, though, that he was beside himself with grief, torn between his allegiance to his mother and his wish not to be humiliated by his wife. I, too, am torn. One part of me feels the steadiness of my impulse to protect and comfort him; the other part lurches unstably from point to point. I move from exasperation at his foolishness to regret that he acted so impulsively in selling his ticket, and suddenly I am frightened. A momentary panic overtakes me as I recognize how close my father's obsessive devotion to his mother came to ending his new marriage.

I return to the diaries. When the expected money did not arrive, my parents altered their plans so that they could remain longer in Paris than they had first intended. ("Still in uncertainty. Back to the hotel in great tension. Could find no peace of mind.") My father sent several urgent wires to his brother Henry in Chicago, asking him to send some money, but his repeated visits to the telegraph company were fruitless. Henry never replied. My mother and Ruth spent several afternoons strolling around the city on their own, while he waited in the hotel lobby for friends or business associates who did not come. In the end, it was his artist friends who scraped together enough money for a return passage on a slow boat later in the summer. ("Everything was arranged, passage and tickets. A great relief to know to go home again.") More money came through after my mother and Ruth left for New York. He sent a telegram by radio to her that she received on board ship, announcing that he had switched his ticket to an earlier and faster boat. When my mother arrived in New York from her honeymoon, she was able to explain to the people who met her that Robbie would be coming soon. He arrived five days later.

There are no songs at all from the period between my parents' meeting and their marriage. The two songs that come after 1930 portray the satisfactions and pleasures that my mother had as a married woman, though they do not speak directly about my parents as a couple. The first of these songs, "Forty Second Street," is an exuberant one. It carries forward the theme of travel and exploration, suggesting trips downtown to Manhattan, where my parents lived for a few years in the early 1930s, when they rented an apartment on East 19th Street somewhere between Greenwich Village and Chelsea. My mother occasionally mentioned the concerts that they attended, the art exhibits, but she spoke most often about the parties that they had then. Single friends and relatives came, as well as other couples — some from the Bronx and Brooklyn, some from Manhattan as well; the small apartment was sometimes so crowded that guests would sit on the fire escape. My mother's salary from Littauer stretched enough to afford at least some food for guests. Many times she told me, the delight at her own practicality evident in her tone of voice, if I heard some people were coming over, Ben, I'd just throw a roast beef in the oven, everyone likes roast beef. (She would serve it, if I recall correctly, on rye bread with mustard.) These evenings were filled with conversation, dancing, and party games as well, of which charades was the most popular. I grew up hearing stories of these games. My father was fond of replicating one particularly successful performance. He would make the introductory gestures, first to indicate that he was giving clues to the title of a book rather than a song or a movie, then to tell that the title was composed of four words, and finally to show that he would depict all four words at once, an act that he accomplished by jumping up and down, his right hand firmly placed in his crotch, his left hand on his buttocks, thus suggesting the title of a recent book, a novel by Sinclair Lewis about the fascist threat in America, *It Can't Happen Here*.

"Forty Second Street," the song from 1932, suggests such happy parties:

> In the heart of little old New York,
> You'll find a thoroughfare;
> It's part of little old New York that runs into Times Square.
> A crazy quilt that Wall Street "Jack" built,
> If you've got a little time to spare,
> I want to take you there.

> Come and meet those dancing feet,
> On the Avenue I'm taking you to,
> Forty Second Street.
> Hear the beat of dancing feet,
> It's the song I love the melody of,
> Forty Second Street,
> Little "nifties" from the Fifties, innocent and sweet;
> Sexy ladies from the Eighties, who are indiscreet.
> They're side by side, they're glorified
> Where the underworld can meet the elite,
> Forty Second Street,
> Naughty, bawdy, gaudy, sporty,
> Forty Second Street.

This song is catchy, with its sudden little variations from the basic steady beat of its four-four time, its clever rhymes, and its images of people traveling from different neighborhoods to the center of the city and mixing together in an exciting world. The song, with its depiction of the simple enjoyment of dancing, makes me think how my mother regretted my father's inability to dance and his unwillingness to learn. This one song of dancing in my mother's book comes from the first years of her marriage, when she did not dance with my father, rather than from the earlier years when she was single and danced with dates and boyfriends. I remember Thanksgivings and other gatherings when my mother would stand up, sing a few bars, and demonstrate some steps of her two favorite dances, the Charleston and the Black Bottom. In these moments she was reliving, I think, the parties of the early years of her marriage: these were fast dances, in which a woman, rather than being held in the arms of her partner, was free to move and to show off for an entire roomful of people. These may have been my mother's performances, the counterpart to my father's witty charades: no wonder she recalled the parties in Manhattan, where she was a hostess, more fondly than the earlier parties in the Bronx, chaperoned by older relatives. Even if my father was not able to dance with her, her marriage did bring her pleasure in dancing. It allowed her to be sporty and gaudy, and, in a rather safe and public way, naughty and bawdy as well.

The last song, from 1938, comes after my parents left Manhattan, first moving to an apartment in the Bronx, where my sister Carol was born on March 20, 1935, and soon after to Brooklyn, where my mother's mother and all my mother's sisters except Ruth were living. This song comes from a little-remembered movie, "Hard To Get," but the song itself is the best known in my mother's book: "You Must Have Been a Beautiful Baby."

> Does your mother realize,
> The stork delivered quite a prize,
> The day he left you on the fam'ly tree,
> Does your dad appreciate,
> That you are merely super great,
> The miracle of any century,
> If they don't just send them to me,
>
> You must have been a beautiful baby,
> You must have been a wonderful child,
> When you were only startin' to go to kindergarten
> I bet you drove the little boys wild,
> And when it came to winning blue ribbons,
> You must have shown the other kids how,
> I can see the judges' eyes as they handed you the prize,
> I bet you made the cutest bow,

Oh! You must have been a beautiful baby,
'Cause baby look at you now.

I like the feeling of openness and enthusiasm that this song, like the other love songs, conveys: you are merely super great, she sings, the miracle of any century. But on listening to it again and again, the song began to puzzle me. I noticed how it differs from the other two love songs. They were songs of reciprocal affection and passion. In this one, though, the singer expresses admiration of the lover's beauty but does not receive any action or emotion in return. Moreover, this song addresses the loved one as "you," unlike "I'm Just Wild About Harry," in which the singer tells the audience about herself and her lover, and "Mountain Greenery," in which the two singers direct themselves to each other and the audience eavesdrops. The audience eavesdrops in this song as well, but in a different way, listening to the singer sing to a silent lover. I was struck even more by how this song is meant to be sung by a man, unlike "I'm Just Wild About Harry," clearly a female song, or the man-woman duets of "Mountain Greenery." When my mother and I leafed through the book of songs, this song was one she sang with particular gusto. Who was singing, and to whom? I was certain that my father had not sung it to my mother. She did not speak of it in an "our song" kind of way, I thought, and, moreover, the song came a full ten years after they met.

I wondered whether some other man, attracted to my mother, sang it to her. I do not believe that my mother, who spoke easily of the boyfriends who took her to movies and plays before she met my father, of dancing with other men at parties after they were married, ever had an affair, but I recall hints of flirtations. My sister Carol once mentioned to me how, when she was a small girl, a piano teacher, Mr. Pimsler, would often come to give my mother lessons when my father was out. On one occasion my mother handed Carol a bunch of grapes in the kitchen to distract her and entered the parlor containing the piano and her teacher. My mother shut the door behind her, the door that Carol somehow knew not to open in the long minutes after she finished the grapes. Was Mr. Pimsler's admiration based on more than his recognition of her musical talents, did he sing her this song, at a time when my father was unemployed, morose, spending long afternoons away at chess clubs or his ailing mother's apartment? My biographer's mind plays with dates: Carol, in 1938, would have been only three, too young to remember this story of Mr. Pimsler, so I check; I find that the song retained its popularity, and Mr. Pimsler could have sung this to my mother a few years later. I think, too, of my mother's insistence that "Mountain Greenery" was Ted and Gertrude's song, as if she were unwilling to include a love song that connected her with my father.

I feel uncertain, though, and visit my neighbor once again. Jane Keller played the song, and I realized that it is simple and happy, with nothing furtive about it. It is difficult to speak the title of the song, which is also the well-known first line of the lilting chorus, without beginning to sing it. The first verse also has this light-hearted quality, a simple melody of eighth-notes running up scales. "The stork delivered quite a prize, / the day he left you on the fam'ly tree": too cheery a tune for Mr. Pimsler in the parlor. The rhythms are syncopated, catchy, and the musician is directed to play *molto rubato*. I recognized *molto* as meaning "very," but I did not know the second word. Jane Keller, accustomed to eighteenth-century chamber music, was also unfamiliar with *rubato*. We looked it up and found that it derived from *rubare*, to rob: "having certain notes arbitrarily lengthened while others are correspondingly shortened, or vice versa," time robbed from some notes and given to others, an expressive, open style.

My mother was the singer, it occurs to me, back in 1938 as in 1988, when Daniel made up the book. This image is one that I can entertain. The eight years of marriage and Carol's birth made her fully confident. She could adopt the male voice of the singer, since she had many masculine characteristics; after all, she earned the money, she made the decisions, proposing and arranging the move back to Brooklyn, to the neighborhood in which her relatives lived. The song, then, is simple and suggests a simple *pshat* reading. The beautiful baby was my sister Carol, then three years old. It was not strange for my mother to sing a man's song as long as the song's baby really was a baby. Though Carol was in her teens when I was born, I have vivid images of her infancy and early childhood, my parents' stories for once corroborating each other. They would reminisce jointly on walks I took with them in the Brooklyn Botanic Gardens, a boulder reminding them of how Carol jumped from it into my father's arms, can you imagine, it must have been thirty years ago. My father, experimenting with photography in that period, had shot and developed many rolls of film. He carefully mounted a selection of the photographs in albums with thick pages of soft black paper. I see the smiling child playing with some Indian toys, feather headdresses perhaps; wheeling a cart; posing in front of a brick building in the arms of one of her aunts.

My mother also recalled these halcyon times and the honor she had in being the first of the Cohen girls to have a child, and how perfect that the first child be a Cohen girl too. Carol's reign as the newest grandchild was brief, since the next two sisters soon took their turns, Ruth having Peter seven months later and Martha arriving to Toots early in 1937. But Carol was somehow special, perhaps also because of the miracle of her rapid recovery from being born a month early and very small, only five pounds, perhaps because Peter was far away with Ruth and Abe in the Bronx. My mother's stories involve not only Carol, called "Cookie" then, but also my mother's sisters, all of whom except Ruth were living in Brooklyn: the sisters fighting for the privilege of pushing her down Eastern Parkway in her carriage; the sisters chattering in excitement at some new accomplishment, pulling herself up on a chair, catching a ball; the sisters rushing in my parents' apartment in the evening, hoping that Cookie had not yet had her bath, so that they could help wash her, sometimes shaping her hair, stiff with shampoo, into coiffures as varied and elaborate as they were evanescent.

The two songs from the 1930s, then, carry forward the sense of exploration and the optimism about love of the four songs from the 1920s. They describe the simple enjoyments of those years, the "dancing feet" at a party, looking at "a wonderful child." They speak of the pleasures that came with marriage — of dancing at one's own party, of having children — rather than of the marriage itself. My mother was fortunate to have the ability to take simple enjoyment, even when faced with many problems, and I am likewise fortunate to have some of this ability myself, in part from her. I am more ambivalent about her ability to remain silent, at times seeing it as a strength needed to persevere, at other times as a cruel denial of others. In any case, these songs show her silences as well: about her father's death and then notably about her husband, the man with whom she moved down to "the heart of little old New York" of the fabulous parties, the man with whom she conceived and raised the beautiful baby she remembers sharing with her sisters, the man whom she loved, who loved her and who failed her in some basic ways.

The book ends in 1938, the six songs giving way to another silence. Perhaps the difficulties of these years overcame my mother's ability to take small singable pleasures. In 1942 Lucius suffered a stroke and became partially incapacitated, requiring my mother to make long train trips to his country estate. Precisely midway through that year, on June 30, my second sister, Judy, was born. Soon after, Carol also became severely ill with rheumatic fever, and my mother cared for all three as best she could, in a state of continuous exhaustion difficult for me to imagine — she always described these months to me as the hardest in her life. Judy, a strong and healthy baby, grew quickly, and Carol remained a bedridden convalescent through most of 1943. In the next year, after Lucius's death, my parents and sisters moved to Chicago, persuaded by the appeals of my father's brother Henry to form a business partnership, perhaps ready to leave the two hard years behind. This partnership, like Henry's earlier partnerships with Max, quickly collapsed, but my father found steady work designing and making fur hats. Despite my father's steady employment, these were unhappy years for my mother: not working for the first time in her adult life, she was bored; separated from her sisters, also for the first time, she was lonely. From this tedium and isolation, from her fear of impending menopause, from the recollected enjoyments of Carol's infancy, or from other impulses, she decided to have a third child. Concerned about the wisdom of this impulse because of her age, she visited the family physician, whose words she repeated often to me, "You're healthy as a nut, Mrs. Orlove. Go out and have a good time." She was forty-one, my father forty-four, when I was born in 1948.

# Chapter 7 COMBINATIONS

The half-full suitcase lay open on my bed. I had just completed the first part of the packing for my departure, folding jackets and pants, then placing them into one side of the suitcase. And now for the second half: I walked to the closet and pondered the shirts that hung in it. Some were new and fashionable enough for me to take back to college, while others, relics from my high school days, would stay behind in my parents' apartment; the ones that could fall in either category required longer consideration. I selected some shirts, hung them on the wooden knobs on my dresser drawers, and began removing them from their hangers and folding them.

Had I left the door closed, my father would have knocked before coming in, since I insisted on having my parents respect my privacy at home. But I must have opened my bedroom door at some point in the packing, perhaps to allow light from the hall to come into my bedroom, which otherwise was lit only by a dim ceiling fixture and small bedside and desk lamps. Because he had not announced his presence, my father did not fully enter the room. He stepped half-way into it, resting one hand on the door frame.

Despite the absence of any spoken words, I could hear him as he shifted his weight from one foot to another, breathing heavily and occasionally sighing. I was as conscious of his presence as I would have been if he were touching me. He was inspecting the job of packing that I was doing, and finding it inadequate. I felt, to use one of the words that cropped up in my family's conversations, "annoyed." I certainly knew how to pack a suitcase, even if I did not do it as well as he could. Yes, he was the one who had taught me the series of steps for each garment—how to check that a shirt was properly buttoned, how to shake the creases out before laying it facedown on the bed, how to make the complex series of folds that turned it into a neat rectangle—but I was doing just fine, and what business was it of his, anyway?

This first scene of our drama must have gone on for at least several minutes as he stood in the doorway and watched me intently while I removed shirts from hangers and folded them. The next move was his. He took his hand from the doorframe and drew closer to me. "Ach," I heard him say, the long guttural sound still not quite a word, but a sign nonetheless of disapproval. I turned and looked at him. Speaking in an ordinary tone, as if we were in the middle of a normal conversation, I asked him whether he would like to finish packing for me. He smiled in relief and agreed, as I knew he would. We moved easily into action. While he refolded the shirt that I had been working on, I selected a few more and set them, along with my sweaters and underwear, where he could reach them, and then left the room.

My recollection of this encounter ends with my leaving the room. From what I remember of my other visits from college to my parents' apartment in Brooklyn, I can imagine several possible denouements. I might have made a phone call to one of my friends from the neighborhood, talking one more time before we both returned to college, or I might have had a cup of tea and a piece of cake in the kitchen with my mother. In any case, I am certain that my father would have taken a while to complete the packing. Once he was finished, I would have thanked him and carried the suitcase to the spot near the front door where it would stand all night, ready for my departure the next morning. The tense event would have been over, though not forgotten, as my writing about it more than twenty years later shows.

In one sense, scenes like this are very common. One recent November I read a newspaper advice column written in anticipation of the Thanksgiving season, when students return from college to visit their parents. The writer counseled the readers to expect conflict over the question of whether the students would now be treated as adults. The students will want to be accorded the rights of adults, the author cautioned, to be permitted to stay out at night without any curfew, but they will also seek the comforts of being cared for as children, the meals and laundry available without question as they had always been. The parents, too, should anticipate a shift in their positions. They will be uncertain whether they should treat the returned students as adult conversational partners, inquiring about their new activities, or as children, pressing them with unwelcome questions about their health, their friends, their grades. The columnist advised their parents to leave the students' rooms unchanged and to avoid intruding on the students' privacy during their visit. Perhaps my annoyance with my father was a normal, predictable dispute that resulted from his simple violation of these principles and from my wish to be treated as an adult even though he saw me as a child.

No, I realized: the incident reflects how different my family was from other families rather than how much we were like them, as the advice column might suggest. The evening has lodged in my memory because of the preciseness with which it illustrates specific ways we felt, spoke, and acted. To draw once again from my family's vocabulary, my father was "upset." There were other words we could have used: "agitated" or "disheartened" would have been more accurate but might have struck us as pretentious. Surely, though, there were families in Brooklyn whose members spoke of each other as being "angry" or "sad." It seems to me that we used the ordinary word "upset" in very specific ways. It was always an adjective, never a verb: "I think Robbie's upset," not, "You upset him." He, too, used it in this way and added a second condition, that it always be stated in the negative. "I'm not upset," he might shout in the middle of a conversation in which my mother had asked him about his day at work, "I just don't think that my boss should have spoken to me that way."

However it was phrased, being upset was a temporary condition for my father, a brief episode that my mother, sisters, and I knew how to handle. No matter what he said, we would agree with him, speaking calmly and continuing what we were doing. Soon he would be better, as he was after he finished packing my suitcase. The indirect manner with which we treated him was entirely in keeping with his own image

of himself. He prided himself on understanding life and acting in the
right manner, with patience and serenity, never showing disappointment or pain.

As a child and teenager, I simply took for granted my father's emotionality and its numerous wordless manifestations in sound: the sighs

and grunts, the disapproving clicks of his tongue against his palate, and, most dramatic, his tears. Since it was sad movies and Passover seders that were most likely to move him to tears, infrequent occasions, and ones at which the friends in front of whom I might be embarrassed were not present, it never bothered me very much when he cried, not merely sniffling, but heaving with impressive sobs, all the while still insisting that he was not upset, just something was very sad, a particular scene in the movies, the recollection of his deceased mother at seders. I could ignore these displays of emotion, but my mother found them intolerable, a particularly deep humiliation if her mother or one of her sisters were present. She referred to his crying as "bawling," and, in moments of extreme anger, called it by a Yiddish phrase, *pishn fun den oign*, which can be translated literally as "to piss from the eyes."

This tendency to break into tears was only one of many traits that made my father seem different to me from the other adults I knew as a child. I came to attribute this difference to his being European. I knew very well the stories of his birth in Russia, his growing up in Germany and Sweden. In Flatbush, the heavily Jewish neighborhood in Brooklyn where I grew up, the other fathers were the sons and, in a few cases, the grandsons of immigrants rather than immigrants themselves. My embarrassment at his difference came not from the dramatic shows of feeling but from more everyday signs. I would be bothered by the books he read in German, particularly by the strange ones with odd thick Gothic letters. When I was in junior high school, I could be mortified by the signs of his Europeanness — his accent, his habit of walking with his hands clasped behind his back, the formality that led him to wear ties on occasions such as school assemblies, when my friends' fathers would not.

Privileges as well as embarrassment came to me from having so European a father, one who could enter many different social circles and whom other adults admired. My friends did not have other European relatives to visit, refugees who lived in Manhattan apartments, with shelves crammed with books of lithographs and sketches, exotic delicious candies, odd fascinating prints on the wall. Their fathers, I was sure, did not take them to bookstores or galleries, or impress the owners with the wide variety of languages that they spoke, with their knowledge of art, history, and philosophy.

Despite these privileges, I often envied my schoolmates for the ordinariness of their fathers. My friends were free, I was sure, from answering the ringing telephone only to hear strange, accented voices who asked for their fathers by unfamiliar nicknames. Their fathers, napping on weekend afternoons, did not twitch and moan in their sleep, troubled by nightmares of distant countries. And, in my imagination if not in reality, their fathers did not have sudden outbursts of emotion, even if these moments were easy for me to handle. When I sensed my father struggling to maintain his composure, I calmed him down, responding to his distress by seeking to end its manifestations. In the instance of the suitcase at least, I also thought that I could trace its sources. I settled on an explanation, telling myself that my presence at home gave him great pleasure and that he would miss me when I left Brooklyn once again to return to college. It seemed to me pointless for him to trouble himself over an inevitable separation. All my friends from high school, all my cousins went to college, and certainly it was better that I go out of town rather than stay home and merely attend Brooklyn College. Did my departure bring up to him his own troubling lack of success, his never having attended college? Why couldn't he just accept my departure, as my mother did, sitting in the kitchen, calmly reading the newspaper?

I had spent the entire evening filled with the anticipation of returning to college. For most of my stay with my parents, the old familiar objects, a dresser, a bookcase, pulled me back to my childhood; now they coexisted with the newer images of my dormitory room, the dining hall, the library that awaited me. I assumed that my leaving for college, just hours away, was equally present in my father's mind. However correct that belief, I now think that I was wrong in attributing his mood to my imminent departure. Had he wished to fuss over my going back to college, he could have chosen among the more common forms adopted by other parents in that situation. But he did not: no insistence that I make a final telephone call to his brothers or sister, no nervous checking of airplane schedules. Nor did he seek, as many of my friends' parents did, to challenge my autonomy once I returned to college. He offered no criticisms of the length of my hair, of the impracticality of the subjects that I had chosen to study. (I had abandoned mathematics, a subject in which I had shown great promise, for philosophy, and then switched a second time, to anthropology, making these choices of ma-

166

———

*Combinations*

jors without any reflection on their possible consequences for my future employment and income.)

I now see that his concerns centered around the suitcase. He would have been equally upset, I believe, if I had been packing not to leave their home but to accompany them on a vacation. His attention was directed not to the end to which the suitcase was a means but to the suitcase itself. I had seen the great seriousness with which he packed, carefully smoothing the lapels of a jacket before placing shirts on it, rolling up a belt two or three times until it had just the right size and firmness to occupy the spot he selected for it. And the stories that he told about his family's travels often began with packing: his mother's grandfather loading his belongings onto the horse-drawn cart that carried him, his wife, and son from the Baltic coast of Germany, torn by the revolutions of 1848, to Russia; his mother's father rushing his wife and young daughters, without time even to arrange to have clothing sent to them, to a priest's house in which they could hide from marauding Cossacks; his mother carefully filling baskets for the long train journey that she and her children would take to Berlin, where his father had fled to avoid forced enlistment in the army with which the Czar was fighting Japan in 1905, baskets that disgorged sausages and loaves of bread for days on end. My understanding of a key element in these dramatic stories — that in each instance these people knew they might never return home — was based not only on the direness of the circumstances they faced but also on the tone with which my father conveyed to me their preparations for the trips. They displayed their wisdom not only in the choice of the moment to leave but also in the selection of goods they brought with them, in the care with which they loaded carts or filled baskets.

For these characters in my father's stories, packing continued to be a crucial skill even after their travels were over and they had settled in some town. Bundles kept cropping up in the long accounts that I heard of the fur business that my grandfather established and in which my father and most of his brothers were involved. In one story, a carefully presented shipment of sample rabbit pelts once impressed a prospective buyer and opened up a longstanding business relation; in another, moths destroyed a sloppy package of fox paws. In these stories and in the recounting of everyday events, my parents spoke of the world beyond the immediate circle of family as filled with dangers and opportunities. It would be better for me to go out into this world with well-packed clothes. A wrinkled sports jacket or shirt might ruin an interview or the promise that a chance encounter might offer. (My father certainly remembered the time that a professor had suddenly invited me, along with a few other undergraduate students, to his house for dinner: how fortunate that I had a well-pressed shirt to wear for the occasion. When I described the evening to my father, he relished equally hearing about the roast lamb that had been served and about the exquisite Englishness of the professor's name, David Henry Peter Maybury-Lewis.) This concern with impressions extended beyond clothes to the suitcase with which I would be seen on first entering the dormitory, on traveling to a friend's roommate's wedding. If I could not learn to take care of such objects as clothing and luggage, then I might miss the chances that life offered.

My father had not trained me well enough for me to take my place in the lineage of illustrious packers. In this aspect at least, he failed in raising me, much as he had failed in other ways: marrying late after several unhappy and unconsummated crushes; having only brief periods of earning an adequate amount of money in the fur business; attracting little attention for his prints, drawings, collages, and other works of art. It was his fault that I did not understand the importance of the properly turned sleeve that would prevent a shirt from wrinkling, that I did not remember to stuff socks into shoes, thus utilizing space more efficiently and preventing the leather from bending and cracking. It is no exaggeration to say that I grew up taking for granted the fact that he was a master packer, and that, though I might never equal him in this regard, I nonetheless might rise to a high level of skill. I believed that children born to other parents were doomed (at least when they traveled) to lives of crumpled shirts and missed opportunities, a fate that apparently awaited me as well.

As remarkable as the significance that my father placed in the suitcase was my accepting it so readily as a gift and as a possession, encumbered as it was with rules for packing. I could easily have been embarrassed by it as a reminder of my connections to an immigrant past, or, more pragmatically, I might have criticized its bulk, its weight, the ease with which its leather might be scratched. Instead, I was pleased by it. It was certainly a handsome object, with its thick brown leather that curved smoothly around the edges, the shiny brass hinges that popped open when a button was pressed. Its origins mattered to me as well. When I had graduated from high school, my parents bought it for me at a store on Fifth Avenue, somewhere in the upper forties or fifties, the most sophisticated portion of a street that was synonymous with elegance. It must have been expensive as well, the result of an unusual moment in which my parents agreed on making an extravagant purchase. I liked it a great deal, willingly lugging it along with me as I hitchhiked across Europe one summer as an undergraduate, and noting with regret its slow demise during subsequent trips to Latin America, as it was tossed on luggage racks atop old buses or thrown, with peasants' bundles, on trucks.

I was fond of the suitcase, though, not so much for its materials or appearance or origins or price but for the combination that my father and I had selected for it. We had carefully studied the little card of instructions that came with the suitcase, first making sure that we understood the procedure by which we would set the three barrels of the brass lock to a specific combination, and then discussing alternative three-digit numbers that we might select. It went without saying that 17 would fit in somehow, since that was the family's lucky number. The number 17 presented itself on many occasions: my sister Carol's happily telephoning my parents from a town in upstate New York, reporting that she and her husband, recently returned to the East from the Midwest, had purchased a house at 417 Hook Place; my father's returning from the public library with a book of poems by 17 Chinese authors. Some part of the propitious character of this number must have derived from its being adjacent to 18, the numerical equivalent of the word *chai* (composed of the eighth and tenth letters of the Hebrew alphabet), meaning "life"; like many other Jews, my parents donated money to charities in multiples of 18 and made toasts not to wealth or even to health but to that most modest and fundamental of hopes, to life, *l'chayim*. However, we had a more personal account of the origins of this particular talisman, tracing it to my parents' wedding anniversary, May 17, and to the address of the house in which we lived for most of my childhood, 659 East 17th Street.

My father and I did not even consider turning to birthdays, telephone numbers, or the other conventional sources of suitcase combinations. We knew from the beginning that we would play with the theme of 17. We entered the project with an animated, almost giddy spirit, as if we were planning a small practical joke on the rest of the world. After discussing several possibilities, such as 289 (the square of 17) and 017 itself, we selected 818. The three digits added up to 17 and could be read either forward or backward. It was a numerical equivalent of one of my father's favorite kinds of word play, a palindrome, or phrase that could be read backward as well as forward. (He enjoyed telling a joke about the first human conversation, in which the two people in the Garden of Eden introduced themselves to each other: "Madam, I'm Adam," followed by the demure reply, "Eve.") Having selected the number, we continued exploring its features: 818 remained unchanged not only when reversed but when turned upside-down or reflected in a mirror. Not quite certain that we had found the perfect solution and reluctant to abandon our game, we reviewed the alternatives. We considered 629, another number whose three digits totaled 17 and that, when turned upside-down, was recognizable, if not unchanged. But the artifice of the substitution displeased us, and we ended our search. It was a simple task for us to read the instructions and carry out the steps of setting the combination to 818.

During that conversation, as in many others, I was aware of the differences between my father and myself. I was the mathematician; he, the artist. I was the one who had once been summoned to City Hall in Manhattan to receive from some deputy of the mayor a prize for a city-wide junior-high-school mathematics competition in which I was tied for first place; I was the one who had taken not one but several years of calculus while still in high school, going to a nearby college for the more advanced courses. In selecting a combination for a suitcase, my father and I could both talk about numbers, but I knew their inner nature, while he merely toyed with their external accidental forms. Surely no attribute of a number could be more mathematically irrelevant, I thought, than its shape. But the fact that numbers had shapes placed them in the realm of art, in his domain of pattern and form, of sculptures, drawings, and collages. Their visual form linked the suitcase combination with the glossy pages of books he had shown me, of reproductions of paintings by Paul Klee, in which a black *o* would fit into a

landscape, a yellow *a* into a geometric design. We could recognize our differences and even enjoy them as a fortunate complementarity.

As I now reflect back on our selection of a number, I am surprised that I did not object even once. In letting him know the combination of my suitcase, I gave up an important area of privacy. Some friends of mine, I knew, had far more intrusive parents, who would systematically search through dresser drawers, but mine could pry as well. When he was in my room, he would sometimes infuriate me by looking not at me but at the papers and books I had on my desk, an activity I referred to as "snooping." Without a secret combination to my suitcase, I would have no place in the house in which I could lock objects — letters from a girlfriend, condoms, marijuana — away from my parents' inspection.

In part I simply trusted them, and in fact it would have been hard for me to shock them. Any rebellious tendencies that I might have displayed were well within the limits established by my older sisters. But even more important was the connection with the number 17 and all that it stood for. It set up a line of difference that ran not between my father and myself but between the entire family and the rest of the world, making us distinct and special. The number 17 itself was invariably an auspicious omen to those of us who knew to look for it and relate stories about it to each other. The combination, itself a combining of my mathematics and my father's art, would somehow bring good things to me when I traveled with the suitcase. It was as if the Orloves were protected by an arithmetical angel who could be summoned by the use of this number.

The particular combination to the suitcase also served a practical purpose. It was not merely an example of a superstition that we had invented and that we played at believing. Suitcases required great care and thought, since they could be broken into. That risk, I learned in cautionary tales from my parents, is what made combination locks preferable to locks that were opened by keys, since such locks could be picked or opened by a thief who had chanced upon a misplaced or poorly concealed key. But combinations, too, were problematic. If written down, they might also be found, just like keys. The best solution, therefore, was to memorize the combination, and to resolve the one weakness in this alternative — the risk of forgetting the combination — by telling it to one or two reliable individuals. For secrets such as these, it went without saying, one could trust family members more than strangers.

In the shared code, I hear echoes of other codes in the family's past. For example, in December 1920, my Uncle Henry, already in New York, wrote a letter to my father in Malmö, using their Swedish names and training him in the art of cryptography.

Dear Salle:

I wrote to ask you whether corn grows with large roots. But you wrote and told me to look it up in the Botanic Lexicon, but there is

nothing there. Corn looks so beautiful and it grows so tall. I understood everything, all of it, that you wrote in my secret code.

Your brother Henrik

This early letter was nothing more than a training exercise, an effort
to see whether the channels were open. Later on, the Orlove men used
these codes. I recall the postcards that my father received from his
brother Boris on which the stamps were glued upside-down. In the
1940s, for example, Boris was returning from a business trip to Lima.
When his ship stopped briefly in the Canal Zone, he sent a card with
an apparently routine message:

> Will be home in four days.
> Regards to everybody.
> Boris.

Any additional information that my uncle conveyed by placing the
stamp in an inverted position, or by failing to put in a salutation, is now
lost, though from piecing together family stories, I suspect that it meant
that my father was only supposed to notify relatives of Boris's arrival
rather than business associates or girlfriends.

In a few instances, my father did explain these codes to me. On another occasion, Boris found himself in a difficult situation while traveling on business in what was then British India and has since become
Pakistan. A man with whom he had previously concluded a business
deal introduced Boris to one of his friends, who urged Boris to buy a
large lot of sheepskins and ship them back to Henry in New York. The
price was low, he assured Boris, and the quality was excellent. Boris was
in a dilemma: he did not want to accept the deal that was being pressed
on him, but he did not want to insult and possibly anger his former
business associate by turning it down. Seeking to prevent Boris from
refusing, his former associate and the associate's friend took him to the
telegraph office and watched while he composed a telegram to Henry.
Boris filled out the text as the men suggested, indicating the details of
the transaction, but added the letters "INTE" after the amount of
money to be cabled for the sheepskins. The two men, puzzled by this
unfamiliar phrase, asked Boris what it meant. They were satisfied, even
pleased, when he explained to them that it was an abbreviation for "in-

ternational," and referred to international money orders that were sent with high priority. Boris and the men parted company amicably. Henry recognized "inte" immediately as an ordinary Swedish word meaning "not"; having lived in Malmö during World War I and just after, my father's whole family spoke the language fluently. Needless to say, Henry never sent the money.

If my father had not trained me to be a skilled packer, I at least joined the tradition of people who protected each other through the use of secret codes. While we were discussing the combination to my suitcase, I imagined a telephone call that I never made, that I never needed to make. I think that he probably imagined it as well: "Hello. Dad? It's Ben. . . . Yes, everything's fine. Listen, I just arrived in Boston. You wouldn't happen to remember the combination to my suitcase, the nice brown one you and Mom gave me? I just can't think of it, for the life of me. . . . That's right, that's it. How could I have forgotten? Thanks."

I, who once resented my father's inspection of shirts in my suitcase, now slowly peruse an entire roomful of his things as I go through the papers that I found in his study after his death, the papers that form the basis of this book. I am literally engaged in an unpacking: of a bookcase that holds catalogs of art exhibits, of letter-filled boxes that he had not opened since he and my mother moved from Brooklyn to California, of a desk whose compartments hold old travel documents and odd notes, of a closet with diaries arranged on a shelf. I seek many things in the contents of his study — a deeper knowledge of his past, an understanding of the signals and codes that I heard as a child, the simple feeling of his presence. I find the goals of my search as much in the way he packed these papers as I do in the words and images that these papers contain.

# Chapter 8 PRINTS

Whandsome-drop-cap When I was a child, I would sometimes hear my parents mention the friends of their youth. They stirred my curiosity with elliptical references to events about which I knew almost nothing, visits to speakeasies, parties that lasted late into the night, sudden weekend trips to the country. Among the names they mentioned, Michael Lenson held particular mystery for me. My parents' other friends would send greeting cards, call on the telephone, or even arrange to meet in Manhattan, but there was never any word from Lenson. As best I can recall, he did not come in to the city from his home in northern New Jersey to see my father, nor did we go out to visit him. The distance itself was a significant but not insurmountable obstacle, since we did range on occasion beyond the familiar orbit of the subway, taking a train from Grand Central or Penn Station to visit relatives and friends out in the suburbs. I was unable to reconcile this silence of Lenson's with the great importance he held in my parents' past. I heard enough stories to know that he and my father had been close friends when they were young, and that my parents had visited him several times during their honeymoon in Europe, while he was studying art in Paris, supported, as I had been told many times, by a fellowship.

What kept Mike Lenson in my mind was not so much the moments when my parents might mention his name as the two enormous oil paintings that he had made, the only large works of art that hung in our house, much grander than my father's framed woodcut and collages. How clear they are in my mind.

The first painting: a woman is seated alone at a table in some sort of restaurant; the entire restaurant is lit with a warm glow — it must be nighttime. Her arms are resting on the table, she has a calm smile on her face, she is looking ahead, somewhere beyond me. As I write now, I realize that I can summon up not only her face and her pose but also her blouse. I am not sure why this piece of clothing should be one of the details most persistent in my mind. Was it that its soft green shade complemented the other colors that I recall: the yellowish light that suffused the painting, the wooden table, her hair of a shade that I would now describe as auburn? Did the slight shimmer of the fabric seem in keeping with the elegant atmosphere of the restaurant? Did the short sleeves set off the confident pose of her crossed arms? I may simply have looked at the blouse, turning my eyes down from her face, too shy to return her self-assured gaze.

The second painting: two women are sitting on the ground in the wilderness, a rocky landscape; the sunlight is strong, even though there are clouds in the sky. One woman is facing forward. She is turning thread on a spindle, her long dark hair hangs loose, her head is tilted, she looks off into the distance, lost in thought. A bright red blouse fits her tightly; I remember the nipple that clearly shows through the fabric of the blouse, the smooth rounded surface of her stomach, the full skirt, bright yellow and green, raised above her knees. The other woman is seated behind the first, facing away from the first woman and from me, so that all that I see of her is her dark robe, her bright headscarf, and her two hands, one holding thread, the other the loom, from which hangs a small clown doll and a pine cone.

I never thought of what I might call the first painting, though, as I think about it now, "The Woman in the Café" seems a fitting title, since the scene is laden with images that suggest France. Or perhaps "Waiting": I now realize what did not occur to me as a child, the woman's pose and expression suggest an entire story, or at least a scene in a movie. She looks beyond the spot where I, the viewer, am standing because she expects someone to come in; she is in love with him, she is entirely confident that he will arrive soon, they will kiss, he will sit down too.

There must have been at least half a dozen occasions, though, when I spoke of the second painting to some friend, calling it "The Two Fates." I felt rather clever to know the reference to the fates of classical mythology, the women whose spinning of thread determined the length of human lives, and to know that there really should be three of them; clever, and a bit smug at being part of a family that had real paintings rather than the reproductions of landscapes or still lifes that I saw on the walls of my friends' houses. I was anxious as well. The first painting was safe art, but the strange second painting, with its heavy symbolism, with its shocking nipple and bare thighs, was not. These moments, when a friend would see this painting on the living room wall, brought the familiar danger that came with being an Orlove. My friend might think of my family not as sophisticated but simply as weird. Better to have a quick joke on hand, and to dismiss the painting that could not be ignored; surely better not to run the risk of linking myself even more closely to it by saying, "You know, a friend of my father's made this painting, and the other one, too, his name is Michael Lenson."

As I was working on the chapters in the first half of this book, I made plans to look systematically through the box that my father had labeled "Lenson Letters etc." In going through the box, though, I was more attracted by the "etc." than by the letters. I spent a leisurely morning examining these scraps: book ads that he had cut out of the New York Times; a sheet of paper on which he had written all 120 combinations of the numbers 1 through 5, beginning with 12345 and ending with 54321, arranged neatly in 20 blocks of 6 numbers each, these 20 blocks in turn arranged in 5 rows with 4 blocks each; an alphabetical list of coins, from airgead, an Irish coin, and bullion to the ancient xunistron, the Tibetan yak-mig-ma, and the zodiacal coins that Moghul emperors made in the shapes of the twelve astrological signs; and one of his very few pieces of mimeograph art (a purple sketch of a fantastic boat, sailing under a sky that has a many-rayed sun in one part, billowing clouds in another). I was especially taken with a few fragmentary recollections from his childhood. He described the times that he saw Halley's Comet in 1910, when he was six years old, and the comet-shaped candies that vendors sold in the street. He recounted a few episodes from the trip that his family took to Russia in 1911 for Boris's Bar Mitzvah, the one time that he returned to the country of his birth after he left it as an infant. The return to Germany left a particularly strong impression on him:

> A stranger talking to father & Boris — Mother stood nearby. The train is staying here for a while Pa said "Go for a walk with your brother & this man" — We left the train, climbed down the steps embankment crossed a field and strolled through the woods — some fields and entered a small village. Suddenly — "I can read the sign here, Bakery, Apothekary" — "Not so loud," Boris hushed me — You are in Germany now — We were smuggled across the border.

I found myself ruminating on this passage: the way that he was exposed, even as a child, to a variety of languages and alphabets; the deliberateness with which his father and older brother concealed their plans from him. Did they think that his excitement at reading the signs could have been the one clue that would have alerted the otherwise successfully hoodwinked officials of the undocumented nature of their reentry into Germany? Did he welcome Boris's reproof as a sign of incorporation into the family's secrets, I wondered, or did he wish that his brother, rather than just quieting him, would also have acknowledged his eagerness to read and his excitement at returning home?

I closed the box up and did not return to it until I began to work more directly on the chapters of the book that included my father's art work. Now more determined in my search for sources, I arranged the Lenson letters and cards in chronological order. The first one, a letter from 1923, reads:

June 21

Dear Bettye & Rob:

I have arrived and found the place to be very nice. Fine lake, and beautiful camp, though it is still unfinished.

I miss you all.

Will write again soon.

Yours,
Mike.

A conventional note sent by someone on vacation — but who was this Bettye? She appeared in most of the other letters and cards from the

1920s, which, like the first, were also brief notes written during summer vacations, when Mike Lenson went away to paint in small towns in the mountains in Pennsylvania near the Delaware Gap. When I eventually realized that Bettye was my Aunt Elizabeth, I was greatly surprised. I had heard stories of Lenson's many girlfriends, but none that linked him with my aunt. In my mind she had always been paired with her husband, my Uncle Irving, a meek lawyer who listened patiently at family events while she told stories of her ailments, of the butcher who did not treat her respectfully, of the noisy neighbors she was forced to live near, presumably because Irving did not earn enough money for them to move to a better area. And yet it was to her, as much as to my father, that Mike Lenson wrote, either addressing letters to both of them, or, when writing only to him, sending "regards to Bettye." The first letter that he wrote after he settled in Paris on his fellowship, dated 25 May 1929, was addressed to "Rob and Bettye." He documents a separate correspondence between him and Elizabeth: "Bettye thank you awfully for your kind letters."

Lenson's tie with Elizabeth, whatever its nature, was soon to come to an end. In a letter of his to my father in November 1929, he asked:

Why didn't you ever write me Bettye married, Rob? I heard of it from a couple of sources, but neither she nor you ever mentioned it.

Possibly alluding to that complaint, he wrote to my father in January 1930:

I had a letter from Bettye. Happily married. I am glad she fell into a little content. We don't have too much of that dished out.

The strongest suggestion of their relationship came still later, in a letter from April 1931, in which he writes of "my attachment to Bettye, which you no doubt suspected."

This "attachment" fits in with the stories my parents told me about Elizabeth as I reached my teens. When Irving took her on a cruise for their honeymoon, she spent the first afternoon on deck, wearing a new bathing suit, and her thighs became so badly sunburned that she would not let him touch her for a week; being excessively delicate, she found it very painful to deliver her first child, Joan, and resolved never to have any more children. Those stories dated to the late 1920s and early 1930s, but Elizabeth's sexual unavailability continued to be a theme: Irving went to the gym a couple of evenings a week, my parents suggested, not only to escape Elizabeth's endless complaints but also to burn off the energy that he could not discharge in the fashion that I was to presume my other uncles used. At family gatherings, Irving was said to get a bit tight after a few drinks and flirt with his sisters-in-law. My mother told the incident that has remained most clearly fixed in my memory. She and my father went over to Irving and Elizabeth's one evening to play bridge. They were in the middle of the game, she explained to me, when Irving slipped his hand under her behind and gave her a pinch; she sat on his hand so firmly that he couldn't move it. She listened in satisfied amusement, as Elizabeth urged him to make up his mind and select a card, before she finally released his hand.

The letters from Lenson also brought to mind another anecdote about Elizabeth, one that my mother would retell whenever someone would mention a couple that had broken up and then attempted to reconcile. Irving had shown a great deal of interest in Elizabeth, my mother told me, and they went out together for a while. She decided to stop seeing him, but he continued to pursue her. She later agreed to marry him, attracted not as much to him as to the respectability of matrimony and his prospects of earning a good income as a lawyer. My mother found a moral in the story: when a relationship has ended, it is virtually impossible to rekindle the flame of romance.

It is this last story in particular that dovetails with Mike Lenson's letters. Taken together, they suggest that Elizabeth had been torn between the exciting artist and the duller lawyer; a Marjorie Morningstar, more or less, in my own family. Perhaps Elizabeth had thought of traveling to France to join Lenson but then had suddenly decided to marry Irving, a choice very much in keeping with her own mother's concern to find a husband who could provide economic security. I could not be sure whether there was any basis for this speculation of mine, since I never found any of the letters that Elizabeth and Lenson sent to each other, nor did my parents ever mention this possibility to me. Their total silence on Elizabeth's involvement with Mike Lenson contrasted sharply with their relish in revealing to me many smaller embarrassing details of her life. They might have felt free to tell me so many spicy stories about her because they respected her other, greater secret. Whatever the details of her early romance, and, in particular, the answer to the unresolvable question of whether Elizabeth was a virgin when she went to the wedding canopy, I certainly was surprised to find that Lenson had thanked her for her "kind letters" in May 1929, not quite two months before she married Irving.

It took a while for my attention to return from these revelations to my father's friendship with Mike Lenson. I wondered whether Lenson had sought him out primarily as a means to get closer to Bettye. Reading the correspondence, though, I decided that Lenson and my father were linked by a bond very much of their own. Once again the most revealing letter came late in the sequence. In April 1931, Lenson wrote from Paris:

Dear Rob,

I will not go into any elaborate and possibly painful explanations. I have not written you in a long time, it's true. I realize that a long while separated, we've had experiences on divergent basis. What I want to say, Rob, is that it is useless to assume that things we've had in common, thoughts friends etc. are still identically the same. Dont, Rob, for a moment interpret as callousness what is a frank statement of fact. I remember well the various incidents that we've lived in common from the earliest visit to your home in 88th St. Lovely nights in the park or about town in company with Moish Katz and Sessit and Charlie. — Many others. In sum, Rob, we're still dear friends.

Perhaps, Rob, the reason for my perturbed state is none of the causes I've mentioned. Rather one I cannot discuss. Or perhaps you've heard. An attachment D'Amour which failed under strain of separation. That had, for a while, almost destroyed my raison d'etré. One must not stake too much on anything. Least of all, the hopes of the future on the whim of a beloved woman.

I leave for Italy in a few weeks. Shall be gone for some months Well, Rob, don't feel hurt at the things I said. Things unexplained in matters of friendship are always painful.

As ever
Mike

This letter did little more than suggest that the friendship had been close, but that Lenson was distancing himself. Apparently, he carried through with his intention to remain separate, since he did not write again to my father for five years.

To fill in this skimpy account, I turned to my father's diaries, which contained a detailed record of their friendship, beginning with the first time they met in a social and athletic club in the Bronx, sometime late in the spring of 1923, before Lenson had shortened his name:

> I met two more boys thru the Wayne Club. Mike Levenson. He is nice. Wants to become a painter. I think he is good. He is cynical.
>
> And Sez [Mike Sesit]. A fine fellow. He uses a fine language. He is strong like Tarzan. He is openminded. Mike is mysterious.
>
> Wednesday Okt. 24th 1923
>
> The 17. Mike was up our house. I showed him some Art pictures. He showed me points that I never observed.
>
> I walked him home. I believe he is an Artist. He has at least Artists temper. We two talked of life and religion. He does not believe in God at all. He told me instances where he defies God. He clenched his fist and his jaw muscles came out. His eyes flashed. I do not think he acted. I like him.

The phrase, "Mike is mysterious," together with "I do not think he acted," gave me a sense of the way that my father, in the first months of a friendship that would last many years, did not feel entirely at ease with Lenson. Later entries show the same uncertainty about Lenson's sincerity and the same wish to become closer to him. As I read and reread the diary entries, I found a fresh understanding of my own discomfort with Mike Lenson's paintings, particularly "The Two Fates." Because I grew up with these paintings prominently displayed in the living room, I must have absorbed some of the ambivalence that my father felt about the man who painted them. My father's immense elation at the possibility that he might be transformed by the art that Lenson opened up for him was balanced by his equally great self-doubts; the exhilaration at being in the presence of an artist led to a sense of his own inadequacy; and, above all, he often questioned the intimacy of his friendship with Lenson. Troubled when doubts struck him, relieved when they passed, he was impelled to write in the diaries because he had no friend in whom to confide. It was painful for me to discover his loneliness and his tolerance of humiliation, so closely intertwined with the excitement that art and artists brought into his life.

> June 9th 1924.
> One evening I took a walk with Mike in the Park. We sat down on a rock. And talked and confided. The night came and enveloped us.
> One Sunday I went up to his house. He had promised to make a sketch of me. He was playing ball on the street. He is quick.
> We went upstairs. I sat down and he started to draw. It was funny. Long sweeping strokes. I rested a few times. While I was posing, my mind wandered far. I remembered of Lotte in Chemnitz, Malmö, When I walked with the old man across the country. Beautiful reminiscence.
> It is a pretty fair likeness although there is something strange about it. He made my face, boyish, soft. Am I really like that, or is this his conception of me.

Another entry, though undated, was written early in 1926:

> I did not see much of Mike before the New Year. We met for lunch a few times and then sat in Madison Square Park talking, Confidential. quiet. Smoked cigarettes to heighten the mood of the situation. I thought the old time was back or rather an improvement of it.
> He was not succeeding with his work for his living. He did not do anything towards Art claiming that he did not have the chance. If I had at least a showing of talent I would try to do some thing. He has talent it could be worked up to something and here he lets it slip past. Does it show a lack of genius, that he does not fight and tries.
> There is a vaine running in him that wants Art and Beauty, but it comes to the surface very rarely.
> I sometimes feel that I could do something. Make a woodcut or mould a clay statue. I must try some time. I believe if one would continuously associate among art it would influence so much to

give the person a kind of ability and power of creation. To be among objects which have been created with love, with every pulse beating emotion at a high pitch to create is impossible not to feel likewise. Every brush stroke or blow with hammer is done with tenderness and feeling love.

Lenson continues to appear in the diary in that year, sometimes in a brief mention of an art exhibit that my father visited with him or of a walk that they took together in Manhattan, and sometimes in longer entries:

Tuesday March 2nd 1926

I went to see Mikes painting. A self portrait. He has a room with another fellow together. It is in an old wooden building on 115th St. They really have two rooms. In the first one a lot of oil paintings. In the back room they paint. More canvases, a few reproductions, plaster casts and dust, Mike was painting. I think the painting to sweet, the pose to proud too goodlooking. But I can't tell him any criticism. What right have I to tell him, I should voice my opinion though. Another fellow painter came up. And he put some life into us. Talked fluently and with humor. It was very interesting and worthwhile.

[April 1926]

Yesterday had lunch with Mike. Would see a play that night.

In the afternoon went to the public library. Wandered from shelf to shelf. Spiritualism Astronomy. Philosophy. How can the mind grasp all that. A book of Art, to be able to create and thus expressions.

I realized how much time I had wasted on nothing and now will do different.

Was walking around, waiting for Mike. Was Hungry. I thought. Now you do nothing. Have all you need. Easy life Some pleasures.

Perhaps sometimes you will walk around and hungry, but then read all those books I have missed. What a comparison between an empty stomach and a full seething brain.

Met Mike had supper. Started talking about Life. Schopenhauer Philosophy. Mike chooses his words well. But I showed him points which he had to accept. And I never thought of those before. Association of thought. One brings the other.

May 22nd 1926.

Last Sunday I saw Mike and Sez. Went to Mike's Studio. Guglichino and two other fellows were there. Had discussions on literature painting etc. Smoked until darkness. The three boys left. Sez read poetry. We left soon too. It was raining. When I walked next to Mike, Sez was talking and I could hardly hear. And visa versa. I felt out of place, superflous.

The following entry mentions Baby, as his cousin Betty, George and Vera's daughter, had begun to call herself. He had returned to spending time with her after his visit to Irene. Elsewhere in the diaries he described the times that he had taken Baby out to the movies, where he had held her hand and kissed her. He wrote of how he hoped that she would love him. She joked and flirted with him but otherwise did not take him very seriously.

September 10th 1926

2. Tischri 5687

I had an appointment with Mike for one Saturday afternoon. I was afraid to be late so I ran. He was waiting. Took my arm. I was happy. We went to his studio. He had forgotten the key. Climbed thru the window. He showed me some of his sketches done at the Artists camp. If he could devote his entire time to it and not worry about anything, he might accomplish something, as it is, it is almost hopeless.

But we had a very good talk. I even told him about Baby. I was conscious of a dry throat and a slight fever.

My father continued to visit Lenson regularly in his studio.

[December 1926]

One Saturday afternoon I walked over to his studio. He was working. I was tired. Layed down on the couch. Mike was playing on his mandolin. I closed my eyes. The tinkling music, warmth of room, I was tired. Later Mike rested on the couch against me.

Later we went for a bite. Mike was satisfied with things. He was sitting and talking for a long time. He was giving up his job. He would do free lancing. It was the pleasure of knowing his own freedom. No bonds or rules.

[early 1927]

Mike asked me to come up on a certain day. He was painting some girl, he wanted me to see her. She is an actress.

Slim girl, very dark complexion sharp profile, when smile, a big mouth, beautiful slim legs a dancers feet.

Mike working rapidly. I did not want to say anything in fear of being thought showing off.

Suddenly left shortly, felt out of place.

My father continued to visit the studio:

Mike suggested I sit for a portrait. I have waited so long for the offer to come from him. Can one really get a thing only by desiring it. It will be a good study. Once, while he was bent over the canvass I looked at him very intently, to hold that instant, he looked up, he was surprised and there was a questioning look between us. Yet neither knew the answer.

Nor, I think, did either know the question. I can think of a series of questions: did either of them know what they sought in their friendship? Were their different wishes compatible? Rereading these passages for what must be the twentieth or thirtieth time, I am still struck by my father's doubts and awkwardness, his willingness to tolerate Lenson's disregard. I also see the close moments that they had together:

November 8th 1927

Last Sunday I went to Mikes Studio, It is all fixed up already. Very pretty, but it lacks something. It has not the same atmosphere of the Studio in 23rd Street.

Mike was happy that I had come. He was all alone. We made a fire.

He expected a girl to come for a sitting. And I should stay. We went for a bite. She was there when he came back. Not goodlooking nor interesting, just a costumer.

In the meanwhile I design a monogram for Mike, he had asked me for it.

Smoked cigarettes, read Swinburne poetry.

After she had gone, Mike still worked on the portrait. I attended to fire. When it got darker, we fired some frankfurters.

Sez came up. And we spent a fine hour in the dark room before the fire and the coals. We all stared at the flames. We hardly looked at each other.

[late November 1927]

I am out of work now for two weeks. But expect to take a job tomorrow. And I think the change will be for the better. So, I had some time for myself but it was very little. But I saw Mike several times. Once I fell asleep in a chair, in the study for 15 minutes. When I awoke he gave me a gentle smile. Our friendship is true and seasoned. It is mellow. Of a fine color. We speak in a soft tone to each other. When we have to ask for something of each other, the words are so gentle and the sentence so tender. Afraid to hurt each other and would rather hurt ourselves.

In the last months of 1927, a new woman appears in the diaries, the sister of one of the friends of his sister Elizabeth: Freda, with whom my father had gone to some concerts and art exhibits, whom he had kissed several times, whom he hoped would like him. An entry from the middle of December describes how he brought her to Lenson's studio. The Charles whom he mentions is Charles Wagner, a poet, a member of the circle of friends that included my father, Mike Lenson, and Mike Sesit.

It was cold, her hand was in my pocket. It took a long time to go downtown. Then we had to walk. It was late, cold windy, getting dark. She was cold.

Mike opened the door for us. Charles was there and Martha. A great blaze in the fireplace. It was worthwhile getting cold for that. She sat in the chair. Warming up. I had thought of being alone with her so that I could speak to her. But now it was impossible.

Mike was working on a big canvas. The warm fire the leaping flames. Not satisfied until everything is consumed. I sat on the floor next to her, in the arm chair before the fire as lovers should. Is she my love.

She hummed the Waltz of The Flowers. I held her hand. I kissed her palm. I was happy. The warm fire. It made her sleepy. I put wood on the fire. I added, what she thought of them. She would tell me when we left, then she whispered in my ear. I think you are nicer than they. I kissed her cheek then. So we sat before the fire. Charles left with Martha. It was very dark, Mike played the mandolin. I put out the lights Freda was sitting on the arm rest of the chair. I took her in my arms. The fire burned and Mike played. The flames sank, it was darker in the room. His face floated with shadows he played softer. We kissed. It was so natural. I had never thought of kissing her in the studio. And here we forgot the whole world. I only know of her in my embrace and her hands around me, holding me to her. So close we held each other.

At the time of this entry late in 1927, my father was entering into another relationship that would prove more serious than the one with Freda. He and my mother had already met, probably during the preceding spring. They were both living with their families in the same apartment building on a wide boulevard in the Bronx, the Grand Concourse, in which my father's family had an apartment on the second floor; my mother's family, on the fifth. My mother, I was told, struck up a friendship with Elizabeth, visited her apartment on many occasions, and became interested in her handsome older brother Robert. The first mention of my mother in my father's diaries, though, takes place in a hotel in the country, where they had each gone separately with friends and relatives for the Fourth of July weekend in 1927. He found her very attractive, and he made excuses that weekend to join her for walks, to play bridge with her, to go to a baseball game together. Later in the year they had gone out a number of times to movies and museums, for walks in the park, to parties; they had had long conversations, they had kissed, but they were both, in the language of my day if not of theirs, "seeing other people" as well. My mother went out on dates with other men, and my father continued to spend time with his cousin Baby and with Freda.

A long entry in his Big Diary describes the transformation in their relationship that took place on January 30 and 31 and February 1, 1928.

In the evening went with Katzy to Tairiris dance recital. In the Subway Katzy wanted to write a note. She did in the [subway stop at] Grand Central [Station] — Will you be my lover. — I had to smile. What a request. Did she know the meaning the full width of it. I could not answer. The crowd and here two young beings. We walked thru streets. She pulled me in a doorway to kiss her. — What matters the dance recital. It was good. Take the bus home, — yes, but it would take to long time, take the Sub and you can come to my house yet. The empty Ave. a few lights and her desire. She tells. I don't know what it is. I am always aware of your presence, when you touch me I must be yours, your embraces and kisses. I can not think of anything else. I cannot sleep. I awake at night and instead of you, my sister lies along side of me.

What can I do. I am to her, as the musician that gives her the music. The poet that gives her the rhythm. Can I give it to her?

At home, she asked me again, on the steps. How could I humiliate her and refuse. Besides I wanted to know what would happen. Everyone was asleep. We sat down. She does not believe in marriage, shall never marry It is silly to be a virgin if she does not believe in it. She wants to know. She trembled with desire. I took her in my arms to comfort her. I touched her breast. I thought she stepped back to free her breast, but with a groan she threw off her clothes. "Will you — Robert." — Nude with passion. How could I? Her unprepared, with my clothes on. In her mothers house, I did not know what. And my ideals of woman, Love and sex. I could not. She knelt before me and her breasts were in my hands. Katzy — some other time. This is passion then. She dressed. Kisses. — I could not leave her go thus. If you want I will do it. No only if you want to too. — Yes. —

So I found out —

(This is a fine way how to tell it. But what's the difference. I will remember it anyway).

Now what shall I do.

The next day. How can I go to business. With such a thing before me. A new door is to be opened. Shall I or not. And where is Love. But she again. Is it not better that I do it, than a rake. We both innocent and thus Sacrifice to Aphrodite. To be pagan. If she so desires, we harm no one. And is it not better than she do it, than some woman who knows who.

I rode down to the Battery and walked around in cold and snow all morning, debating, figuring, accepting, wondering, disgusting, desperate. I would go to Mike. I felt miserable, cold and hungry.

A man was stretched out on the ground his blood making a crimson stream on the wet, black sidewalk and the snow. Mike wondered, what's the matter. I told him, and also, that I had decided to go thru with it. I was in earnest. So we prepared and he told me. Disgusting. I was ready to quit. And this is what the poets sing of. I did not understand that they feel differently and then take the essence of emotions of different times and blend them together, as a painter blends his colors and paints a canvas selecting the objects of different places, to form the harmonious. And here I had dreamt and was to be rudely awakened. Another day and I would know. I had deliberately decided to do so and I was.

I could not refuse any more. Saw Katzy and she asked me to come up to her house. She came close to me. Do you want to stop it. I don't want to hurt you. She came close. Embraced me. She was undecided herself. Call me as late as possible, for otherwise I would go mad. So we decided.

I spent the afternoon with Mike. Were at the Library. I looked up Birth control index and the cards were very much thumbed.

Mike left me, shook my hands, soll sein mit Glick [good luck to you].

One of the things that had made me decide, was the thought of us two meeting at twilight, and walking thru the darkening streets, filled with the knowing of a fulfilling. And around us humanity would mill not knowing nor guessing.

I took the streetcar to Gramercy Park. I had called her to meet me there. When I spoke to her, she gave me the thought of a cat I had seen once during a heat nothing else but the instinct of sex. I was late. I ran around the corner and she came toward me. "I am so sorry." She took my arm. Her presence put all fears away. I was aroused. A woman. To give each other to each other.

But it was early, and we walked around for nearly two hours thru dark streets, places I had never seen before. All deserted. I was under a strange spell. All the noises that passed me, I imitated. A cars horn, streetcar, cats, peoples conversations. We went to the italian place — Napoleon — where I had once been alone, and once with Freda. We ate but little. Were too tired to eat, and the nervous tension of what was before.

I was so sombre, she looked at me. I did not like the look. I could still return. This responsibility she would have a hold on me. Would I not hurt her. Myself. What of the days afterwards. What if disappointed hurt. To take a fine emotion and put it into such a violent act. She understood my thoughts.

We were at the Studio. Embraced. Do you know what you are about. Yes. And I shall never be sorry.

So I made a fire. I was like mad.

Broke the wood, poured the kerosine. Burn, flame, burn. And now what.

But it was good to sit by the fire. I took my shirt off. The bare chest to the fire. Her hands tore at my flesh. Here take my body — Her breathing. Go Katzy.

I undressed behind a big canvas, she was already rolled into a blanket. Give me one, I could not appear nude before her. Not yet. I was ready to cry. Like going to death. Why I should be so serious I don't know. I felt terrible.

We embraced. She walked to the couch and I followed.

(How can I here describe it. Or need I more knowledge to draw the essence out of)

The embrace of arms, bodies and legs, there was no fury, no passion no desire only sad duty.

She laughed loudly, Oh God, how horrible. I almost choked her. Her body swayed, trembled, Drowning. How her head was flung back in utter yielding to passion, and then her eyes would open shiny & black. I held her. Cries, whimpers, groans sigh. I sigh and bewailed it inarticulate. She pressed me to her heart. Comforted. You are not sorry. I left her. Made more fire. Came back to cover her up, but she embraced me again.

So this is what it is. How silly, how ridiculous. I laughed, again. And again. She became frightened. It was cold. So we went to the fire. In one blanket. Embraced. Small talk together. Her warm body, her flesh. Nature is only senses. She felt that I had done so for her sake, she asked me. But I denied it. I asked her, I am glad that you asked me, that you want me, she said. So I got what I asked for.

The fire had died out it was dark and cold in the room. We dressed and left.

It seemed all so incomplete and unfinished to me. The same to her. She said. "I have to rewrite all literature now, for they have given the wrong version. We laughed and joked.

I fell asleep in the subway. Later on she told me, that she hated me for that. I did not even lean my head on her shoulder. Go and understand woman.

I went into my apartment and she had to walk three flights yet.

And so I learned and know but it was not what I had dreamed of. I felt more chaste than ever before. The day afterwards I felt strangely free. I walked erect, with my chest filled with air. Buoyant. It seemed like a joke.

I met Katzy after work. She looked pale. We walked to 9th Ave. L. She told me that her whole body was broken up, her legs were out of place. She felt bad, as I feared she would. We rode on the open platform. Suddenly I saw tears in her eyes. Katzy — It was windy. But soon she dried her tears and changed. She was glad to be with me. The day before I had told her that one has to develope a taste for it, like olives. But today that it was like cutting the pages of a book, before one can reade and enjoy it. I thought of never asking her. But when she asked me to burn the note I knew that I would not, for that would be like finishing it all, and felt that it was not time yet to do so.

It took me several tries before I could read this passage completely, from beginning to end. I found my eyes jumping ahead, skipping over the words that described my parents' naked bodies. I got up from my desk, paced around my study, had a second cup of coffee, went to the bathroom to urinate, and finally composed myself. I sat down, took a deep breath, and read through this section twice. Once I had accustomed myself to the extraordinary nature of this diary entry, I found, to my surprise, that it seemed very familiar to me. I had grown up with my mother's brief statements and my father's longer, more reflective searches for a proper wording. I recalled as well the way that my father would often demur to my mother's proposals. Only after some insistence would he agree to go out to dinner at a Chinese restaurant, to take a walk in the park on a weekend afternoon, to send a birthday check to a grandchild. This was the way, too, that they made the big decisions in their lives, to have children, to move from New York to California, to have their bodies cremated.

The one element that puzzled me came at the end of the account. "I went into my apartment and she had to walk three flights yet." Why did my father not walk my mother up to her apartment on the fifth floor? After having made love for the first time, surely he would have wanted to remain with her as long as possible, or at least he would have been gentlemanly enough to give the appearance of not wanting to leave her. He had violated one of the most fundamental, if unstated, rules of dating that I remembered from my teens and early twenties, the requirement that the boy walk the girl to her door. Perhaps my father wanted to withhold this little bit of attention from my mother, much like the numerous moments, recorded in his diaries in the following months, in which she was troubled by his refusal to say "I love you" to her; perhaps he was simply peeved at her anger that he had fallen asleep on the subway. Well, no, I thought later, perhaps there may have been some other explanation altogether, my mother and father might simply have been trying to avoid their own parents. My mother's mother might have been waiting up, a widow with six unmarried daughters, living only one floor below the top of the building, she would have been alert to footsteps in the hallway; my father's parents, accustomed to their sons coming and going at all hours, would not have stayed up for my father, and, since they lived only one floor up from the lobby of the building, there were more people passing by their door anyway.

Reflecting on this question again several months later, I realized that my mother may not have wanted him to walk her up to her apartment.

She was the one, not he, who had the brief moments of privacy in ascending the flights of stairs, the chance to reflect before entering an apartment with parents and siblings. I have no diaries of hers, only my imagination to direct me, to lead me to think that she climbed the stairs confidently, that she let herself quietly into her apartment, that she had called a few words to her mother, who was already in bed, that she undressed quickly, that her sister Ruth, with whom she shared a bed, had already dozed off but woke up. I have wondered whether they exchanged only a few words before they both fell asleep or whether they talked at length. The first somehow seems more likely to me, but I will never know.

I do not know whether my father was following my mother's wishes in not accompanying her to her apartment, but he certainly did not carry out her request "to burn the note" that she had handed him in the subway station. The note was one of the first items I found when I began going through his desk in the months after he died, in the period when I was avoiding the closet that held the urn with his ashes. The locked upper part of his desk contains a little cabinet, about five inches wide and seven inches high, with a little door. This cabinet held three small old books, all bound in leather (a French book, printed in 1812, of chess techniques; a 1908 English edition of the *Rubaiyat of Omar Khayyam*; an undated, privately printed book of erotic poems, illustrated with engravings, which my parents probably bought in Europe during their honeymoon in 1930), and an envelope on which my mother had crossed out the printed name of her employer, Lucius N. Littauer, and written:

12/25/36
To my first and only love
from Katzy.

My father had replaced the original contents of the envelope (probably a Christmas gift of money, since his work in the fur business was going very poorly at the time) with the note, which he had saved. It is written on a piece of looseleaf paper three inches by five. The six holes in the paper are torn, showing that my mother had ripped the page rather than removing it by opening the binder. She must have pulled it out with one firm gesture, since the holes are torn evenly.

Robert, dear:
         Will you be my
lover? Do not speak.
Write your answer.
                Katzy

A brave note, I think, rather than an imperious one. Perhaps her courage was beginning to fail. She may have asked him to write rather than speak because, already knowing my father well, she thought that he would turn down her request if he spoke but would consent if he waited a bit. I think I detect these growing fears in the steady hardening of tone in this brief note, moving from the tenderness of the reversed words, Robert, dear, to the openness of the question, and then to the peremptory closure of two simple direct commands and the unadorned signature. But there is only so much analysis that even the most eager biographer can do on a document that is fourteen words long. I can only be certain that the note itself was successful, whatever it was that my mother felt while she was writing it.

The diary entries later in 1928, though not as long as the description of their first lovemaking, give many details of my parents' lives. They argued, one becoming angry with the other for some lack of consideration or affection, and then they would make up. They strolled through Manhattan, visiting art galleries and museums, walking through parks, meeting friends to have a meal or go to the movies. And they kept returning to Mike Lenson's studio, making love with as much passion and more satisfaction than the first time. On occasion, they also made use of one apartment or the other, when they were certain that their families would be away. I can trace their lovemaking not only in the entries in my father's diaries but also in a series of circles and squares that he drew around certain dates in the calendar printed on the inside front cover of the Daily Reminder. The first of these dates, marked with a circle, was January 31, 1928, the first time that they made love. By comparing the later marked dates with the corresponding diary entries, I confirmed my hypothesis that these signs marked their lovemaking. I wondered why he kept so careful a record of this aspect of their relationship. It seemed to me that he was uncertain about so many things in his life that he must have drawn some reassurance from these marks. He could look at them and tell himself precisely how many times he had made love to a woman. As his biographer, I have benefited from these marks. Even though I was willing to read descriptions of my parents' lovemaking, some residual sense of prudishness or embarrassment would have kept me from tallying up their sexual acts: this night they did, this night they didn't. Thanks to my father's systematic recording, though, I can easily note that they made love ten times in the four months that followed their first encounter.

I pause, I look up at the ceiling, I feel a fondness for him, a fondness based both on an acceptance of our similarities and on my relief over the differences between us. The first time that I made love is described in no journal, marked on no calendar. I cannot recall the precise date, but only the month and year, October 1967, and that only because it immediately preceded the November in which my nineteenth birthday fell: the impending arrival of another birthday that deepened my despair, that condemned me to another year, perhaps even a lifetime, of virginity, to a lack of knowledge of the most fundamental of all human experiences. This sense of incompleteness and failure, akin to my father's self-doubts, was as acute as the sexual desires that came over me.

I feel fortunate, though, that no impulse led me to write a description of my first time in bed with Betsy. The pleasure and intimacy, sufficient in themselves, required no recording. Some details of that evening, though, a month or so after we met at a dance, are still fresh in my mind. My initial awkwardness and subsequent elation resemble his — and those of many other men, I am sure. The account of that night that I have kept in my memory, that I look back on as if it were a sort of video to be replayed from time to time, is like my father's in another way. It is not limited to the bedroom but continues with my walking out with Betsy (the strict rules that governed the movements of college students in those days required that she should be out of my dorm room by a certain hour, 11 P.M., I believe, and back to the last bus that would take her back to her college in time to meet the 12:30 curfew). My father wrote that he felt free; I recall rapture, wordless delight, a sense of tenderness that extended beyond myself, beyond Betsy, to every person we passed on the way to the bus stop, as if I were recognizing for the first time that all of humanity had attained, had always been in, a state of grace.

Such flashes of recognition, I might add, came more easily in those years than in earlier or later times. Several weeks after that first night, in a coffeehouse with Betsy, I was struck by the power of the phrase "make love, not war." I do not know how I might have explained at the time the link between lovemaking in a college dorm and the end of the war in Vietnam, but I did not question this slogan, whose fundamental truth was suddenly, brilliantly evident to me. Nor was I likely to be asked for such an explanation in that era, a time of sensation rather than thought. My father, a more introspective person in a more analytical period, left a far longer written record. (And here I feel a lack. I can recall only a few elements of the ending of our time together: an uneasy afternoon with Betsy in Manhattan, both of us at a loss for words and caresses, it must have been during Christmas vacation; some tentative phone calls; the decision not to see each other for a few weeks. I would like to know more.)

And yet my father's account of his early lovemaking, for all its detail, was not entirely explicit in its meaning. I tried to figure out if there was some logic to his almost alchemical system of circles and squares. I did establish the significance of the dashes and semicircles near a few dates, partially surrounding them rather than completely enclosing them as the squares and circles did. These marked the times when my parents' lovemaking did not reach what my father termed "consummation," either because of his impotence or because someone interrupted their privacy, as happened one evening in March when my parents believed that they would remain alone in his apartment. At the sound of some people coming in the front door (my father's parents, as it later turned out), my mother, demonstrating once again her presence of mind, grabbed a coat, put it on, dashed out the window to the fire escape and climbed up three flights of metal stairs to the fire escape outside a window in her family's apartment.

However, the difference between the straight dashes and squares on the one hand, and the curved circles and semicircles on the other, remains a mystery to me. If they were an effort to keep track of my mother's menstrual periods to avoid a pregnancy, I could not crack the code, and, at any rate, there would be no need to use straight and curved lines to distinguish among the incomplete and therefore riskless acts. At one point I wondered whether these different shapes recorded emotional tones rather than specific sexual acts. I thought that the squares might have marked encounters that left them happy and the circles ones when they were sad, but I could find no regular correspondence of this sort. I finally decided that these straight and curved lines were spontaneous, unreflective gestures of my father's hand as he drew on the calendar. I took them as an indication that he recognized—consciously or unconsciously—that there were some aspects of his experience that could not be captured by words alone. It struck me as entirely characteristic of him that, once he decided to record the times when he and my mother made love, he did not settle on one simple mark. In their playful alternation of simple forms as well as in their brevity, the squares and circles may have been for him, as they definitely are for me, a refreshing balance to the serious deliberation of the Daily Reminder and the wordiness of the big diary.

About five months after they first made love, my father reflected on his life:

July 11th — 28

It is my birthday and I am twenty four years old. And I have nothing to show for my having lived so long.

I am of importance to my mother. A girl loves me now so I am of importance to her, and Mike is my friend. But his Life is so filled up, with more important things. That I would soon fade out.

So of what importance am I.

My father measured his life by the passing years, he noted that he was entirely lacking in accomplishments, and then he defined himself not by the feelings that he had for other people but by the feelings that they had for him. His mother came first, and Mike Lenson got the longest of these brief summaries. Katzy, reduced to "a girl," is the only one who did not even merit a full sentence of her own.

I have spent a good deal of time puzzling over this passage. Did he think of Katzy as a casual fling? Was he so bound up with other people that he did not have very much emotion to spare on his first lover? Despite the fact that I am not much inclined toward conventional Freudian categories, the phrase "Oedipus complex" kept running through my mind for a while. Could I discern some general incestuous impulse not only in relation to his mother but also in his attraction to his cousins Irene and Betty? My father certainly adored his mother and detested his father, toward whom he had felt explicitly murderous impulses, as described in greatest detail in a diary entry from 1925:

> The innumerable scandals I don't want to repeat. The evil influence that the old man [his father] had over the whole family was and is terrible. His acting, behaviour, speech was insane. Mother suffered dreadfully. And there are no excuses for his doings.
>
> Only one incident do I want to put down. He had been raving all evening. The answers and curses were working on all. His hollering frightened Milton [then eight years old], who cried for the old man to be quiet. I could not stand it. I told him if he did not shut up I'd beat him up. He did not listen. I jumped at him and hit him at the face. He rushed to the window and screamed for help. I wanted to pull him back. He screamed more, I was ready to throw him out thru the window. Henry told me to let him have his way, because it must take an end. People came up from the street. The old mans behavior was disgusting. The janitor said. You always make trouble. They ought to kill you.
>
> Afterwards Henry told me not to take those things so much at heart. Mother is used to it long ago and she does not feel it so much. I was trembling and could hardly speak. I was choking. I wanted to speak, but the emotion was too strong. I jumped up, screamed a few words, and sank together sobbing and crying.

Was my father so bound up in his hatred for his father, in his veneration of his mother, that he could not become deeply involved with Katzy? Another vaguely Freudian idea, related to this one, came to mind, the "latent homosexual." Perhaps my father, so closely identified with his mother, was more in love with Mike Lenson than with Katzy; perhaps Katzy, like Elizabeth, was an acceptable female intermediary for the attraction that my father felt toward Mike. Did erotic impulses underlie his attentive recording of the gentleness with which he and Mike spoke to each other, of the occasions when Mike touched him, of the time when they rested together on a couch? Were these impulses the source of his eagerness to pose as a model for Mike, of his fears that Mike might lose interest in him, of his disdain for the women who always seemed to flock around Mike? I scrutinized the photographs that show my father and Mike together to see whether they reveal any sexual feeling between the two men, but these pictures only heightened the ambiguity of the question instead of resolving it. These possible erotic impulses, though, if they did exist, never surfaced consciously for my father.

This attraction to Mike makes me realize how often I have noticed my parents' reversal of gender roles. Stated most simply, my father had many traits often deemed to be feminine — gentleness, sensitivity — that contrasted with my mother's conventionally masculine qualities of resolution and determination. Firm, well-defined, my mother faced difficulties by choosing a course of action and sticking to it in stoic silence, while my father, overwhelmed with emotion and indecision, would often break into tears.

Faced with this reversal, I have occasionally indulged in a fantasy: what would have happened if my father had been born a girl and my mother a boy? I can imagine that my father's mother, at her sixth delivery, would have been delighted to be told that she had a daughter, since her first three children, all boys, were healthy and strong, while her fourth and fifth, both girls, died before they reached a year of age. Did my grandmother ever wish that she had had more daughters besides the two whom she bore, Elizabeth and Gertrude? Did she recall the woman-filled house in which she grew up? Did part of her anger at her husband stem from her jealousy over the fulfillment of his wish for sons? These thoughts, I believe, are more mine than hers: she valued my father's devotion, she built — especially after Gertrude's marriage to a gentile and then her death — a strong bond with Elizabeth.

For my mother's mother, the wish for a son would have come later in her life, I think, after her husband died and she was left a widow with six young daughters. She might have found solace in the strong male presence of a son, and who better to propose for this position than my mother, the eldest, the one who was willing to leave school and to go out to work? There is a hint of this reversal in my mother's story of seeking out a synagogue after her father's death: despite his opposition to religion, she said, she wanted to say kaddish — the prayer for the dead — for him, so she and her sister Ruth went from synagogue to synagogue, only to find, to their anger, a series of orthodox congregations that informed them that this ritual obligation could not be fulfilled

*Michael Lenson (left) and my father on a trip, Lake Champlain, New York, 1928.*

by daughters. But my mother's mother, like my father's mother, drew comfort from the children she had. She recognized, I believe, her good fortune: not all widows had children whose wages helped support them, had as cozy a home as the one with the six Cohen girls.

My speculation moves forward in time. What if my father had been a woman, my mother a man, when their families lived in the same apartment house in the Bronx? Would they have been attracted to each other? Would I have been born? I cannot get this fantasy in focus: I would need to adjust my parents' ages, making Francis older, Roberta younger, and their heights as well, so that he could be taller, and she shorter. I would need to invent a job for him (he would not have been a secretary), some more active involvement in art for her. The fantasy that I find satisfying, I realize, is the one of my grandmothers' acceptance of their children. Through that fantasy I come to accept my parents as well. Passages in my father's diaries have stirred me once again into recognizing the reversals in my parents' lives, into understanding that these reversals made me feel, as a child, that my family was different from the families of my friends, that I was an outsider in the neighborhood, in the world. I invent feelings of loneliness and grief for my grandmothers, and then I make my parents console them. Like my imagined grandmothers, I draw comfort from the strong strange people my parents were. I would not change them.

I would not even undo my father's tangled attachment to Mike. It, too, was part of who he was. When I am faced with these homoerotic possibilities, I turn to a third Freudian concept, "sublimation"; I note that whatever sexual stirrings my father felt in Mike's presence found their outlet with women. Mike's lending of his much-used studio and his wish of "soll sein mit Glick" gave my father courage when he left for his fateful appointment with Katzy.

As my father's biographer, I can invent scandals that suggest that he most desired his mother or his friend rather than my mother. These alternative accounts did shock and intrigue me at one time. My dissatisfaction with these scandals and with the psychological terms that summarize them comes from their tendency to take a complex whole and reduce it to a mere instance of some well-known syndrome, to the operation of a simple dark sexual force. They do not do justice to the power and the uniqueness of the constellation of ties that linked my father to his mother, to his friend, and to his lover. These terms offer a pat analysis of the tension that colored all three of these relationships, a combination of admiration, passion, tenderness, and affection, undercut by gnawing self-doubts. I seek not to classify my father's fears and his yearnings for intimacy but to witness them, to sympathize with them, and to comprehend how they led him to persist in his efforts to become an artist.

These struggles of my father's, reflected in his diary entry on his birthday, were shaped by two events in the months that followed. I will take these events out of chronological order and begin with Mike Lenson's departure for France in September 1928. As described in the longest published essay on his work that I have found, a four-page article in the Sunday magazine section of the February 8, 1970, issue of the *Newark News*:

> Mike, more or less on a dare, submitted a few of his art creations to the committee of the Chaloner Prize, which meant four years in Europe, all expenses paid, to the winner, and to his own astonishment won it. "The checks kept coming in," he said, "as I studied in Paris and Rome."

The tone of surprise also appears in the letter, dating from August 1928, that he wrote to my father from the Adirondacks, where he was painting and offering art lessons to guests at a nearby country club:

> I will be happy. Rob, what has happened to me occured only in books. I will live the next four years so that I will have a store of beautiful memories to last me the remainder of my days.

My father's diaries describe how Mike Lenson left the following month; first came a party in his honor on September 16:

> A crowd of relatives in B'klyn. Mike was amiable. His brothers. He said, only his friends will remember him.
> I kissed him. It was a virtous kiss.

and then the actual departure on September 21:

> Went to the ship to say final farewell to Mike. A family crowd. And a useless prolongation. Mike was tense and anxious to be off. Am

glad that I spoke to his father. Was the first to kiss Mike. Am glad
of it. Then the rush to catch a last glimpse.

The other change came earlier, as shown by an entry in the Daily
Reminder only six days after my father's birthday, on July 17:

I went up to K. house. She told me of her worries. It would be like
killing our firstborn. But let us wait.

By the end of July she was convinced that she was not pregnant.

K. came up [to the shop where he worked]. I was glad to see her.
Everything is all right, Lover.

Despite this scare, my parents apparently did not always use contra-
ceptives, as a diary entry on August 5 suggests:

K. called up. Met me at the Bridge. Don't smile so. — We loved
each other. I hope David was not conceived, because of my
excitement.

I cannot imagine why my parents assumed that the child they might
have conceived would be a boy rather than a girl, nor do I know why
they would choose a Jewish name for him but not follow the Jewish
custom of naming him after a deceased relative.

My father's concerns were well founded, since a pregnancy did result,
documented in an even more laconic fashion by later diary entries: August 22 has a marginal note: "A week overdue"; August 24 makes reference to "the medicine" that he obtained; September 4, to a "message"
that "she is feeling splendid." The first longer account appears on September 10; it contains his nickname Salo:

She was strange. Spoke of outside things. Then of David. — At the
stairs. The Goodbye. Upset. Crying. Turning to me embracing. On
the roof. I don't love you. Don't want David. Speaking. Unhappy
tears. Embrace. Finally a smile. Stroking my lips. Salo Lover.

On September 12 they planned to see a doctor on the following
Monday, September 17, right after the farewell party for Mike Lenson:

Found out that nothing but an operation would help. I knew it.
Saw her in the evening. What are we going to do? She would go

with me. It was a quiet evening. It stilled all my fears of her not loving me. I knew but I did not believe. But she was willing to undergo anything for me.

And yet after all that peaceful talk were embraces that made me swoon. I felt as if she were the Lover and I the maid.

They were able to arrange the operation very quickly. The entry for September 18 reads:

Made many calls to day. How are you. I need your help doctor. We went up. He was so kind and understanding. — I love you.

The other doctor, in a keyed up desperate mood and yet annoyed by the repetitions. The nurse so sad at these denials of giving life. K.'s firmness. Everything will be all right — yet there were tears in her eyes. One's first born. —

The tears in her eyes, I believe, did not course down her cheeks. "Firmness" is the precise word to describe my mother's fortitude and self-sufficiency. I cannot help wondering what would have happened if she had not had the operation. I imagine that they would have married and that they would have been unhappy. They might have had another child or two, but I do not believe that I would have been born. My thoughts, though, do not linger on my near-encounter with nonexistence but on my mother, on that determined woman, half my age as I now write, whose fears and loneliness I wish I could have assuaged.

The diaries record the effects of this crisis not only in the written entries but also in the series of circles and squares. Before August 22, when my father recorded "A week overdue," the intervals between love-making were two weeks or less; afterward, the gaps were longer. There are no marks of any sort in the months of September and November, and none in December until the last week, when an odd cross hangs down from 26. The entries in the diaries suggest the intensity of these last months of 1928. My parents took walks, mostly through parks, and had long conversations, with moments of great tenderness between them as well as some sudden fits of jealousy. They discussed their future in great detail. By the end of the year they decided on a plan of action, an arrangement that I had never heard of before, even though I thought that the 1960s and 1970s had witnessed every possible sexual and domestic configuration: they saved some money and borrowed a little from friends to buy some furniture and pay the rent on a small room where they could be alone, though they continued to live with their parents. This room of their own seems to have provided a satisfactory replacement for Lenson's studio, which became unavailable to them after his departure for Europe. A circle surrounds December 29, and the following months contain many more circles and squares, with no semicircles or dashes at all.

The diary entries for the last months of 1928 also contain a number of short references to my father's art. He took a number of photographs, made a few sketches, and attempted a couple of sculptures, but he wrote most often of his prints. He focused on his own art with greater attention than he ever had while Mike Lenson was still living in New York. In the month of November, for example, he wrote, "I read, made some cuts"; then, "I have been obsessed w/ buying a few things for my prints, so today I bought them, even though the money means a lot to me today"; and later, "Tonight I made my first portrait."

My father's diaries from this period gave me a new understanding of his prints. I had grown up with the phrase "woodcut," which I took to refer to the framed black-and-white picture that hung in the house on East 17th Street. I also recalled the set of tools with which he had made his prints, the small knives, chisels, and gouges that he kept in a box at his basement workbench. I would not dare to pick up or even touch these instruments, with their terrifyingly sharp metal blades. Once or twice he demonstrated their use to me, gripping a chisel firmly and sliding it into an old square of linoleum with a gesture whose strength and steadiness awed me. As I listened in fascination to my father's explanation, I discovered that the process of making the block required a mental control as impressive as this physical one. The block was a double inversion of the print, reversed right and left, and white and black as well, since the roller would ink only the portions of the block that had not been cut away. The action of the knife was to mark the areas that would remain white on the printed page, the exact opposite of the pencil that wrote black on the white page. Here was another of his astonishing capabilities: to see everything that was not going to be there in a picture and to draw that with a knife.

This power of his was most clearly manifest in the framed print,

Landscape
with Bridge
*by my father,
linoleum
block print,
1933.*

about the size of a sheet of typing paper, that hung in the living room. When I was growing up, this print was the clearest visual image that I had of his childhood in Europe. I see it plainly: on the left is a hamlet of four or five little stone houses, a barrel next to an open door, an old wooden fence; on the right, some tree-covered hills; in between, a stream, crossed by a footbridge leading to a path on which stand a man and a boy. It takes a moment to see them: the man is fishing, the boy watches him, and in the background, the sky is filled with swirling clouds whose immensity brings poignancy to the smallness of the houses and the people.

This print depicted not only the landscapes of a Europe that he had left in 1921 when he came to New York but also a second, more recent world that had also disappeared, the time in his life when he had made prints. In my mind, the print, like Mike Lenson's paintings, was genuine art, the kind of thing I had seen in museums, in galleries, in heavy art books with glossy pages and colored reproductions. The sketches and collages that he made when I was growing up, the sculptures he assembled from wooden blocks and bits of metal and plastic, were interesting and attractive, but they were not serious enough, not demanding enough in technique really to be art. I would occasionally wonder why he had stopped making woodcuts but did not ask him directly about it, much as I had been curious about the ending of his friendship with Mike Lenson but never spoke about it.

As I read through the accounts of my father's art work in his diaries, I thought of this familiar woodcut and of the larger set of woodcuts that I had found in the earliest stages of going through his papers. On some occasions during the first year after his death, I had been content to stand in the doorway of the study and feel his presence as I looked around the study. I found the room quiet, calm, very much the way it had been when he was alive, his papers carefully arranged in piles on the small table and bookcase. At other times during that year, a sudden impulse of curiosity would direct me to explore some portion of the study, and I would read through a set of notes he had left piled on a small table or examine the contents of a desk drawer. On one particular morning, though, able neither to draw comfort from the orderly silence of the room nor to focus my attention on a particular set of papers, I walked slowly around the study, ill at ease. I paused briefly by the bureau, gazed out the window for a few moments, stopped at the bureau again, and then crossed over to the bookcase. I skimmed idly through a collection of Chinese poems, translated into awkward English, I flipped through the pages of some old German books printed in Gothic script, knowing that I could not read them, and then I squatted down in order to look at two boxes on the bottom shelf. I placed them on top of the bookcase and opened one, then the other, to find unexpected treasure, a collection of my father's prints.

I wrote "Robbie's woodcuts!" on the boxes and sat cross-legged on the floor, the boxes next to me, lifting out the crumbling yellow prints one by one, arranging them in neat piles on the rug. A dim recollection of these boxes came to me; perhaps they had been on a high shelf in a closet in my parents' bedroom in Brooklyn, but I had never seen any of these woodcuts before: dramatic faces, scenes of New York, of Europe. For a long moment I looked at a scene of a village square. It reminded me of the framed European landscape that I had known since childhood, with its nostalgic evocation of a place that seemed to have so much more history than America did. This one, though, seemed not to be of Eastern Europe but of some Mediterranean country, with strong sunlight on a street running down from the square, on houses that had shuttered windows. A policeman was standing idly in front of a café while a woman at a pump in the square was filling a two-handled clay jug. The two enormous trees looked like olive trees rather than anything that grew in Russia or Germany.

I began to sort through the other prints. I was delighted to find more prints of the familiar village scene with the bridge, but others did not appeal to me: a skyscraper shooting upward, the perspective greatly exaggerated and unevenly rendered, so that the building looked twisted rather than tall; a nude woman, one leg thicker than the other; a still life of plants on a table with some irregular splotches of light gray among the shadows—perhaps my father had not succeeded in inking the block evenly or in transferring the image to the paper. I picked one print to look at more closely, to see whether I would come to like it better. This portrait of a man, for instance, I thought, there might be something more to it than first met my eye; yes, my father must have liked this one, he had put his initials in the corner. Trying to come up with some reason for the way that the man's head is tilted to the left, I thought that he might be remembering something—or is he gripped by some strong emotion? There is no way to tell, the face does not show feelings but simply my father's lack of skill; I do not think he intended the flare in one nostril to be so pronounced, the eyes to be slightly crossed, the bottom lip to be pulled inward on one side and puffed out on the other.

I closed the first box of prints and reached over to the other. One folder held a set of small prints, none more than five inches on a side. One landscape appealed to me, unmistakably New York: Manhattan as seen from across the Hudson River, tiny ferryboats in the water, skyscrapers outlined against enormous billowing clouds. I soon found myself looking quickly through these smaller prints as well, disappointed by expressionless portraits of faces, by the nude women (one with distorted hips and buttocks, another with oddly bulging arms), by the Christmas card that included YULE GREETING at the top, Robt. S. Orlove at the bottom, and some awkward haloed figures outlined against a grove of trees in the middle. And suddenly, a head of a man, turned to the left—I immediately recognized the face. The handsome young man was my father himself: the thick black hair, the large but well-shaped ears, the dark eyes, the passionate mouth. The paper had faded to a soft beige color, giving his skin a realistic tone. If he had been looking directly out of the print, I might have found his presence overwhelming and would have been unable to keep looking at him. Since his head was slightly turned, though, I could gaze steadily at him. It was as if I had entered a room in which he was standing, but he had not yet noticed me. Indeed, he seemed lost in thought: I was struck by the determination in his broad forehead, his strong chin, the way he held his head up. I, too, was lost in thought, absorbed in the firm look on his face. I realized that I had opened my mouth and tensed my vocal cords, as if I were about to speak to him. I sighed and put the portrait in the folder. I shifted my weight, stood up, and tried to take a step toward my desk, only to find myself staggering forward and grabbing a chair in order to steady myself. I had been sitting cross-legged on the floor for so long that my feet had fallen asleep. I stomped up and down a few times to restore sensation. In control of my limbs once again, I walked across the room and put the boxes back on the bookcase.

Several days later, it occurred to me that I could select a few of my father's woodcuts, have them framed, and hang them in my living room. I knew that I wanted to have my own copy of the landscape with the bridge, and there might be another one or two that I might like as well as that one. I wanted to have a large print of my father's on my living room wall. The New York river scene and the self-portrait would be too small, even if they were framed with wide mats, but I could go back over the others that I had looked at before and check through the rest of the second box.

On my next visit to my mother, I settled down on the floor of the study once again. I was disappointed to notice that all the copies of the landscape with the bridge had one area or another where the inking was incomplete. I finally selected one in which this defect seemed least noticeable and then looked at the other prints. I considered selecting another landscape, since they seemed more pleasing at a second look. The print of the Mediterranean village caught my attention once again. The contrast of the deep shade under the trees, the bright sunlight in the street winding down from the square, reminded me of village plazas I had seen in Peru, in the lower mountain valleys where the climate was warm enough to allow trees to grow. I began to imagine the conversation I might have had with him if he had shown me this print before

*Untitled self-portrait by my father, linoleum block print, c. 1930.*

he died. Appreciative of coincidences and recurrences, he would have enjoyed hearing how the print made me recall myself, years earlier in Peru — which village was that, Mosocllacta or Sangarará, where I stopped to look across a square and saw a scene just like the one that he had drawn, decades earlier and on a different continent. I would have told him how the European policeman idling just outside the café made me think of a Peruvian counterpart, standing in front of a *tienda*. The local women in Peru had struck me as purposive as well, carrying a load of onions to a market rather than filling a jug at a fountain like the woman in the print, but with the same efficient movements. In each scene the woman was the one point of action in the shady and silent plaza.

And then I began to realize how delicately I would have had to proceed in this conversation about the print. I could not have pointed out to him the poor quality of the inking, particularly the faintness of the

212

dark areas, even though I knew he would have been aware of them. Nor could I have asked him about the edge of the print that was slightly ripped. He would have taken that question as an accusation that he had not packed it carefully, or that he had allowed someone else, looking at it another time, to tear it. I certainly would not have mentioned the way that the two main branches of the larger tree looked very much like upraised arms, an effect exaggerated by the shading on the lower portion of the trunk, which gave it something of the appearance of a pair of legs. He could not possibly have intended this woodcut to look the way that it did when viewed at a distance, like an illustration for a fairy tale in which a giant was partially disguised as a tree.

My mind came back from these imaginary tactful evasions of sensitive issues to the task of selecting a print to frame. Whatever I might have said to him about this woodcut, it would not have gone together well with the other print I had already selected, the scene of the Eastern European village with the bridge. The landscapes resembled each other too much, and the poor inking in the second one would have called attention to the same defect in the first. I went back to the second box. It held some sketches by other artists, including a few by Mike Lenson, and a book of notes that my father had written as well, but it had only a few woodcuts. I did not like the first ones that I saw: some more Christmas greetings, an abstract design of vortices and waves. At the bottom of the box I found a large sheet of thick paper on which my father had pasted two smaller prints. It took me a few minutes to realize that this yellowing piece of paper, with an irregular left edge and straight lines for the three other sides, had been a page in a notebook in which he had glued his woodcuts. The left edge would have been held in the binding of the notebook. I could see a faint crease where he had bent it back and forth before tearing it out of the book. The upper print shows a Pueblo Indian village, a large multistoried adobe structure, the upper houses built on top of the lower ones. A simple print: no person, no other object interrupts the building under the open desert sky. The walls of the houses are set at right angles to each other and to the flat roofs, creating sharp edges that separate brilliant sunlit surfaces from ones in deep shadow. A few of the walls are interrupted by a window or two, plain rectangles that repeat the angles of the walls and relieve the otherwise stark monotony of the light and dark surfaces. These windows give a sense of scale, of the thickness of the adobe walls, of the great height of the village. My father must have liked this print a great deal, since it is one of the few that he signed, ORLOVE. The lower wood-cut is also an open-air scene, on a smaller scale. The trunks of three trees reach from the bottom to the top, sharply outlined against a sky with billowing clouds. A small figure of a woman stands silhouetted against the sky as well: her posture, her skirts, her hair suggest that it is a windy day. I could just discern the slight downward tilt of her head. She seems to be thinking deeply about something, while remaining aware of the windy day and the dramatic cloudy sky. Even though I had not seen this print before, I knew at once that the woman must be my father's sister Gertrude; I had seen a series of photographs on which the wood-cut is based, taken when my father accompanied Gertrude to the country house in the Hudson Valley, the house I now know to be the one of her friend, or lover.

I looked at the sheet, taken in by the visual power of the prints and their strong associations for me. The Pueblo village scene reminded me of the kachina that he had on his desk, of his books of Southwest Indian art, of the times he took me, when I was a child, to the American Museum of Natural History, with its Indian artifacts and dioramas. When I saw the portrait of Gertrude, I recalled how deeply he loved her, how pained he had been by her unexpected death at the age of twenty-seven. I noted a flaw in each (the shadows on a couple of the adobe walls were not quite at the correct angle, and one section of Gertrude's skirt was awkwardly rendered), but these did not detract from their appeal. Their defects did not come to mind as I looked at these woodcuts, with their intense moods, with the dramatic clouds and sky that set off the poignant figure of his sister and the powerful Indian village. I considered cutting the prints out of the sheet and framing them separately. Suddenly, a thought came to me: I could frame the entire sheet.

A few weeks later, I spent more than an hour talking over different possibilities with an assistant at a frame shop. We first considered placing the sheet with the two prints directly behind a mat but then decided to add one more element. We "floated" the sheet in front of a black background, so that its jagged outline would be as sharply defined as possible; we placed the floated sheet and its black background behind a mat of a yellowish beige color, close to the tone of the notebook page,

Cliff-dwellings *and* Figure Against Clouds *by my father, linoleum block prints, 1932.*

and then enclosed the matted sheet in a simple black frame. I had gone very far from my original notion of framing the two prints separately.

This sheet became the subject of conversations — not an imaginary one with my father but very real ones — in which I would stand next to a friend, a few feet from the spot on my living room wall on which the framed sheet hung, and explain the story, with very little variation from one occasion to another: these are two of the woodcuts that my father made when he was young, I really like them, look, here's a Southwest

Indian pueblo, and this woman is his sister Gertrude, she died very young. At this point I would pause, briefly leaving my listener alone to admire my father's work, and then continue: I found this sheet among his papers, it was a page in a notebook he kept. Look, you can see how smoothly he glued each of the prints in, but how he didn't exactly line them up, the top one is tilted at a slight angle. Here my listener and I would bend at the waist to look more closely at the page, or take a small step forward. I would go on: I can't really figure out if he meant to take good care of these prints. He had hoped to be an artist, to show his prints at exhibits and to sell them, but he didn't have much success, and he ended up just putting them in a notebook. And look how the paper in the notebook has deteriorated, the edges are breaking off, I wonder if he used cheap paper because he felt his work wasn't worth much, or if he just didn't have enough money to buy better paper, he made these during the Depression. You know, I would continue, it's funny, I actually like the way that the paper has turned yellow, it gives the prints a soft tone, and that's why I framed it this way. My listener and I would now straighten up or take a small step back to our original position, to get the entire framed object into view once again. After a final pause I would offer my summary: I decided to float the whole sheet against this black background, it really gives me a sense of the period in his life when he made these prints. At this point the listener would offer a brief expression of interest, which I would acknowledge with some murmured reply, and the conversation would end. Having begun to move back from the framed prints on the wall, we continued our return into whatever it was that we had been doing when I began my story.

However curious my listeners may have been about my relationship with my father, I was just as pleased not to go on. Like my imaginary conversation with my father about the Mediterranean village, these conversations might quickly lead to more difficult terrain where I could not speak as easily. I could not maintain the confidence in my voice if I were to continue: You know, my father framed only one or two of his woodcuts, he never had these framed. I don't think that he felt that they were good enough. He never even showed them to me, or the others he made. When I was growing up, I had no idea that he had made a lot of prints, I was surprised when I found two whole boxes of them. And the truth is that most of them really weren't very good at all. The two on this page were the only ones that I wanted to have framed. The others are over at my mother's apartment, they're still in the boxes that he put them in.

With the framed sheet in view in my living room, I began to pay even more careful attention to the references in his diaries to his wood-cuts. The first notes that I found were lists of prints he had planned to make. The first was simply a pair:

*Subjects for Cuts.*

------------

A young woman steps out of a curtain of overhanging, blossoming branches. She is nude.

An old woman steps out of the curtain like overhanging branches of a willow tree. It is a grey autumn day.

------ . ------

The second series, an effort at a woodcut-novel like the ones made by Franz Masereel, an artist whom he greatly admired, treats a similar theme in more detail:

*Series of cuts.*

*The six ages of man.*

In twenty pictures.
Showing only heads, with expressions fitted to the emotions.

Head of a woman, in agony : Birth.

------ . ------

Baby sleeping
    " feeding
    " crying

------ . ------

Child laughing
    " ~~asking~~ wondering
    " weeping

------ . ------

Youth looking intent
    " ~~thinking~~ pondering
    " kissing = the only cut with two faces.

man. proud —
worried depressed
thinking

—— . ——

mature. serene
sad
worried

ʻ
—— . ——

old man, senile
dozing
pained

—— . ——

a death mask

I realized that I was relieved that he had not made these prints. Even if he had executed them well, they would have been depressing, with their emphasis on worry and decline. I was chagrined to admit that he might have been right not to pursue his printmaking any further, despite my efforts to rescue the few good woodcuts from oblivion and put them on display.

One summer morning, I was reading through my father's big diary. As was often the case, I was torn between my self-imposed responsibility to read it word by word and my impulse to skim through the long tedious accounts of his mother's complaints, of his doubts that he would ever find steady work. One section, from April 1929, caught my eye:

> I had always thought and dreamed, that I would be able to ac-
> complish something in one thing or another. Photography, reading,
> writing, linoleum cuts, archery. Now it is chess. I like it, and believe
> that I play original.
>
> But I have found out that deep study and perfect control are nec-
> essary for mastery.
>
> This, chess has taught me.

I recalled the many times I had seen my father play chess when I was a child: the long interval of intense concentration as he sat, leaning slightly forward, and then the moment when he reached to the board, picked a piece up with his thumb, forefinger, and middle finger, and placed it in its new position on the board. He never interrupted the steadiness of his movement, not even when he took an opponent's piece. On those occasions, he would swing his arm down, and, as his hand neared the board, he would rotate his wrist, smoothly sweeping the captured piece up in his ring finger and pinkie and pressing it against his palm just before he placed his own piece in the exact center of its square. His motion continued as he quietly settled the captured piece in some inconspicuous spot on the table and then folded his arms. This courtly reserve, this utter absence of gloating, bespoke a seriousness of purpose that I could barely fathom.

I entered a calm reverie, seeing the chessboard in my mind, my father gazing down at it, while I sat wordless at his side, trying to fathom his thoughts. Suddenly the phrase "linoleum cut" from the passage in the diary came into my mind. Now wait, I thought, he made woodcuts, not linoleum cuts, didn't he? Did he also make linoleum cuts? Perhaps some of the prints that I thought were woodcuts were in fact linoleum prints, made by cutting the reversed image into a sheet of linoleum rather than a block of wood. I sat up and began to look through his big diary purposively, searching for the word "woodcut." I did not find it at all, and it appeared only once in the Daily Reminder volumes, in 1926 when he felt the impulse to make some work of art, a woodcut or a clay statue. However, he did use the phrase "linoleum cut" on many occasions. I went back to the two boxes and came across some notes he had typed, LIST OF LINOLEUM CUTS. It included forty-eight prints, with the dates he made them, their titles, their sources, and their dimensions. The realization came to me: there had never been any woodcuts at all.

I was puzzled rather than surprised or shocked. I did not doubt this new truth but simply wondered how I had come to firmly believe that my father had made woodcuts if he did not use the word at all in his own writings. I wondered whether I had been lied to when I was a child. Someone must have told me that these prints were woodcuts, I thought, but, try as I could, I was unable to recall how the landscape with the bridge had been described to me. I realized that I had hardly heard it spoken of at all. It was simply a familiar object on the wall, and I had come to know very early that my father had made it when he was young and that he was proud of it. In my eagerness to be proud of it as well, I must have assumed that it was a woodcut. I certainly knew about both sorts of prints, and the differences between them. There were any number of sources from which I could have picked up the notion that woodcuts were a higher form of art than linoleum cuts. Some of his art books contained woodcuts; I recalled in particular a volume of Dürer's work. I knew that counselors at day camps taught linoleum printmaking in the periods dedicated to arts and crafts, an easier activity than making woodcuts. Outside the realm of art altogether, I associated wood with living room floors, linoleum with the humbler floors of kitchens.

Why am I not upset, I asked myself. Shouldn't I be disappointed to have these works reduced to mere linoleum block prints? And shouldn't I be furious at my family for turning me into a liar? In calling these prints woodcuts, I had invented falsehoods about my father, a distortion of reality far more insidious than the common situation in which children hear, learn, and repeat the untruths that others have made up. I had unconsciously volunteered myself as an accomplice in deception. How I fled from inquiry: as a child, watching him cut into a linoleum block with knives and gouges, I did not ask the entirely natural question, "Daddy, is this how you made the picture we have on the wall?" As an adult, my memories of seeing him with his tools and a linoleum block were kept in one part of my mind, the notion of his print as a woodcut in another part, hermetically sealed off from the first.

I reflected on my lack of anger. Perhaps I had already come to accept the ways we tried in my family to aggrandize ourselves, so that it did not seem important to me to maintain the distinction between those statements that were exaggerations and those that were outright falsehoods. Perhaps I derived comfort from participating in the family's custom of speaking imprecisely and favorably of my father's art, of sheltering him from the critical voices in the wider world and in his own doubt-filled mind. To be angry is to want an alternative, to believe or to hope that alternatives are possible: I may be unable to conceive of a life without this web of stories and memories.

Nonetheless, I was not entirely at ease. I would occasionally think about my misapprehension. I tried, unsuccessfully, to reconstruct some situation when I might have spoken of his prints in front of relatives who might have known that they were linoleum prints. It would have made a difference to me if I could have been certain that I had called them woodcuts, and that this error had remained uncorrected. To check a hunch, I looked back through the other folders that I had made during the project of writing this book, and I could not find one that I had labeled with an exclamation point other than "Robbie's woodcuts!" Against what challenger, I wondered, was I still shouting rather than stating the nature of these prints.

These doubts were still in my mind when I came across another passage in my father's diaries from January 1933:

> I feel a certain strength in me, new and different. Even such a little thing as my monogram, gives me pleasure.
>
> I could never make a design out of the combination of an R and an O. But now I have it, thus
>
>
> The O is a circle lying down and the R is the compass measuring the enclosed contents. I have the R stepping out of the circle. But I don't feel strong enough to believe that I can leave the inherited Or- love behind and step out as myself, as
>
> Robert.
>
> That is for my prints.

This passage brought to mind how my father had given himself the name Robert on coming to America. Beneath its apparent playfulness, this arrangement of initials conveyed serious meanings. The *R* stands straighter than the *S*. Unlike the *S*, wobbling on its curved base, the *R* can take firm strides forward, away from the limits of the family and down a path of its own making. The only one that bore the monogram was a portrait, the distorted man's face, and there was not a single one that he signed as Robert.

I came across another passage in his diaries from October 1933 that helped explain why he did not make more use of the monogram that he liked so well:

> Close within myself, the thoughts whirl and jump from one pole to another. The problem is, what is it all about.
>
> I sit back and reflect calmly. The incomprehensible purpose of

existing. I know of no way out. If I could find a place for myself, an occupation that would take up all my interests and at the same time give me satisfaction of doing that work there I might be helped.

So far, the only escape would be in creating pictures. This has given me the greatest gratification. But I know that I am no artist. I may be able to see beauty, but to reproduce or create it is not in my scope. I am not talented.

No, it will be nothing more but a weak desire, and I shall play with it, as the dilettante that I am. How strong is my character?

I was not surprised to hear my father call himself "not talented," since he often doubted his abilities, but I was puzzled by his statement that he was able only "to see beauty," not "to reproduce or create it." I tried to explain to myself why this wording stuck in my mind. It really is not such an odd turn of phrase, I thought, perhaps I am reading something into his words that is not there. After some reflection, I came up with only one reason for noticing this particular phrase, and not a very satisfactory one: I would have expected him to contrast the word "see" with the equally simple word "make," to wish that his ability to see beauty would give him the ability to make beautiful things. Was he implying that to "create" beauty was to invent something in his imagination, a higher form of art than to "reproduce" beauty, a simple copying of beautiful things that he saw? A few days later I found a second passage, from the end of December 1933, that indicated that my intuition was right, that he was hinting at something in that first passage.

The desire to record graphically, either in words or in pictures, things I see.

I can trace the entire evolution of it. Out of an admiration of pictures, came the desire to be able to do likewise. And the first impulse was to copy, what I had liked so much. Once I knew it, understood it, I grew further. I could select my own pictures. I had developed a taste and only certain incidents would give me the same effect. I began to have my own technique. And above that has come the ability to create my own visions. I believe they are good.

At the moment I am at a dangerous spot. I am taking to much for granted. I have made several cuts during the summer, and they have found some sort of appreciation. After all, even if the method applied, is my own as best I was able, which makes it individual, while the design was by some one else M. Lenson in this case. Can I do artistic work.

This brings another point to the for. I don't believe that I ever will be able to produce a fine line drawing, or a delicate block. I haven't had the training nor the skill. I begin to realize that I ought to study drawing, so as to be free to express personally my own conceptions.

So therefore not having the skill I must naturally believe that the idea rates higher than the action. The meaning of a picture is more important than the manner employed in portraying it.

Once again he described copying as an inferior form of art. He spoke of moving beyond making copies to develop his personal taste and technique, so that he could create his own visions. He still doubted himself, though. At best, he could apply his method to a design by someone else. If he had his own technique and method, though, why would he not feel himself to be creative, to be truly an artist? He still did not speak plainly, but at least he left some more direct clues. What made him doubt the value of the linoleum cuts — which were based on his own method and which other people liked — was that the design was by someone else: Michael Lenson in fact, whom he called by a distant M. Lenson rather than his more usual and friendly Mike. Lenson's name in one sentence, and his doubts, "Can I do artistic work" in the next. Having shown how Lenson brought forward his feelings of inadequacy, he was finally prepared to give a specific description of the obstacle to his artistic development. "I begin to realize that I ought to study drawing, so as to be free to express personally my own conceptions." Here was the problem: Lenson could draw and my father could not.

I went back to the boxes of prints and looked through them once again. This time I noticed other sketches and photographs. Near the bottom of the box I found the photograph on which the distorted portrait was based, along with the tracing paper on which he copied the outlines of the face to transfer to the linoleum block. This paper had many tiny holes in it: he had attached the tracing to the linoleum block and laboriously pricked the design with a sharp pin through the sheet onto the block before he could begin gouging out the linoleum itself, before he could begin eliminating the evidence of the copying itself by cutting out the pinpricks as he carved into the block.

I found a few more photographs of faces and of paintings, and then a very familiar image, a sketch, very much like the landscape with the bridge. Quickly, without thinking, I put the sketch back in the box and stood up. Could I have really seen it? I went back and started looking through the box, finding myself distracted by other prints, then forcing myself to locate the incriminating sketch once again. In the box I found another copy of my father's print of the landscape, and I compared it with the sketch. They were identical except for a small area in the upper left-hand corner, a portion of a cloud in the print, but which in the sketch contained an inscription: Lenson 31 /.

I kept looking from the print to the sketch and back again. Finally, in a state of great agitation, I put them back in the box, then began to worry that I had not packed them well, and took them out again. It finally occurred to me to consult the list that my father had made of linoleum cuts. The print corresponded unambiguously to one of the entries for the year 1933:

> Landscape with Bridge    Lenson — Cassis France 9¼ × 12.

No other landscape had as prominent a bridge; none of the others had those precise dimensions. I looked Cassis up in an atlas and located it in the south of France, just east of Marseilles, a part of Europe that my father had never visited but in which Mike Lenson had traveled extensively. Checking closely, I found details in both the print and the sketch that were unambiguously Mediterranean: the stone walls of the peasant houses were certainly not Slavic or Germanic, nor were the roofs, with their clay tiles and their slopes too gentle to bear the weight of winter snows. And the print entitled "Shadows and Sun" must be the village scene with the woman at the pump. That was a reasonable title for it, and it was the only piece exactly 10 × 8¼. It, too, came from Lenson's travels, in this instance to Palma de Mallorca in Spain. I discovered that the prints of women were also derivative: Lenson's name invariably appeared in the list after the titles "Seated nude," "Nude," "Nude by window." When my father made these prints, he was capturing the moments when women had stood unclothed in front of Lenson rather than him. I recalled the hints that the model for "The Woman in the Café" had been one of Lenson's lovers, and it occurred to me, as it must have to my father as well, that among his other lovers might have been the women who posed for the works that were the sources of my father's prints.

I had indeed uncovered a secret. The notion that the print was a woodcut might have been an invention of mine, but I was sure that I was not the only one to think that the landscape with the bridge, the most important of all my father's prints, had been an original work of his. I confirmed this point when I next spoke with one of my sisters. I had lost the last shred of the possibility that the print was what I had always assumed it to be, a nostalgic evocation of his childhood memories of Europe.

This second disillusion might also have angered me. What prevented this reaction, I think, was not simply the familiarity of the experience, the fact that I had already given up other beliefs about my father much like this one; it lay more in the gain that compensated for the loss of a myth. The hidden connection to Lenson's sketch revealed one of my father's most private areas of vulnerability, an aspect of his past more intimate than any fondly remembered childhood scene could be. Concealed beneath the layers of self-doubt that he had shown, he had kept another such layer secret, the one in which he admitted to a fundamental inability to create, in which he acknowledged his enduring dependence on Mike Lenson. By choosing this linoleum cut as the one that he would frame and hang on his wall, he declared it to be the high point of his printmaking. If his sole intention had been to make my sisters and me believe that he had seen the village, the bridge, and the man and boy with his own eyes, he could have destroyed Lenson's sketch, and, if he had been working systematically, he could have erased Lenson's name from the list of prints as well. Instead, he preserved these tangible reminders of the origins of this print, reminders that became for me a sign of a personal, if wholly private, integrity that balanced the duplicity with which he abetted the family's false version of the print.

When the shock of this discovery wore off, when I found that I could accept both the old and new accounts of the origins of my father's print, I was able to look steadily at Mike Lenson's drawing rather than just to glance at it long enough to establish it as the source of my father's print. I soon realized that I liked my father's version much better than Mike

Lenson's, a reaction that, I believe, does not merely reflect filial loyalty but genuine differences between the two identically sized images of the same scene. The sketch, with its soft charcoal shadings, is a pleasing rendition of an attractive landscape. The sharp contrasts of light and dark give the linoleum cut more emotional power. In my father's work, the bare-limbed trees stand out more clearly, and the huge clouds fill the sky instead of merging into a haze. The peasant houses look worn rather than mellowed by age. Filled with waves, the river flows with real force. In Lenson's drawing, the man and boy, small figures along the river, are an element of minor interest in the landscape. The more dramatic setting in my father's print brings them more sharply to attention. Rather than blending into the countryside, they must face its challenges. I find myself admiring their capacity to endure the hardships of nature and the passing of time. However much my father's print is a secondhand work, there is still a great deal of him in it. Even if it depicts a scene from an imaginary journey of his rather than a real one, it captures the intensity of feeling that he had experienced, that he wished to portray, and that is missing from Lenson's pretty drawing.

As I reflected on the two versions of this landscape, I felt sad. In this print, and in other works like it, my father must have seen a confirmation that he was, as he phrased it, "able to see beauty" — that is, he could look at drawings and paintings made by others, and use his personal taste to select the most beautiful ones, which would serve as sources for his prints. And yet this print also confirmed his limitations. Able only to copy the designs of others, he was not truly an artist. I wished that I could somehow leap across the decades and console him, that I could point out the evocative power of his prints, that I could encourage him to make more of them.

I found some solace a week or two later when I looked at the list that he had made in 1934 of his linoleum cuts. In the entries for 1932 appear the two on the sheet that I had framed, "Figure against clouds," based on a "photo," most likely one that he took, and "Cliffdwellings," attributed simply to "copy." I thought of the time when my father reviewed his prints, selected some of them, and assembled them into a notebook. Somehow, he must have been able to set aside the conflict between his doubts about his true creativity and his hopes that he would transcend the stage of copying other people's work. He must have drawn some satisfaction from this dramatic rendering of the massive Pueblo buildings, from the passionate figure of Gertrude standing between two trees, silhouetted against a cloud-filled sky on a windy day. He longed for a public display on the walls of a gallery, where others could admire his work; he settled for a private exhibition in the pages of a book. I do not know whether, as he pasted in his prints, he hoped that the notebook would mark a first stage in a printmaking career that would have further accomplishments, or whether he assembled it as the final archive of a period in his artistic life that he was closing. I can at least be certain that he was not filled with despair. If he had been, he would have destroyed his works or simply have left them all unsorted. He was at least able to distinguish between the ones he liked less and the ones he liked more, and to deem some worthy of preservation. This sheet had once led me to criticize my father for using cheap paper, for not lining the prints up when he pasted them in. I had come to view it differently, knowing that he often felt that his prints were not worth saving in a notebook at all.

The entries in his diaries suggest that 1934 was a year of intense reflection for him about his marriage and life, as well as the year of cataloging his linoleum cuts. In January, looking back to the anniversary of the day he and Katzy first made love, he wrote:

> In a few days it will be six years I have tied up my life with Katzy and many experiences and impressions have taken place. And I still let time pass unutilized.
>
> All this is possible, only due to Katzy's earnings and her shouldering all responsibilities. She lets me go along as I see fit.
>
> So many times have I considered what and why Katzy helps me and every time have I sunk lower in my own estimation. I felt like crawling in the dust.

His bleak assessment of his economic dependence was accurate. Her steady employment for Lucius N. Littauer provided the regular income that met their economic needs, while his occasional jobs in the fur business brought in relatively little money. His despondence, though, seemed to go beyond his inability to find regular work. His birthday in July brought another point of reflection:

> Arrived at my thirtieth birthday. Had looked forward to it, as a point where I'd know what I am about.

Six months ago it seemed it would be a decisive turning point. I thought it possible to have my life in order and to go on towards the definite goal.

It was such an adolescent view to take.

Time just goes on, and there is not much to spare to live for oneself.

This retrospective impulse continued past his birthday. Early in the fall, he wrote:

Am staying at home bringing this book up to date. Perhaps it will relieve me of some of the tension.

My diaries are before me, almost every day notes since 1928. And it has been an everpresent misery and depression. Not as if it has been six years, but one day of agony. How can such misery last so long.

The spasmodic optimism had nothing concrete to back it up.

It has all been a rising and falling of emotions.

But of accomplishments, there are none.

He even doubted the importance of his diaries:

Are all my thoughts, my desires, even this writing a means to escape myself, escape the knowledge the mess I am in, part because of the condition and part because of my lack of tenacious trying, seeking attempting.

How much he had changed in his twenties, and how little. There had been many beginnings in 1928. That was the year that he first made love to a woman, the year that he first made prints. And yet he had not advanced since that year. Though he and Katzy had continued as lovers and married in 1930, he still felt weak, frightened of her sudden bursts of anger and her long resentful silences, disheartened by his inability to earn money. And he had recognized his failure to progress as an artist, his continuing dependence on others, especially Mike Lenson, as a source for his prints.

Despite his "everpresent misery," he did continue to visit art galleries at the time. Perhaps the pleasure that he took in his ability to see beauty, and the sheer abundance of his free time, overcame his pain at seeing other people's success. His earlier interest in photography, a medium that he had judged inferior to printmaking, reawakened, as one entry in September 1934 shows:

> Went to Photographic Xhibit. The men are perfect technicians, but no artists. The execution is excellent, but no original thoughts to express. Just commercial illustrators.
>
> Why cant I try my hand at things, I have certain ideas about.

Apparently this visit led him to review his own work. He went back to the photographs from their honeymoon. A week later, he wrote:

> Some friends were over in the evening and I projected some of the European pictures.
>
> I am disappointed with them. They are not at all as good as I once thought.
>
> The enthusiasm blinded me in the beginning. What is worse, is, that I dont take any more pictures, and find out just what I can do. It is easy enough, to say, while looking at something completed, I can equal or better this.

That winter he continued to think about photography:

> It almost seems as if I have neglected photography.
>
> I think about subjects for new pictures. It seems silly to make prints after the photographs I took in Europe. If I have something to say. It should be of the present environment and present condition instead.
>
> But I am waiting for better weather until I go out to take shots.

The good weather came soon:

> Went downtown and took photos. It was a brilliant day, fit for such a purpose. Took people at work, it is different than shooting buildings. I was so intent, I muttered to myself. It was cold out, but the fresh air was invigorating. I was full of activity.

Other entries, interspersed with this shift from linoleum cuts to photography, describe a change in the marriage as well:

> For many years I would make notes on pieces of paper thinking that I would either write them into the book at a more convenient time, or elaborate the ideas further. But I never did that either.

There was quite an accumulation, haphazard and no dates to tell to what time the thought belonged.

There was a mass of scraps covering the period of the beginning of my relationship with Katzy.

I have felt that I will never reconstruct that time in a consecutive order. But I was also disturbed by this mixture of notes.

I finally did go thru them thoroughly. I destroyed most of them. There was no need to keep them. They had become dead things.

I want to get everything in order, my interests, my thoughts, my entire life.

I want to be unhampered by all this old apendage.

Unhampered — and freed. It is from the last months of 1934 that I found the one mention in all his diaries of an impulse to make a picture with my mother as the model:

Katzy was resting on the sofa. The room was in darkness. One lamp only threw light on her nude body. The shadows reflecting were lovely, the modeling of the ribs, the full breasts, highlights on the thigh and shoulder. I almost began a drawing.

Ribs, breasts, thighs, shoulders: I do not know if it was his eye that moved back and forth over Katzy as she rested, or his mind that moved over the image of her as he wrote. And yet I imagine that even if his eye moved, he stood motionless, delighting in his wife's body until he recognized his wish to make a drawing. It seems unlikely that he ever carried out this impulse on another occasion, since I have never come across any such drawing, and since he doubted his ability to sketch. Perhaps he considered taking pictures of Katzy, although I think that nude photography would have embarrassed both of them. At any rate, the attraction between them not only shifted into the possibility of artistic creation but moved in other directions as well. He and Katzy decided to have a child. Carol was born on March 20, 1935. Since he had abandoned his system of indicating lovemaking with circles and squares in 1933, I cannot pinpoint the dates when she might have been conceived. Had it not been for Mike Lenson, with his encouragement and his available studio, my parents would not have become lovers as soon as they did; perhaps they never would have at all. In a similar vein, I wonder whether they would have begun having children if my father had not given up linoleum cuts and renounced his dependence on Mike Lenson as a source for creativity. In admitting artistic stagnation, he could recognize the stagnation of his marriage as well.

There were evidently many moments in which his new daughter brought him great delight. The photographs that he took of Carol in her first three years of life suggest to me not only the interest and pride that lead many parents to take pictures of their children but also a great burst of artistic energy on my father's part. Certainly, the album into which he assembled them reflects his originality. He mounted portions of contact sheets, so there are strips of tiny photographs, an inch and a half by an inch. He cut the background from other photographs so that my sister's head is silhouetted against the black paper of the album. The brief captions ("1936," "Feb—1937"), written in white crayon, also stand out sharply.

He carried techniques from his prints to the photographs—the contrasts of black and white, the concern for a balanced composition, even the feel of the surface, since the matte finish of the photographs (only a few have a glossy finish) has a soft texture, much like that of the paper on which the linoleum cuts are printed. He also experimented with features of photographs that were unavailable to him in printmaking. There is a slight blurriness to some of them, a consequence of not focusing precisely. I think that this effect was deliberate, since he used it to emphasize a pensive mood, precisely the times when Carol would not have been moving, when it would have been easiest for him to focus the lens sharply on her. The themes of the photographs are unusual, too. In addition to the commonplace shots of a child smiling, playing, petting an animal, he has recorded Carol sleeping, Carol crying in apparent frustration, Carol simply staring off into space. I wonder whether he realized that he had captured some of the "six ages of man" that he had intended to portray in a series of twenty cuts. He does have the baby sleeping, feeding, crying; the child laughing, wondering, weeping. Instead of moving steadily toward the decline in old age and the final end of death, he stopped, captivated by the possibility of recording the many moods of earlier periods.

I am particularly taken with a photograph from 1936. Carol is crawling up a flight of stairs. Another parent might have photographed the triumphant grin of a child as she reaches the top of the stairs, but my father recorded her midway in her ascent. Her knee is raised to begin the climb to the next step, but she has paused to look around her. She turns her head back, and she is looking off at some point beyond the edge of the photograph. Her smile suggests that she likes the view from this new perspective. I think that my father felt a great empathy with her at this moment. It is, at any rate, a more evocative portrait of a face than any of his linoleum cuts. Freed from his dissatisfactions with his prints, my father eagerly explored a new medium; freed from reliance on others for his subject matter, he depicted a subject that was very much of his own making.

## Chapter 9 LIGHT-MACHINE

T he one major gap in my father's papers begins in 1938. His album of photographs of Carol tapers off in that year: he put in thirty pictures a year in 1936 and 1937, a dozen in 1938, and then only nine for the entire period from 1939 to 1945. (My mother's book of songs closes in 1938 with a celebration of Carol's early years as well, "You Must Have Been a Beautiful Baby.") In November 1938, exactly ten years before I was born, he finished his book about his mother. After completing an account of a visit that he made to her in a Jewish old age home, he found enough relief from his sense of guilt and inadequacy that he no longer needed to write about her. His own diaries also slackened off at the same time. Having abandoned his system of squares and circles in 1933, he slowly left off writing altogether. The first long stretches of blank pages in the diaries appeared in 1936, and by 1940 he was writing only brief, sporadic entries.

One of the reasons for this new scarcity of documents was that my father was working more regularly. He spent a good deal of time in the fur district in Manhattan, sometimes making patterns for stuffed animals, more often buying and selling furs. He would visit his father's shop, using it as a base from which to handle orders for his brother Henry, who was still in Chicago. At the shop or in the street he would run into acquaintances and chat for hours, staying abreast of the gossip and rumors of the fur trade, and setting up business deals of his own.

An occasional holiday would break this busy work schedule, giving 233 him an opportunity to consider different ways to spend a bit of free time. October 3, 1940, was the first day of Rosh Hashanah, and the Jewish firms in the fur district observed the holiday:

> Since business was closed stayed home. Put the house in order, took a nap. Went to the Museum to see the silk screen prints. Liked one that showed a row of old trees, overhanging a road. A quiet day. I did not know what to plan for the following free day.

Unlike the reform Jews of German extraction in other lines of business further uptown, the predominantly conservative and orthodox fur merchants of Polish and Russian origin observed the second day of Rosh Hashanah as well. The entry for Friday, October 4, reads:

> Decided to visit father at the temple and took Cookie [Carol] along. We called for Elizabeth & Joan. The old man was very impatient. In the synagogue I wondered about the traditions of the jews. While looking about noticed those old and weary faces. When leaving, he made a date for next week. Insisted on my coming.
>
> At supper had a phone call to come to the home. Katzy & I rushed uptown. We saw mother and Elizabeth sitting together and I knew then that my father had died. I had not even given it a thought before. There were no sensations, perhaps it was due to a shook [shock]. He had had a quick attack and was gone within ten minutes. Thrombosis of the heart. George came later. I was going to stay with mother. Katzy went home alone. I would never have believed I would ever spend a night in his bed. I looked thru his effects, destroying all of his papers. Others do not have to see them. He had made all the arrangements for his funeral. Beyond this there was nothing of any importance.

I find myself wondering whether he simply threw his father's papers out, but the word "destroying" suggests some form of actual violence: did he tear them up or throw them into a furnace? Did he sleep poorly in his father's bed and get up in the middle of the night to start rummaging through the papers, or did he sleep soundly, awakening in the morning filled with the resolution to search out all of his father's papers and destroy them? Whatever the specific details of his actions, my father was motivated, I believe, by anger against his father, anger against the strength of this man who, despite the fact of his death, threatened to keep on burdening his son with obligations. My father's decision that others did not have to see his father's papers, though, was not only an act of rebellion or an attempt to gain power over his father by learning his secrets and then not revealing them. It also seems to have been an act of detachment as well, a calm willed excision of a painful past, like the earlier destruction of the "mass of scraps covering the beginning of my relationship with Katzy."

The thoroughness of this detachment appears in his accounts of the following days. Relatives gathered on Saturday and attended the funeral on Sunday, waiting two days rather than the usual one after the death to follow the religious requirements that burials not take place on the Sabbath. The family began to sit shiva, the seven days of mourning, at Elizabeth's apartment rather than at the old age home where my father's mother lived. After a visit of a few hours at Elizabeth's on Monday morning, he returned to work and continued working through the week. He did not mention attending services on Yom Kippur, nor did he write of going to synagogue to say kaddish, the prayer for the dead, for his father, a gesture that his mother would have felt to be appropriate. His father appears only once more in his diary, on Sunday, October 13, the first day after the shiva ended:

Had to go to the Bronx again. Mother had to be at the home to make some arrangements for herself and the locker [his father's storage area] had to be looked into. I helped her pack her few poor belongings. She has to vacat their old room. She was under mixed feelings. She may not have cared for or respected the old man, but he had given her protection and a means to live. But he never knew how to give it to her.

In the locker where the few miserable things he had saved. Ridiculous things he had hoarded. Bottlecaps, buttons, pencil stumps, and the endless, old and troublesome papers. He used to say, only paupers own nothing.

After leaving mother at Elizabeth drove home furiously. I think that I shall weed out some of the papers I have accumulated. Make some room.

Katzy had prepared a bath for me.

This last sentence is important to me. Without it, I can only infer a period of relative calm in my parents' marriage from the infrequency of diary entries and from the supposition that my mother must have been pleased that my father was bringing in more income. In the laconic account of the preparation of the bath, I think, too, that I detect a moment of great sympathy between my parents, my mother recalling her own grief at her father's death. The final entry in the Daily Reminders, a few years later, consists of another brief mention of a gesture of my mother's:

Katzy bought a bottle of french wine to celebrate our wedding anniversary.

In her generosity, in his easy acceptance, I sense their growing ease with one another and with their lives.

Some fragments suggest that my father traveled to Chicago on business with some frequency in the early 1940s. I know of one such trip only from a piece of cardboard that I found between the pages for December 4 and 5 in his diary, a Pullman train ticket, NEW YORK to CHICAGO, Ill., printed on one side, DEC — 4 '41, stamped on the other. The following pages are blank, lacking an account both of the trip and of the bombing of Pearl Harbor a few days later. A letter of his to my mother provides details of another such trip: the long days of meeting people in the fur trade, the time that he took one evening to carve a little horse out of wood for Carol. He emphasized that he was sleeping on a narrow single bed at Henry's. The good provider and concerned father, the faithful husband awaiting his return to his matrimonial bed, he sounded relatively untroubled in his marriage. Nor does this letter express much concern about his art. The few photographs that he took were mere snapshots of relatives, and the wooden horse sounds more like a simple plaything than an expression of his inner feelings.

In 1944 my parents finally moved to Chicago, where my father joined Henry in business. This departure, I think, might have taken place earlier if it had not been for several events. They felt a great responsibility to find jobs and an apartment for Adolph and Carola Weingarten, cousins of my father's on his mother's side, who arrived in New York in February 1942, after many difficulties in arranging their departure from Europe. I recall many stories of their flight: their hardships in Berlin, as

Jews and as Communists, after the Nazi takeover in 1933; the difficulties of their escape from Germany to France; the nightmarish quality of their stay in Marseilles in 1941, not knowing whether the Vichy government would allow them to leave or whether the American government would let them in. As a child, I did not take seriously the stories about the dangers that they had faced, because they seemed so settled in their apartment on the Upper West Side, in a solid brick building whose elevator struck me then as particularly European and that is still clear in my mind: a round cage within a cylindrical wrought-iron grille of a style that I now know to be Art Nouveau; the openness of this structure allowed a gradually shifting view as the elevator ascended from the marble lobby to the floor, the fifth, I believe, on which Adolph and Carola's apartment was located. I only found out later how narrowly they avoided the camps. The meeting at Wannsee in January 1942, in which Nazi leaders established the Endlösung, or Final Solution, took place while they were still in Marseilles, and by the summer of 1942 the Vichy government was turning over Jews of French as well as foreign citizenship to the German rulers of occupied France.

In June 1942 my parents had another child, a girl. Since Carol had been named for my mother's father (Carol Louise for Chaim Lazer), it was my father's turn to pick the name for this new baby. As the first child in the family born after my grandfather's death, she could have been called Barbara or Beverly as equivalents of his name, Benjamin. Instead, my father decided to commemorate his sister Gertrude. Because my mother also had a sister Gertrude, a woman who was alive and well, it would not have been seemly to call the new daughter simply Gertrude, so she became Judith Gertrude instead.

Soon after Judy was born, Carol came down with a serious illness, which was variously described as St. Vitus' dance and as rheumatic fever. Though the most severe phase passed quickly, her convalescence was slow and coincided with the gradual deterioration of the health of my mother's employer, Lucius N. Littauer. These were the months that my mother always remembered as the most difficult of her life, in which she had to care simultaneously for a sick child, a new baby, and a dying man. My mother made several trips a week to Manhattan. Littauer's chauffeur met her at the train station and drove her to his country home in New Rochelle in Westchester County, where she would take dictation and attend to office business before the chauffeur brought her back to the station. I felt like I lost my father all over again, my mother said, describing Littauer's death in 1944 at the age of eighty-five. Soon after that, my parents, freed of obligations, moved to Chicago.

The diaries, which say little about the late 1930s, come to a complete halt in the 1940s. The Daily Reminder volumes for 1944, 1945, and 1946 are entirely blank. My father made no diary entries after leaving New York for Chicago. These years marked the least introspective period in his adult life, and, I believe, the least troubled as well. Carol had recovered from her illness, Judy had grown from babyhood, and my parents now saw their own household as complete. He trusted Elizabeth to take responsibility for their widowed mother, Adolph and Carola were settled, and my parents had no serious responsibilities in New York. They also had few financial worries, in part because of the inheritance that Littauer left to my mother. Though my parents had always rented apartments in New York, they were able to buy a three-story house in Chicago. They lived on one floor and let out the other two, a steady source of money during the wartime period of scarce housing and high rents. He continued to earn income, even though his partnership with Henry ended — only a few months after it began, if I recall correctly, though without the rancor that had marked the earlier splits between Henry and Max. Through the contacts that Henry had established in the fur business in Chicago, he met a man who manufactured fur hats. Though my father had had more experience with stuffed animals than with hats, he worked for this man sporadically for a number of years, designing hats and making patterns for them in the fall season, cutting and sewing a few custom hats himself at that time, occasionally stopping by the shop at other times. My father told how this man would seek him out: my clients are begging me for hats, Mr. Orlove, could you please come in, just tell me what you want me to pay you.

He often refused these requests. He valued his free time, which was principally taken up not with art (a few family photographs aside, I have not found anything from this period to which that term could be applied) but with chess. From his stories, from a few photographs, from chess columns in newspapers of the period, I have gained some glimpses of the unfamiliar world of downtown chess clubs, where men, dressed

238

*Light-machine*

in ties and jackets, would gather and engage in silent games, lasting hours, with near-strangers. These clubs were the setting of some of my father's stories of the period, in particular his favorite one of all. He once beat the reigning city champion of Chicago three times in a row. As the afternoon wore on, kibitzers gathered around the table. My father remained calm as his opponent's surprise turned into raw fear. The greatness of his victory, I gathered, was most clearly demonstrated in his opponent's stammered refusal to play a fourth game, in his hurried departure from the club.

If my father found this life satisfying, my mother did not. The phrase with which she described this time in her life — "I wasn't cut out to be a lady of leisure" — pops into my mind. Caring for her two daughters did not take the place of the lively atmosphere of Littauer's office, nor did the friends she made in Chicago compensate for the absence of her sisters, from whom she had never previously been separated. She had even more time on her hands once Judy entered school around 1947. Faced with an empty apartment, with free time, my mother decided to have another child. My father was initially hesitant, unsure about this step as he had been about many others, but I gather that once he agreed, they had no difficulty conceiving me, and no concerns about the pregnancy. Present-day expectant couples in their forties, as my parents were at that time, seem to worry more than they did about miscarriages and birth defects. My parents spent the summer midway through the pregnancy with my sisters at my Aunt Gert's house in Connecticut, on an unpaved road, miles from the nearest telephone. And they were confident enough to choose, and to announce widely, the name that I would be given: Barbara, carrying forward the B of my father's father's name. I do not know why they were so certain of my sex. Perhaps they assumed that their daughters were destined, like my mother and my father's mother, to have only sisters, perhaps they took seriously the interpretations that relatives offered of my position and movements in the womb. They may have had more individual reasons as well, my mother hoping for the arrival of another Cohen girl, my father doubting that he had the virility required to sire a male offspring.

It is, I believe, no exaggeration to say that they were overjoyed to have a son. In his state of elation, my father was overtaken by an uncharacteristic fit of Slavic nostalgia, during which he announced that I would be named Vladimir Nikolai. Nonsense, my mother said, no child of mine will go through public school with a name like that. Call him Benjamin after your father, she continued, and give him any kind of crazy middle name you want. And so I became Benjamin Sebastian, my father at that moment deciding that he would found the tradition that the men in the family would have S as their middle initial, following his own example, Robert Solomon. (I have been glad to carry on this tradition with my first son, Jacob Samuel, and with my second as well, Raphael Solomon, born after my father's death.) Once, perhaps in fifth or sixth grade, I pointed out to my mother that my father's proposal might not have worked out as badly as she anticipated. I would have become Nick to the world and kept Vladimir a secret. She responded to this suggestion with an arch harrumph, indicating her unwillingness to entertain the thought that my version was correct, and, I suppose, indicating as well her confidence that I would come to appreciate the way in which she had shielded me, even at birth, from one of my father's flights of fancy.

The plan in which I would have called myself Nick came from the efforts that I took never to reveal my middle name to my classmates in elementary school. Even my first name was somewhat unusual. I disliked being called Ben Franklin and sometimes wished that I had received Mark or Barry or Steven or any of the other common Brooklyn names of the era. Had the strange and pretentious name Sebastian ever leaked out, it would have certainly made me the object of derision. I could anticipate the punning taunts: spastic, bastard. And yet I was resigned to my middle name. It was simply another strange thing about my family that I had to conceal. Only in my twenties did I come to like my names. Uncommon enough to be distinctive without seeming peculiar or requiring explanation, Ben appealed to me for its sturdy simplicity and for its evident but not excessive Jewishness. Later, when I did field research in Peru, I began, almost by accident, to use my middle name, and it stuck. Everyone in town, from the bishop in his residence at the edge of town to the beggars on the street corners, knew me as Sebastián. As the months went by in which I hardly spoke English, as the Berkeley to which I mailed packages of field notes grew more remote, my new identity centered on this name. When I returned to the United States, it took me a while to reaccustom myself to the thought that I was Ben. This future, though, was remote when I was born in Chicago. Ben and Sebastián lay in some unimagined future, Barbara joined David in the realm of my parents' named but unborn children, and I entered the family as Benjy.

In the years after my birth, my parents began to talk of moving from Chicago, impelled by my mother's continued dissatisfactions and by my father's concern that he was not earning enough money there. We left Chicago when I was two and a half, just a bit too young to retain any memories of that city. After considerable introspection, I have decided that the only image that I can summon that might count as a recollection, the view out of our living-room window, is one that I do not really remember but have only invented on the basis of hearing stories about my interest in watching cars on the street below. What else I know about these first years of my life definitely comes from such stories. My parents agreed, for instance, that I uttered my first word, "light," when I was playing in my room late one afternoon. My father was delighted that I had demonstrated philosophical tendencies at an early age by naming an abstract quality linked with spirit and knowledge. My mother, by contrast, was impressed by my practical nature. It was dark in the room, she said, and I just wanted someone to turn on the light. Only after years of repeated tellings of this story did it occur to me that both accounts could be correct, or that I might have had something else in my mind at the time, so that both of these accounts could be false. I cannot weigh these alternatives, since I can recall neither the moment nor the room. The first image that I can bring to mind is of a moment less than a month after we left Chicago for New York. (We combined this move with a vacation, driving first to California, where we stayed for a few weeks before reversing our direction and continuing on to our destination, New York.) My single memory of the trip is not of the prairies that we drove across, the mountains, the Pacific Ocean, or the Mojave Desert that we crossed in August on our return, but rather of a basket of kittens under a kitchen table, which I was able to describe in sufficient detail when I first recalled it years later that my parents could quickly place it in the house of a friend whom we visited in California.

I also recall the very end of the trip, stepping out of the car onto East 17th Street when we finally arrived in Brooklyn, though I have no way of substantiating this claim, only my conviction in the accuracy of the image of the huge mass of our newly purchased house in front of me. Though not as enormous as it seemed to me then, the house was in fact quite large, three stories high, with a large porch that ran the width of the house and continued partway around one side. It seemed endless to me, filled with many corners: the entry hall table that accumulated fascinating objects left by family members as they hurried in or out, the landing between the first and second floors where I could sit and play, the linen closet in the bathroom into which I would climb so that I could pound the back wall and hear a dull thump. I was delighted when I was told that this sound indicated the presence of a hollow space, part of a dumbwaiter shaft that a previous owner had closed off. This explanation confirmed my sense that the house might contain other mysterious recesses.

The size of the house was important to my parents as well. However much they liked the formal style of the house and the solidly Jewish and middle-class character of the neighborhood, the Midwood section of Flatbush, I think that they were particularly drawn to its six bedrooms, the precise number that they needed. My Aunt Gert, the only one of my mother's sisters still unmarried, had been living elsewhere in Brooklyn with Gussie, my mother's long-widowed mother; they both moved in with us, taking the two bedrooms on the third floor. Carol, then sixteen, the oldest of the children, took the front room off the living room on the first floor, and my parents, my sister Judy, and I had the three bedrooms on the second floor. As the youngest child, I was given the bedroom right next to my parents. Connecting my bedroom and theirs was a tiny room with a sink. This room, which could not be reached from the hall or from any other room, must have been designed to allow one person to wash up while another was in the bathroom down the hall. I never used the room for this purpose, though. Instead, I treated it as a kind of secret passageway to my parents' bedroom, disguised by doors that looked as if they opened onto closets. When I woke up lonely or frightened in the middle of the night, I would rush to my parents' bed through that room, a shorter and more private route than the one through the hall. The room had a small leaded window above the sink. On some nights, the moon would shine through the window onto the floor, leaving a pattern of light and shade that I recall with great clarity, although I cannot be certain whether I saw it many times,

242

—

*Light-machine*

or whether I had seen it only once or twice and then dreamt about it afterward.

My father must have felt surrounded by my mother's relatives in the house. Not only were her mother and sister under the same roof, but several of my mother's other sisters also lived in the neighborhood or a few stops away on the nearest subway line. We spent our summers with my mother's family as well, at Gert's house in Connecticut. When my father was working, he would commute to the city, joining us only on weekends. The nametag that gained me admission to the town beach on the nearby lake read Benjy Cohen. To answer the questions that I immediately asked and to assure my participation in the deceit, this subterfuge was explained to me: my Aunt Gert was the one who owned the property, and only immediate family members of such residents were allowed to use the beach for free. Others had to pay a great deal for this privilege, or they might not be admitted at all, so we simply changed our names. As a child, I relished the notion of tricking doltish authorities, of the family sharing a secret that we revealed to no outsiders. It now strikes me as implausible that the town officials who issued these nametags really believed that my sisters, my cousins, and I were the numerous offspring of my aunt, a single woman. The whole charade was probably an unnecessary continuation of the habit, vital to survival in previous generations, of circumventing officials by rearranging family ties.

I do not recall my father, a man sensitive to being slighted, ever expressing resentment over this loss of the family name. His acceptance could have come from many sources: his knowledge that this change was strategic and temporary, his recognition that it made it easier for us to spend summers in a way that we all enjoyed, his familiarity with such ploys. Or it may simply have been that these years in the early 1950s were happy ones for him. He took satisfaction in the economic security that came from the ease of finding employment in the fur district in Manhattan. He shifted from job to job, as owners of shops hired him as a toy designer and a patternmaker, and also, on some occasions, as a foreman or supervisor of cutters and sewing-machine operators. As soon as I entered kindergarten in 1953, my mother also returned to work. The New York City Board of Education hired her as a clerk, though her position would now be called a secretary. (My mother used this language of a preprofessional era when she spoke of her work as well: she had a job, not a career; she earned money rather than an income; and bosses, rather than supervisors, were the ones in charge.) For the first time in their marriage, my parents were on a relatively equal economic footing.

It was not just the steady money, though, that let my father accept this seasonal loss of the family name. If his children were being absorbed into an extended family of Cohens, they were also becoming reacquainted with the Orloves, brought together by the death of my father's mother in the summer of 1950. Howard lived in Queens; Elizabeth and Milton, in the Bronx. Though we did not see them as often as we saw my mother's sisters, we visited them more regularly than when we lived in Chicago and were able to get to know them, their spouses, and their children. Henry also came through from time to time, and even Boris, the business traveler, appeared in New York occasionally, staying in his townhouse in the Upper East Side while he and Mildred were still married, in the Hotel Saint Moritz on Central Park South after they divorced, always bringing exotic presents from his trips: a copper filigree ornament from India, a tiny silver saucepan from Paris, and, one of my favorites, a pottery bull made near Lake Titicaca that he purchased in Lima, the first Andean object to enter my world. The snapshots that show my sisters and me with our cousins suggest to me that my father sought to record this welcome reestablishment of ties among the Orloves.

I might easily have not paid much attention to his art from these years. I had first found a set of the drawings that he made at this time when I began going through his papers, early on in my exploration of the contents of his study. Despite their bright colors and simple abstract geometric shapes, none of the drawings held my attention for long. They seemed like exercises rather than finished products. He experimented with using a ruler and compass, with drawing freehand; he tried crayons, pastels, watercolors, felt pens, but did not settle on any one medium. I looked at these drawings long enough to note that he did not sign or date them or give them titles. They probably did not matter much to him, I thought. I returned them to the heavy cardboard box in which he had stored them, and moved on to other papers.

Nor did the drawings impress me several months later when I came

*My father's brother Boris in New York, 1961.*

across them again, looking for letters or notes from Michael Lenson that my father might have placed with them. Once again, they struck me as undeveloped, more like the doodles in his notebooks than his more serious works, his prints and photographs. It seemed to me that he had toyed with drawings and then dropped them instead of pursuing them intently.

One morning, about a year later, when I was working on a chapter of this book, I completed a draft of one section earlier than I had anticipated. I had no work planned for the hour that remained before my self-imposed noon deadline, so I walked around the study, straightened some piles of papers, and then thought to look at the drawings again. This time, too, they failed to hold my attention. I decided to return to a task I often postponed, the transcription of my father's diaries. Now in a hurry, I replaced the drawings in the box, put the box back on the shelf, and sat down in front of my computer. My eyes traveled back and forth between the screen and a volume of the Big Diary. After a few minutes, when I looked down at the keyboard, I noticed a small red lump just above the knuckle of the middle finger on my left hand. I stared at the glistening mass for a few moments until I realized what it was: blood oozing from a wound slowly enough that it had begun to congeal before it ran down my hand. I was startled and a bit confused. I had cut my hand when I put the drawings back in the box, I decided; 245

but had the wound really been minor, or had I blocked the sensation of pain that it must have caused?

Taking care to keep my finger horizontal so that the blood would not drip on my keyboard, on my clothes, on the rug, I walked out of my study to the bathroom. I washed my finger off and then leaned my head down to examine it more closely. The rough edge of the box had not actually cut into it, I saw, but rather had only scraped off some skin, a layer so thin that the wrinkles that connected my pores were still visible. Minute droplets of blood seeped out of the moist surface of my exposed flesh. These red points grew and merged, forming two tiny ovals, very close to each other but separated by a bridge of intact skin. I must have scraped my finger twice: did the edge of the box vibrate slightly when I first hit it, or had my hand been shaking? These thoughts, in fact all thoughts, left my mind as I stared at the broken pale skin, my attention held by the slight sheen of the twin red films.

The realization that blood might start dripping onto the sink brought me abruptly back to my senses. I pulled myself up and washed my finger off. After patting it dry with toilet paper, I covered the scrapes with a band-aid, and walked back to my study. Despite my efforts to return to work, I was unable to continue the transcription. I looked at my hands, idle on the keyboard, the band-aid forming an odd companion to the gold wedding ring on the adjacent finger. Suddenly I was filled with an urge to find out whether I had bled onto my father's drawings when I put them away, to see whether the flaps of my skin might have become attached to them. Holding my hand carefully, I opened the box once again and examined the drawings. Many of them contained bright reds, usually in straight and curved lines, and a few had dots, larger and more regular than any that would have formed from my abrasion. It was very unlikely, I realized, that any of these spots were my blood, nor could I expect to find the little bits of my flesh that had scraped off. My curiosity flagged and was replaced by a sense of repugnance. I put the drawings away once again and walked out of the study into the kitchen, relieved to have lunch alone without having to confess to the embarrassing episode or to invent a lie with which to explain the band-aid. As I slowly ate my sandwich, I resolved that I would wait for a calmer time and then return to the drawings.

That time came a few weeks later. Determined to look at the drawings carefully, I tried, without success, to divide them into different categories, to note some aspect of line or form that would allow me to begin writing about them. I finally took one at random, placed it on my desk, and sat down to describe it.

Here is what I wrote: Like many of the drawings, this one is small. It measures about five inches by six. Near the center of this white sheet of paper is a black circle, drawn freehand, with broad quick strokes of a felt pen. The circle is just under three inches in diameter, entirely filled with an intense shade of yellow, except for one rectangle, taller than it is wide, of an equally intense blue, placed within the lower right section of the circle. A black dot sits on top of this blue rectangle. The drawing holds my attention as I look at the whole black circle, at the blue rectangle, then the black dot, then back to the whole circle again. I see the intense colors, I see the black lines, I see the whole. I can see why my father did not give this drawing a title. To have called it "Circle #6" (his drawings include other such colored circles) or "Round Design" would not have added much to it. Nor is the drawing a representational depiction of people or objects. If the black dot were larger in proportion to the rectangle, it could perhaps be taken as a head on a blue body; as it is drawn, though, it is too small to be realistic, so "Figure" or "Man" would not be appropriate titles. I suppose the drawing could have been called "Monument," if the black dot were understood as a sculpture on a blue base. These one-word titles, though, would be wrong in implying that the drawing is a picture of some blue and black object or objects in front of a yellow background. There is no suggestion of depth or scale, and not even enough of a hint of mass to warrant an abstract name like "Presence." The drawing simply is what it is, a bold arrangement of a few strong colors and shapes.

This brief essay accomplished its aim of allowing me to contemplate the drawings, to see them in their own terms rather than as tokens in my struggles over exploring my father's papers. Later that week, I spent a quiet morning drinking tea and looking through them. At first I considered the possibility that the drawings marked a sharp change from the prints and photographs that he had made decades earlier. There was only one geometric form among all his linoleum prints, an odd giant comma with many details, somewhat like the principal motif on a paisley scarf. Even this figure — much more complex than the simple shapes in the drawings — may have been a stylized wave, an object rather than an abstract shape. The use of color was also new, appearing previously only in a few sets of photographs that he took with Kodachrome film in the late 1930s. I reflected on these shifts, at times admiring him for his courage in striking out in new directions, at others regretting his dilettantish hopping to new types of art before fully realizing the potential of any of them.

After a while, though, I realized the continuities from his earlier work to his drawings. Like the prints and photographs, they show the sense of balance and design (evident even in his boyhood attraction to the classical facade of the Leipzig City Hall), they demonstrate his desire to portray the simplest inner aspects of beauty. The contrasting areas of black and white in the prints of buildings are often geometric, whether the rectangular forms of skyscrapers or the triangular shadows on the walls of the Pueblo dwellings. In the photograph of my sister Carol climbing the stairs, each step on the staircase is a defined rectangle as well. Moreover, the drawings resolved an old dilemma of his. In shifting from printmaking to photography, he had gained by making original designs rather than copying other people's works. The simple mechanical nature of photography, though, meant that he had given up working with his hands: the construction of the image that he had found satisfying and to which he returned in his drawings, once again able to experiment with different patterns in his efforts to render his powerful moods in visible form.

Despite the similarities between his earlier art and his drawings, the shift from realism to abstraction was a major change. It seems to me that his art might not have taken this geometric turn if the family had not moved to New York. Part of the appeal of this "what if" kind of question that often comes up when biographers think about their subjects and, more generally, when people think of their parents' lives, is the impossibility of describing alternative worlds, in this case the one in which we remained in Chicago. Nonetheless, the flourishing art world in New York in the 1950s offered him a stimulus that he otherwise would not have received. The Museum of Modern Art, which he visited regularly, had a much larger and more diverse collection of twentieth-century paintings available for viewing than the Art Institute of Chicago. He was now able to see many works by his great favorite, Paul

Klee, as well as by Miró, Mondrian, and Leger. He was taken with the simple forms and evocative colors of the work of Josef Albers, a long-established artist, who continued his series "Homage to the Square" through this period. More contemporary work also interested him. American abstract expressionism, concentrated in New York, was in full swing. Jackson Pollock's drip paintings might have been too messy for him, and Willem de Kooning's work was too crude, but he found other artists to inspire him. Ad Reinhardt's controlled forms and colors, the echoes of Chinese calligraphy in Franz Kline's figures, and even Mark Rothko's thick, rough-edged shapes excited him with their newness, their energy, their purpose.

In New York, my father had more opportunity not only to look at art but also to talk about it. I recall the artbooks at Adolph and Carola's, the thick covers, the heavy sheets of glossy paper with reproductions of European paintings, African sculptures, Buddhist statues. It was through Adolph as well that he got the idea of making sculptures by casting molten lead into molds that he carved, since Adolph, along with some of the other German refugees, carried out the custom of melting lead at New Year's and pouring it into water, divining the events of the coming year in the forms that it took as it suddenly cooled. He also discussed chess with Adolph, a topic not as far removed from art as might be thought. *Die Philosophie des Schachs*, the philosophy of chess, from where does this German phrase spring unbidden into my mind, a fragment of their conversation that I overheard, a book that one of them lent to the other? I recall how my father would sometimes leave a chess-board out in the living room in our house, having copied the early moves but not the later ones, in a game that had been published in the *New York Times*. The pieces remained for days in a particular configuration that had lasted only minutes during the actual game. I had assumed that he meant to study it to learn tactics, to try to recapture the thoughts of the great players, to talk the game over with Adolph, but it now occurs to me that he may simply have liked the way that the board looked. Gazing down at the pieces, whether in the games that he reproduced or in those that he and Adolph often played, my father saw, I believe, something beyond the possibility of different moves: a series of interlocking regions or shapes, some of them filled with an intense conflicting energy, others nearly empty of force, together making up the sixty-four squares of the board, patterns much like the ones in his drawings.

The trends in the New York art world did not hold as much appeal to Mike Lenson, living in New Jersey in the 1950s. After his return from Paris in 1932, he had achieved some success as a painter of murals in public buildings, such as the Newark City Hall, a post office in West Virginia, and the New Jersey pavilion in the 1939 World's Fair in New York. Although he continued to paint until his death in 1971, it was for these murals and some social realist paintings of working-class families from the 1940s that he was known. He is listed as a mural painter in the 1991 edition of *Who Was Who in American Art*; the last exhibition of his mentioned in the seven-line biography was in 1946, though he had had one-man shows, which received generally negative reviews, through the early 1960s. A gallery in Manhattan included him in their autumn 1988 issue of *American ArtNotes* as part of "the artistic legacy of the 1930s and 1940s."

An article on Mike Lenson in the Sunday magazine section of the *Newark News* on February 8, 1970, offers a view of his life as an artist after the 1940s. It discusses the lectures and classes that he gave in New Jersey and the reviews of art shows that he published in local newspapers. One such review in the December 21, 1969, issue of the *Newark News* panned "New York Painting and Sculpture 1940–70," the show with which the Metropolitan Museum of Art opened the celebration of its centennial. This show, the first major retrospective of postwar art in the most established art museum in the country, marked the acceptance of avant-garde art by the establishment, but Lenson did little more than offer "a plea for people and content" in the midst of the different schools of abstract and pop art with which he felt little sympathy.

The 1970 article also includes nineteen color reproductions of recent works of Lenson's. The one mural illustrated in the article shows five women, one girl, and one infant. This painting was evidently completed in the late 1960s, since that is when the building in which it is located was constructed, the headquarters of the New Jersey Federation of Women's Clubs. These women are pretty enough but lack any emotion. They do little more than represent aspects of women's clubs: one is picking flowers; another holds a book; a third, in a robe and mortarboard, must have just received the diploma that is in her hand. The other paintings have conventional themes and little power: portraits of his sons, of a girl feeding pigeons, of famous British poets. They do not appeal to me as much as some of his earlier paintings, especially "The Woman in the Café."

I can imagine several sources for this flatness of Lenson's work. Living in the suburbs, he may have been cut off from the vitality of the urban art world. The teaching and lecturing with which he supported his wife and two sons, born in the mid and late 1940s, may have absorbed most of his efforts. I keep thinking, though, that in settling down to a life as a husband and father, he may have given up the charged visual and erotic relationships with the women who modeled for his earlier paintings. At any rate, the women of the New Jersey Women's Clubs lack the allure of "The Woman in the Café," the mystery of "The Two Fates."

Lenson, who rejected the new art of the period, and my father, who was intrigued by it, had drifted so far apart that my parents did not even invite him to my sister Carol's wedding on September 1, 1956. The wedding was not large as such affairs go, probably not more than fifty people, but it was much bigger than the other events in our house. Our Passover seders were small, and we usually went to a Cohen sister or to one of the Orloves for Thanksgiving, so the parties in the house were infrequent, small, confined to a single room: a half-dozen or so of my classmates in the dinette for my birthday, a sleep-over party to which Carol invited her college friends, and which I would join early in the morning, happy to serve as a kind of mascot to the teenaged girls in pajamas crowded into her bedroom.

Carol's wedding was the single occasion on which people filled the entire house. Guests spilled out from the two big rooms on the first floor into the dinette, the porch, the front steps. The staircase was occupied by women going to and from the room on the second floor where Carol was dressing and into which I, just seven at the time, was still young enough to be admitted, even though I was male. The caterers could barely get through the crowd to bring the trays of appetizers and drinks from the garage and kitchen where they were working. Of the one brief period of quiet in all this hubbub, the wedding ceremony itself, I recall only the beginning, Carol walking down the stairs and across the living room to the wedding canopy set up in front of the fireplace, and the end, the moment that I had anticipated, the excited shouts when Joe's foot came crashing down on the wineglass, and the guests pressed forward to kiss the bride.

At some point after the ceremony, I was drawn into service as a waiter. The guests were amused to give orders for drinks to me, one of the few small children at the wedding, and even more amused to see me carrying them back. Elizabeth in the living room in an elegant dress, my cousins Paul and Martha chatting on the railing of the porch — the memories that I have of this time when I moved through the celebration delivering drinks have blended so thoroughly with the wedding photographs that I was later shown that I cannot separate the images that I had seen myself from the ones that the photographer recorded, with a single exception, my father's expression as he reached down to receive the drink I handed him, the broad wordless smile on his face as he gave me a long steady look before he returned to his conversation and I scurried off to take someone else's order.

As my biographical eye moved from the earlier portions of my father's life to this period in Brooklyn, it gradually dawned on me that one of the greatest crises in his life occurred in the ten years after Carol's wedding. His work, his family life, his art were all going smoothly in the mid-1950s; by the early 1960s, they had each begun an apparently irreversible decline. I was surprised at myself: why had this crisis been so unclear to me at the time? The years from 1956 to 1965 ought to be the period of his life that I knew best, and my memories of his daily life during these years should be far richer in detail than the occasional documents that I found for other times. This decade of my life ran from the middle grades of elementary school to my graduation from high school, when I went off to college. Living at home with my parents, no longer so young that I saw my parents as figures of mythological proportions, I should have had an intimate knowledge of the conflicts that troubled him at that time. Instead, this period seems more remote to me than the 1920s and 1930s, and the shifts that took place at this time have been among the hardest for me to reconstruct. After some reflection, the reasons for this difficulty have become clear to me. My concern at the time had been not to study each of the family's members on their own terms but to establish a place for myself in a changing family —

and outside the family as well, in the circle of my friends in the neighborhood.

One shift, at least, was undeniable. The house at 659 East 17th Street seemed empty after Carol's wedding, since Gussie and Gert also left around the same time. When they settled back in New York after Labor Day later that September, having spent the summer at Gert's in Connecticut, they returned not to our house but to the top floor of a three-story house several blocks away at 1061 East 17th Street. They were joined by my mother's sister May, her husband Abe, and their son Chuck, who moved from their apartment in Coney Island to the second floor of that house. These moves, I now realize, must have required a good deal of coordination among my mother and her sisters, as well as a thorough search of the neighborhood for a house in which two apartments were available at the same time.

As I look back, the reasons for Gussie and Gert's move remain unclear, though I have later heard different versions that propose one or another of the sisters as the protagonist of the action and that center on the difficulties of sharing something—kitchens or household expenses or the tasks involved in raising children or the responsibilities in providing companionship for Gussie, who was seventy-one at the time of the move. (Another equally plausible version centers on Gert's wish for greater privacy in conducting her relationships with men. This story gained favor after Gert finally married in 1972, at the age of sixty-one, two years after Gussie died.) At the time, though, I did not reflect on the causes of the move, since I was so shaken by its consequences. My mother, busy at work, and Judy, involved in her own activities with her high-school friends, could not compensate for the loss of the female attention and affection with which I had earlier been abundantly supplied. The house itself seemed empty. Some of the furniture had been removed from Carol's bedroom on the first floor and from the bedroom next to mine, into which Gussie had moved a year or two earlier when she and Judy switched rooms. We neither used these half-empty rooms on any regular basis nor closed them off altogether, so they acquired an eerie feeling, as if they had been struck with a plague of silence. Judy took over the entire third floor, which she had previously shared with Gert. It became a kind of teenage territory into which I rarely ventured. Even the kitchen seemed somehow diminished. It was in this room, as the four of us ate our meals with less conversation than when there had been seven people at the table, that I had a particularly acute sense of the family's having shrunk.

This sense of abandonment became more acute two years later, when my parents decided to sell the house, now far too large for their needs. We moved in the summer of 1959. Our new house at 825 East 13th Street was only six blocks away, and the house itself, with a large porch, three stories, and a full basement, resembled our old one as well. The block, though, was a step or two down in a social hierarchy. The single-family homes had been divided into apartments, and we rented the first floor. The block was more crowded and less refined. Some of the women wore housedresses when they walked to the grocery store and the laundromat, and there was an Irish bar on the corner. The bustle on the street included the other neighborhood children, who played jump rope, stoopball, ringalievio. On the new block I rarely joined in these games, which I had learned when I visited my cousins Jackie and Amy in Bensonhurst. Unlike my cousins, these children were troublemakers, roughnecks who spat, cursed, and got into fistfights. On Halloween, they not only went from door to door asking for treats but also wandered the neighborhood streets late at night to carry out tricks as well, whacking each other with stockings filled with chalk. Feeling entirely out of my element on the new block, I kept up my ties with my old friends for a year at least. I was able to finish sixth grade in my old elementary school, which now lay at some distance. When we moved west of East 15th Street, we crossed into another school district, but some relative must have pulled strings to allow me to finish up in my old school. I went many blocks out of my way to walk my friends home before I would swing back around to our new house.

It was this move and the consequent need to find new ways of remaining in touch with my friends that led me to ask my parents if I could have a Bar Mitzvah. My elementary school friends had started Hebrew school when I was in third grade, as was the custom in the neighborhood synagogues affiliated with the conservative movement. My parents, who did not belong to a synagogue and never attended services, had not mentioned a Bar Mitzvah to me. As I heard my friends speak more of their own, though, due to come in a few years, I wanted to have one as well. My parents were happy to go along with my wish.

It took us a while to find a synagogue that would allow me to enter their religious school. I was already too old to enter a conservative program, and the orthodox yeshivas on the edges of the neighborhood were out of the question. We finally settled on a reform temple, Beth Elohim, which was willing to admit a sixth-grader to their religious school, with its relatively undemanding curriculum. The congregation included a number of families of German Jews who lived in the elegant brownstones near Prospect Park. I never felt comfortable with my fellow students, who intimidated me with their fancy sweaters and their easy references to the private schools that they attended, particularly the Ethical Culture schools popular in their set. To compensate for this isolation, I sought academic success. My efforts to memorize the Bible stories and to pick up some bits of Hebrew were rewarded with praise, high grades, and a few bronze medals with blue-and-white ribbons at graduation.

In my second year in the new house, I faced another exile. The district boundaries for junior high schools often coincided with the elementary school districts. Without exception, my elementary school friends all went to one junior high school. I had to attend another, filled with groups of children who all seemed to know each other already from the elementary schools that they had attended. A complete stranger in this school, I experimented with my identity. I solemnly announced to my old friends from elementary school and to my relatives alike that I had become Ben and was no longer to be called Benjy. For much of seventh grade I imitated the flashy dress that I associated with the Italian boys: bright shirts, tight black pants, pointy shoes. I even began to develop a taste for rock and roll, which I would listen to on the radios that the tougher boys would smuggle into wood shop, a defiance of authority that impressed me greatly. I listened attentively, even though they played them at a volume so low as to be nearly inaudible. My contacts with such rebels were limited, though, since I was mixed with them only in manual arts and gym. These two courses, aimed at developing our bodies rather than our minds, were atypical both in segregating the sexes and in integrating academic levels. I attended all my other classes with the other children who were part of a special program that compressed the usual three years of junior high school into two. In my second year in junior high school, I had returned to the tastes of the honors track. I listened to folk music, then beginning its revival, and I dressed in the

Ivy League style of khaki chinos and button-down shirts, though, unwilling to adapt myself fully to these fashions, I refused to wear loafers.

My Bar Mitzvah also took place that year. I invited only three friends to that event, one from elementary school, two from my junior high, and none from religious school. The children of the substantial members of the congregation celebrated their Bar and Bas Mitzvahs in the main temple, a grand neoclassical building, but mine was held in the smaller chapel of the religious school. The brief ceremony struck me as a poor display, inferior to the Bar Mitzvahs that I saw in conservative synagogues, where my friends chanted rather than read their Torah portions and recited apparently endless strings of blessings to much larger groups of people. I was contented nonetheless. I had planned and accomplished my initiation, not into manhood, but into the neighborhood.

This sense of acceptance continued with me the following year, when I entered high school. Most of the students from my junior high school went to one high school, Erasmus, but I lived just within the boundaries of the district for Midwood High, where I was reunited with my elementary school friends. We spent time together both in school, where we were part of an honors program, and outside, since we visited one another a great deal, often sitting around and listening to the music that captured for us, as music often does for adolescents, our barely expressible moods and desires. Our two great favorites were the Beatles and Bob Dylan, both early in their careers, both of whom, in different ways, brought us the promise of freedom. We enjoyed the Beatles for the unaffected happiness of their songs, for the simple lyrics and steady rhythms that suggested dancing, parties, love. By contrast, we admired Dylan and carefully traced his shifts from folk to protest to rock, from acoustic to electric instruments. We were in awe of his absolute commitment to honesty, his rejection of all personal and political hypocrisy, his visions of freedom and transfiguration. His songs were all the more important to us for the effort that they required to grasp the profound truths that lay in his dense and obscure imagery.

We not only listened to the music but imitated it as well. A number of my friends played guitar or harmonica, instruments that will undoubtedly seem as corny to my children as Mike Lenson's mandolin does to me. One or two wrote songs, but a more common form of written expression for us was the poem. I can quote a few because I have saved the 1964 issue of *Patterns*, our literary magazine. A good deal of it was printed in boldface and italics. The magazine's Faculty Advisor, Abraham Singer, lent support to our efforts at experimentation by permitting the art and production editors to use a variety of typefaces and layouts.

Torment and self-doubt were quite in fashion:

> And then I looked down
> To the ground
> And saw my face reflected
> In the puddle of water.
> It was harsh, my face,
> And streaks of tears
> Blotched it red;
> And the ripples
> Helped by some fallen leaves
> Distorted it even more.
> It was lonely and sullen,
> My face;
> And the wind
> Tousled my hair
> To upset the image again.
> It was harsh, my face.

Another poem also records solitary gazing:

> I sit alone
> And watch
> The two burning candles
> on either side of the table.
>
> But my eyes are not drawn
> to the yelloworangewhite
> tongues of flame
>
> But rather to
> the light grey shadow

Stolen by the tall blue candle
From the fire-gleam
of the thin black candle
And cast upon the wall.
I see the shadow of the curiously
shaped bottle
and the shadow of the candle
in the bottle.
And the shadow of the rivulets of wax
On the sides of the bottle
and candle.

But the flame, its Life, is a ghost
And casts no shadow.

These poems capture the moodiness characteristic of adolescence and of the era as well, since hippies had not yet replaced beatniks as the models for cultural alternatives. For another literary expression of our sense of our lives, I turn not to a published source but to my memory. Every year, the sophomore, junior, and senior classes each put on a musical show called "Sing," with dialogue and lyrics written by the students. One such Sing was based on the extended comparison between getting into college and getting into heaven. I can still recall the melody of one of the songs and its opening lines as well. I am certain that I remember the first four correctly, but I may have altered a word or two in the fifth:

Heavenly gates
Can't just be walked through.
Saint Peter waits
Eager to talk to
Illustrious applicants seeking admission on high.

We knew that this heaven was divided into many levels. The uppermost was commemorated in a song of two verses, the first of which was sung to the melody of "Gaudemus Igitur":

Harvard University
Shrine of all things scholarly

Harvard University
May we prove worthy.

The second verse was set to a snappy show tune:

> Harvard is one school and Radcliffe's another,
> Their friendship is something to see,
> But if Radcliffe and Harvard are sister and brother
> Then, brother, they're living incestuously.

The other end of heaven was described in lyrics written to Brahms's Third Hungarian Dance. To this melody, one of the standards of classical music radio stations and of the piano teachers of my neighborhood, were set verses that depicted someone who received one rejection letter after another. The only line that I remember is the final one, which described the worst fate we could imagine, acceptance into the safest of all "safe schools":

> Brooklyn College, that's where I'll get my degree!

The bits of lyrics that I recall from this Sing capture our sense that our time in high school was finite and that we would leave for a higher existence. (No song spoke directly of those destined for the hell of not going to college. We could barely conceive of the sins necessary for this fate, such as very low grades, bad scores on College Boards, and parents who were unwilling or unable to pay for college.) Graduation was a kind of death, in which we would leave our childhoods, our parents, and after which we would be reborn into heaven. Bernstein, Falk, Gershek, and Tetenbaum, the four members of the Sing Lyric Committee listed in the school yearbook, gave this afterlife a very hierarchical organization as well as its decidedly non-Jewish gatekeeper in the awaiting Saint Peter. The brightest and the luckiest of the "applicants" were sent to Harvard, the greatest university, described in a song whose first verse spoke of high culture, of a place redolent of age and tradition, where people knew Latin (rather than going to Hebrew school, I suppose); the second verse promised the sexual freedom that we were sure would come with distance from our parents. The most unfortunate among us would remain in Brooklyn College, right in our neighborhood, still living with parents.

There was, indeed, a good deal of competition in high school. We received numerical grades on a scale of 100 rather than the cruder letter grades with no distinctions finer than a plus and minus. Our graduating averages were calculated to a thousandth of a point. (Merely the third in our graduating class, I felt great envy of those who were ahead of me; among the facts engraved in my memory is the valedictorian's graduating average, 97.027, nearly a half-point higher than mine.) Rather than simply describing this competition, though, the songs undercut it through humor and through the evident willingness of many students to put a great deal of time into the show rather than into their homework. One side of our lives was made up of our obsession with grades, but this very obsession led us, perhaps unrealistically, to minimize the importance of anything other than grades and College Board scores to the college admissions process. This obsession freed us as much as it bound us, since it made anything other than courses and tests irrelevant. We might have believed that college admissions committees would have been impressed by time spent on the literary magazine, on the class shows, and on the many other extracurricular activities methodically listed in the yearbook — clubs, teams, student government, and two other magazines, a science journal that bore the post-Sputnik-era title of *Andromeda*, and the resolutely liberal *Road Ahead*, a magazine with a "policy of stimulating discussion of important problems relating to the student and the world in which he lives." Some activities, though, were not mentioned in the yearbook and could not have impressed St. Peter's earthly counterparts on college admissions committees. Interspersed with ads for pizza parlors and drugstores, a note in the back of *Patterns* reads:

> The Midwood Peace Group
> is a discussion group on
> peace and current issues
> that tries to do its small part to promote
> peace and justice in the world. All are
> welcome. For further information, call:
>
> UL 9-1165

The Midwood Peace Group, to which I belonged, had a dozen or so core members and another dozen or two who sometimes came to the evening meetings that we held in each other's homes. We would not have admitted that we enjoyed displacing our parents from the living rooms, since we took ourselves and our purpose of opposing the war in Vietnam very seriously. Of our numerous discussions, I recall only two. One focused on the propriety and significance of encouraging our members to wear buttons bearing the familiar peace symbol. Our decision not to push each other toward this daring gesture is also reflected in the blank upper-right-hand corner of the ad, from which the dangerous image had been removed at the last moment. In the second debate, related to the first, some members who wanted to march in an antiwar demonstration in Manhattan asked permission to carry a Midwood Peace Group banner, a proposal that the more cautious members of the group opposed because it would compromise their autonomy and would submit them to a danger no less severe for its vagueness: "getting us into trouble."

The attraction of the demonstration, as I think back, lay as much in its location as in the views that it sought to present. Eager to explore beyond the limits of our neighborhood, we were drawn to Manhattan, only a subway ride away, where exciting events such as demonstrations might occur. Our favorite spot was Greenwich Village, where we would sip espresso or Italian sodas in coffeehouses while eyeing the people around us, and where we listened to guitar players in Washington Square. We occasionally went to the Bleecker Street Cinema (my friend Eric Weitzner and I once sat through an Ingmar Bergman triple feature, elated to be watching black-and-white foreign films with subtitles, confused and intrigued by the obscure symbolism and the Nordic gloom) and more frequently visited Folk Dance House, where we would meet other young people from the entire metropolitan area and show off our skill in the Balkan dances then popular.

The Village was also our connection to Dylan. We were thrilled with the single reference in one of his songs to a part of our lives. This reference appears in "Visions of Johanna," a very urban song whose meanings we debated (who was Johanna, we asked, and was the song really about her or about visions, all the time longing to know what it would be like to make love at all, let alone in a loft, as described in the song):

An' the all-night girls, they whisper of escapades out on the D train.

We wondered whether it was the whisperings or the escapades that took place on the D train, since this was the subway line, also known as the Brighton Beach train, that took us from Flatbush to the Village. But we were not all-night riders. It was usually well before midnight that this train brought us back — talking about the music we had heard or the way someone had danced — back to our parents, waiting up for us, back to our familiar bedrooms with our book-covered desks.

We had been right. As we discovered when we gathered back in Brooklyn during our semester breaks and vacations, all colleges were heavens, wonderful parentless realms filled with possibilities. The Midwood Peace Group had prepared us well for the demonstrations that awaited us on campuses across the northeastern United States and in the Midwest. We were eager to try out new experiences as well. These were the late 1960s, a time to expand our minds, to enjoy our bodies, to change the world.

And I had been admitted to the highest heaven of all. One morning an envelope, embossed with a crimson seal, arrived in the mail from Cambridge, Massachusetts. I turned it over several times before opening it, as my parents watched in unbelieving joyous wonderment. We knew how to read these divine signs: even unopened, this envelope revealed its message of invitation in its thickness, in the numerous forms that it contained for prospective freshmen to complete.

Harvard did not disappoint me. I strolled in delight along the paths between the old brick buildings, I reveled in the book-filled shelves in the vast libraries. I joined happily in the endless conversations in dorm rooms, along the Charles River, over coffee in seedy restaurants. And I danced. In my freshman year, I would go with some friends from my dorm to the mixers, a common occasion in those times of sex-segregated colleges. Of the ones held at Radcliffe, known by the vaguely Anglophilic name of "jolly-ups," I retain one image in particular, a classmate of mine on whom I had a great and secret crush. Now she was not discussing Donne's metaphysics in our English section, her eyebrows knotted in concentration; she swayed, absorbed in the rhythm, her long hair unbound, her forehead shiny with sweat, a wide grin on her face. In my sophomore and junior years, through a friend whose older sister was active in Students for a Democratic Society, I would occasionally be invited to parties off-campus, a long walk from my dorm to old frame houses in working-class neighborhoods near Central Square; in awe of the older and more radical people at the party, I usually stood to the side and watched the dancing on the first floor, the occasional couple heading upstairs. I only rarely joined in the former, never in the latter, but welcomed this glimpse of adult life nonetheless. The best parties came during my senior year, when Abe Goldman, Jon Kamholtz, and I shared a triple in a turn-of-the-century apartment house that the university had purchased. Our suite consisted of three small bedrooms, a bathroom, and a living room with leaded windows, hardwood floors, and a fireplace: a living room barely large enough to hold the eight or ten of us who would crowd in some nights, dancing without pause for hours on end.

One of the most critical moments of my years at Harvard took place during my first week there, when I saw the announcement of the current set of freshman seminars, an early taste of the close attention that undergraduates received from instructors. Those who wished to apply for the limited places in these seminars had to select a few of the numerous offerings and be interviewed. I signed up for two that seemed very serious and adult (film criticism and psychoanalytical theory) and, on a lark, wrote my name down for another that struck me as absurd, an examination of the African Bushmen in the Kalahari Desert. When I spoke with the professor in charge, Richard Lee, I was captivated by his research. He had spent several years with a completely preagricultural people who lived from the animals they hunted and the plants they gathered; he drew upon his material to reconstruct aspects of the earliest phase of human existence. I enjoyed the broad view of human culture that the readings and discussions offered. I looked forward to the weekly meetings and spent a good deal of time with the other students outside class. As the year wore on, this seminar proved to be a cozy refuge from the harsher aspects of life at Harvard. The relaxed discussions were a comfort after the aggressively competitive intellectual atmosphere in mathematics and philosophy classes, in which my success was not automatically assured, as it had been in Midwood. In the prospect of a field that absorbed me, I found some relief from the gnawing uncertainty about the future that awaited me after the next graduation. The amicable tenor of the other students made up for the arrogant self-assuredness of some of the wealthy students from old families, whose disdain for me far exceeded that of the German Jews at Beth Elohim. (Was the story that we told each other true, that one of our classmates represented the tenth generation of his established Boston family to attend Harvard? The college had been founded in 1636, so this possibility was entirely plausible.) Late in spring, after we turned in our final papers for the seminar, we had an afternoon of sheer rapture. Dr. Lee took us all for an outing on a small river at some distance from Boston. As farmhouses on the banks came into view, as leafy branches passed slowly overhead, the three canoes moved idly along, gathering, dispersing, gathering again. We chatted, we sang, we floated in silence. Surely there was no better spot on earth.

My interest in anthropology continued in the next two years. The various courses on kinship, religion, archaeology, and primate behavior drew on my background in mathematics and science, and, though I did not realize it at the time, on my family's awareness of the centrality of kinship to human existence and on the exposure to non-Western art and philosophy that I had received from my father. Moreover, like virtually all the other undergraduate anthropology majors, I was guaranteed the opportunity to conduct field work overseas — a level of opulence that is virtually unimaginable today. I spent one summer in a shantytown in Rio de Janeiro, another with Indian peasants in southern Mexico. Latin America was a second heaven, a greater and more unexpected one than college had been. Landing on my own in these unfamiliar settings, barely able to make myself understood, I was somehow able to build ties with a few people — a tailor and a storekeeper in Rio, one large rural family in Mexico — and spend long easy days with them, accompanying them in their work and in their meals, conversing about their lives and mine. This exploration fascinated me, moved me, confirmed for me my involvement with the left-wing politics of the times. I did not hesitate in applying to graduate school in anthropology.

My parents accepted this choice of profession. They viewed with equanimity my abandonment of mathematics, in which I had demonstrated such brilliance, first for philosophy, then for anthropology. Only later did it occur to me to wonder why they did not wish to see me select a more practical field, such as medicine or law, or a more established academic discipline, such as physics or economics. They may have felt that Harvard students were guaranteed success whatever their majors, and trusted that the future would work out. I think that they sensed as well my enthusiasm for my courses and my field work. My mother was glad that I took pleasure in traveling, and my father was interested to hear about other cultures.

Most simply, my parents knew that I would not have taken any objections of theirs very seriously. They knew that my attention, which had begun to turn away from them when I was in high school, was now moving even further afield. As I look back, I am struck by how unaware I was of my parents at the time. If I were conducting an anthropological research project about my family, I would find myself to have severe limitations as an informant about this period in the 1960s, and the years before as well. The first interview or two would be enough to establish that I did not see my father clearly or objectively. I knew him closely rather than coherently, I would decide. Personal concerns led me, like many children and adolescents, to see parents in a fragmentary and incomplete way despite my proximity to them. I might be able to provide myself with many concrete incidents about my father, but not with an overall view of his life in these years.

I would turn to written documents to fill in the picture, but here, too, I would face similar difficulties in establishing the general pattern. My father's notebooks from this period are quite different from his earlier diaries. They contain abstract musings on Art, Meaning, Time. I could not decide, on the basis of these notebooks, whether he was content enough to engage in intellectual reflections, or whether he tried to find refuge from his inner troubles by removing himself from everyday life.

The one source that could fill this gap is my memory of my mother's words. I recall hearing her tell her sisters, "I never got to have my menopause because Robbie was too busy having his." The phrase suggests a transition, a crisis, sudden flashes, emotional outbursts — normal for women, abnormal for men. I can recall some of his signs of distress: complaints about his boss at work, painful grunts at the dinner table as his indigestion troubled him, nightmares that made him moan in his sleep. But what was the transition, the crisis that brought so belittling a phrase to her mind?

Once I looked back over the family tree that I had constructed, I could see the events that made up the transition, or, rather, a transition composed of two parts. In the first, my father became a father-in-law and a grandfather. After Carol and Joe were married in 1956, they moved to Iowa, where they entered graduate school and soon began having children: Aaron David in 1957, named for uncles of Joe's who died in concentration camps (his Hebrew initials, *aleph dalet mem*, spelled out Adam, the name by which he is known in the family, the first man, son, grandson), Daniel in 1958, Rammy in 1961, Sara in 1963. Judy married young, even younger than Carol. She was nineteen in 1961, when she and Paul Glattstein, whom she knew from the neighborhood, had their wedding, a small ceremony in the rabbi's office of the temple where I was preparing for my Bar Mitzvah. They moved several times — to Indiana, upstate New York, Pittsburgh — as Paul finished his engineering degree and took jobs. Their children also came soon: Mira in 1962, Seth eighteen and a half months later, in 1963. "*Se le vino un chorro de nietos*," I explained to a Peruvian friend of mine in Davis, talking about my father; "grandchildren poured down on him," though a steady rain might have been a better image, since my sisters had more or less followed my father's parents in spacing their children every two years.

This acquisition of sons-in-law and grandchildren was balanced by losses. My father became the oldest of his siblings, even though he had been born sixth, right in the middle of the set of eleven — or, more to the point, fourth among the eight who had survived past infancy. Gertrude's death at twenty-seven in 1937 and Max's at forty-eight in 1946 had seemed untimely, and the remaining six assumed that they would have more normal lifespans. He certainly did not expect the news when Henry's wife, Jane, called him from Miami Beach in 1959. She had been in their home, she told my father, when she heard the phone ring in the next room. Henry answered it and began arguing with a business associate of his. She heard shouts, then a crash, then silence. She ran in to find him on the floor. Henry had literally dropped dead, a month short of his sixty-fifth birthday.

Among the documents in my father's desk, arranged in an envelope marked "BORIS' last notices," I did not find a telegram describing my uncle's death, so it was probably by telephone that he received the news about his brother in 1963. Boris, whose business dealings had not been going very well, died in Hamburg, also of a heart attack, also a few months before he turned sixty-five. Divorced from Mildred a number of years before this time, he had designated my father as his next of kin. Boris did not leave any money for his burial, and there was very little money left over after his debts were paid, so the arrangements fell to my parents. One of the documents in the envelope was a Western Union money order for $111, made out to Department of State, Special Consular Services. The attached message reads:

FOR CREMATION BORIS ORLOVE HAMBURG AIR SHIPMENT REMAINS
TO ME STOP

In the space in the Western Union form marked "sender's full name" appears Robert S. Orlove, but the handwriting for these words, and for the rest of the telegram, is my mother's. I was surprised only for a moment: I soon recalled how she handled the family's routine financial matters, balancing the checkbooks, preparing the income tax returns, and how incapacitated my father could become at such times. I think that she would have checked the businesslike text with him and that they were in agreement that Boris be cremated. It certainly would have been far more expensive for them to transport Boris's body to New York for burial, more distressing to have him buried in Germany. I wonder, though, whether they were as upset as I was by the document from the Office of Parks and Cemeteries in Hamburg that confirmed this decision. The name of the location, Krematorium Hamburg-Ohlsdorf, reminded me of other German crematoria. I found something chilling in the German term for cremation, *Einäscherung*, "into-ash-ing." Even the simple registration number on the certificate, 6611/63, brought to mind childhood images of tattoos: on the arm of the thin quiet man at a candy store on Foster Avenue who took my coins when I bought comic books; on the arm of the plump woman, probably a good bit younger than I am now, who placed loaves of bread in the slicing machine at a bakery on Avenue J. I recall the matter-of-factness with which my friends and I noted these tattoos: "she has numbers" was all we needed to say to refer to these marks.

It may not have been the troubling image of the cremation at all but rather the simple image of his brother dying alone that led my father to seek more information about his last moments. He wrote to the agency that had arranged for the cremation:

19. Sept. 1963

Most honored Mr. Orlove　!

We hereby confirm the receipt of your note of 25 August 1963. According to your wishes, we have called on the owner of the Hotel Frieden and we have also readily obtained information about your deceased brother. On 1 July 1963 your brother checked into the above-named hotel for the second time and lived there until his death. It was well-known that he had a heart condition. However, he did not have specific complaints. He slept well, and also ate well, and was a warmly-received guest, who often chatted with the other guests and felt at ease in the hotel. On 24.7.1963 your brother came into the hotel around 10:30 P.M. and went into his room. He probably had not drunk any alcohol, as we were also told. He soon felt nauseous. On the way to the bathroom he collapsed. The doctor who was immediately consulted gave your brother an injection and arranged for his admission into a hospital.

The report of the police authorities responsible for the case indicates a sudden heart attack. Your brother thus did not suffer.

Your brother had probably engaged in commercial activity (rugs).

The American consulate was informed of his death and received a watch and a ring from the police-station responsible for the case to pass on to his heirs.

We hope to have served you with this statement and remain

yours faithfully
[illegible signature]

This account raises questions as well as answering them: were there other evenings when Boris did return drunk? In addition to the fatal heart attack, was there an earlier, lesser one that gave Boris nausea and made him collapse? Did Boris's room have a private bathroom, or did he go down a corridor to a bathroom he shared with other guests? Was the doctor really consulted "immediately?" There was no way to address these doubts, nobody to whom my father could turn for further information. And he already knew another, striking fact: Henry and Boris, born four years apart, had also died four years apart. If the Orlove men were destined to die just before they turned sixty-five, my father would have had only six more years to live.

If my mother simply meant "menopause" to refer to a change of life, then the term applied well enough to my father, for whom the gain of sons-in-law and grandchildren and the loss of older brothers marked a shift from middle age to old age, a shift (at least in the premature deaths of his brothers) that he may have resented, as women often resent menopause. But my mother meant something more, using her wit to cloak her anger. She deemed his fits of crying and outbursts of anger to be signs of the irrational moodiness and unpredictability often attributed to menopausal women. She was unprepared when this man, who had been very emotional when he was young but more even-keeled in later years, once again made demands on her that left her unable to attend to her own needs.

My mother may also have been alluding to the fact that menopause ends. I think that she was telling her sisters that my father's crisis, however unmanly she considered it to be, was over. She no longer needed to neglect herself, disregarding her own menopause, to take care of him. Another phrase of hers that sticks in my mind confirms this possibility: she would tell many people, more distant relatives and neighbors as well as her sisters, "I told Robbie to take early retirement."

This second phrase was certainly true, at least in the simplest sense, for he stopped working well before the normal retirement age of sixty-five. I did not notice this shift when it happened. I had always been accustomed to his periods of unemployment, lasting weeks or months. The fur business was seasonal, a fact whose normalcy my mother would corroborate with tales of her uncles who worked in the garment district and were laid off each winter. The family took for granted that my father would "take some time off" after the Christmas rush and at other times as well. I think that the intervals between his jobs increased, and that he gave up looking for new work in the early 1960s. Among his papers I found editions of the *Official Directory of the American Toy Fair* for the years 1958, 1960, 1961, and 1964. These books, four inches wide, nine inches high, and just under an inch thick, must have fit easily into the coat or jacket pockets of the visitors to the fair, which was sponsored by the Toy Manufacturers of the U.S.A., Inc., and held in Manhattan each March. The even-numbered pages of these directories contained brief descriptions of the thousand or so exhibitors; the odd-numbered pages were left blank so that prospective suppliers or purchasers could write notes on them. Since my father rarely discarded notebooks, I think that these four directories indicate the years when he attended the fair. They suggest to me that he worked fairly steadily through 1961. The trip to the fair in 1964, a few months before he turned sixty, was probably a nostalgic look at his former line of work rather than an active search for a job. The entries that he made in these books indicate his activities in the years after his retirement. He visited art galleries, he strolled through museums and parks, "seeing beauty," as he had phrased it earlier.

In the Cloisters, a set of medieval buildings transported stone by stone from Europe to a bluff in Manhattan overlooking the Hudson River, he found some labels whose terms fascinated him as much as the medieval art to which they referred:

> At the cloisters
> Roundel
> Champleve
> Pyx
> Mazer
> Chasse
> Pricket

He had a similar reaction in a park, rearranging the names of flower varieties into a kind of poem-collage:

New Iris flowers in the Botanic Garden in Brooklyn.

———

The flowers are planted, to a certain order, their colors a glowing palette. Their names by necessity follow a random order. A mental arrangement gives a meaning to their poetic selection.

———

Inimitable — Magier — Swan Wings — Snow Peak — Golden Niphetos — May Wonder — Queen of Night — Poet — Maskarade Santiago.

When my mother would explain how she told my father to take early retirement, her intention was not, I believe, simply to allow him to satisfy his curiosity by exploring the city's cultural facilities. She may have been offering him some sort of apology for her first cruel remark. To speak of his retirement was to give his work history the outlines of a career, a suggestion nearly as generous as the use of the term "menopause" was mean-spirited. By using the words "I told Robbie to take early retirement," my mother indicated that she was the one to take the initiative in his giving up work. I think that this implication is accurate: she may well have reached this decision after she compared her lot to that of other women. Her sister-in-law Jane had married a successful businessman who died before he reached the conventional age for retirement; after Boris's death, my mother must have sensed the risk of heart disease among Orlove men even more acutely. It was not only the threat of widowhood that she had in mind, though. Several of her sisters were married to professional men, good providers who were so worn down by the stultifying civil service careers for which they had opted during the Depression that they offered little companionship. At some point in the early 1960s, she may have assessed her lot. After Judy's wedding in 1961, she no longer had the responsibility, which had weighed so hard on her own mother, of seeing her daughters well married. A move in 1962, though of only one block (from 825 East 13th Street to 845 East 14th Street), put her on a more pleasant street, away from the bar and the noisy children's games. Her income was adequate, her health insurance and pension would complement the social security payments that she and Robbie would receive, and there was no reason for him to remain at work, troubled by conflicts with his employers.

In this phrase of my mother's, I hear the suggestion that my father retired from art as well as from employment. Through Adolph's contacts in the German refugee community, he was even able to display and sell a few of his drawings. By the end of the decade, though, he seemed to take less pleasure and satisfaction in them. He made fewer drawings as he began to conceive of a new sort of art project. When another connection established through Adolph gave him the chance to have a few of his works included in an exhibit of some note, his main efforts had already shifted away from his drawings. This exhibit, held on May 6 and 7, 1961, was a fundraiser for *Dissent*, a left-wing cultural and political magazine. The brochure lists a number of leading painters among the contributing artists: Adolph Gottleib, Franz Kline, Willem de Kooning, Robert Motherwell, Barnett Newman, Larry Rivers. Despite this opportunity to hang his works next to those of famous artists and to meet them at the opening, my father did not press ahead with his drawings. He did not let this exhibit distract him from the project that he was working on at the time, his final attempt to achieve some public recognition for his art through his "light-machine."

In the years before this exhibit, he had begun working with scraps of colored plastic that he had been given by his brother Milton, then employed as a salesman for a small plastics manufacturer. He became interested in the patterns made by light reflected off these pieces, in the varied abstract shapes reminiscent of his drawings. In his study, he glued bits of plastic to wheels and connected them to small motors and belts that made them revolve. He then rigged up lights to cast beams of light on these rotating pieces of plastic. The last stage of his work consisted of experimentation with different sorts of screens to capture the slowly shifting reflections. His final choice was a thick sheet of translucent plastic onto which he shone the images from behind.

I recall the moments when my father would set up a working model of his invention on the dining-room table for the family to view. It would take him a few minutes to find the proper position for the light-machine on the table. He would turn out the lights and, with a flick of the switch, set it in operation. I was mesmerized by the figures that would appear on the screen. My memories are a bit vague, and the shapes themselves were ill-defined, but I believe that I can recall an irregular oval of soft green that slowly concentrated into a narrow spot and then fanned out, a yellow line that gradually ascended from the bottom and moved off the top of the screen, a red ellipse that expanded before fading out. I now wonder whether this interest of a twelve-year-old provided my father with encouragement or simply reminded him of the great distance that still lay between him and fame. I suspect that he would have wanted me to watch the machine for even longer periods, but I was in the second year of junior high school at the time, busy with my friends and my preparation for my Bar Mitzvah, and unaware of his concerns.

In his desk, I found some photographs of the machine in operation. Two of the photographs are virtually identical. He must have stopped the machine to capture an image that he liked a great deal, and tried different apertures or shutter speeds to let different amounts of light onto the film. Had the machine been in operation, the image on the screen would have shifted a bit in the time it would have taken him to advance the film to the next frame. This favorite image of his has three shapes, one large and two small; the other photographs have single shapes. Despite these differences, the photographs all show irregular curved forms. The slightly fuzzy outlines and bright centers of these shapes have a yellowish white color, and their softly illuminated interiors are muted tones of reds and greens. They make me think of the many times I saw my father's eye caught by shifting curved forms: how attentively he would pour half-and-half onto the ice cubes floating at the top of a glass partly filled with cold coffee, watching the white liquid drift and mingle with the brown before he would stir the two into a uniform shade of beige with his spoon; how he would pause on a walk in a park in winter to look at water in a stream moving under a thin layer of ice; how his attention could be wholly absorbed by the screen of a television set tuned to a science program on which appeared images of jellyfish serenely pumping their way through a tropical sea.

In the locked drawer of his desk I found carbon copies of a letter and a description of the machine that he sent Mr. Wolder, as well as a diagram.

825 East 13th Street
Brooklyn 30, N. Y.
March 29th 1961

Stanley Wolder, Esq.,
521 Fifth Avenue
New York 17, N. Y.

Dear Mr. Wolder:

As per our discussion, I am enclosing herewith a detailed description and drawing of my invention, the model of which I demonstrated to you at your office.

It is my understanding that you will have a search made to deter-

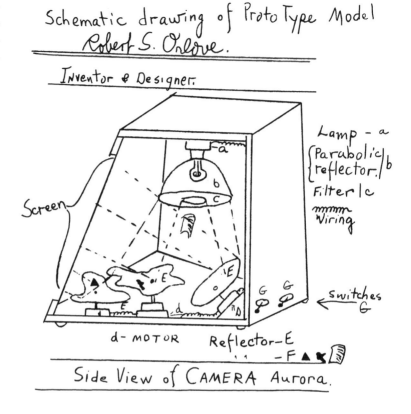

Schematic drawing of Proto Type Model
Robert S. Orlove.

Inventor & Designer.

Lamp - a
(Parabolic|c
{reflector.|b
Filter |c
Wiring

Screen

Switches
G

d- MOTOR          Reflector-E
                              -F ▲ ⚡ 📄
Side View of CAMERA Aurora.

mine its patent possibility. I trust that you will be able to prosecute this search promptly.

Please acknowledge receipt and keep me advised of all developments.

Very truly yours,
Robert S. Orlove

My mother must have composed and typed the letter. When she worked for Littauer, she had become familiar with the proper phrases to use in business correspondence. The concise nature of the letter also makes me think of her. Each of the four sentences is necessary, and no extra flourishes are added. Her authorship is also suggested by the neatness of the typing and the absence of spelling errors, in contrast to the phrasing and the typing in the description of the machine, clearly my father's work:

Herewith a disclosure of the device described below.

Invented, developed and designed by Robert S. Orlove,

825 East 13th St. B'Klyn. N.Y.

THE PRINCIPLE:

By rear illumination to disperse light particles and thru recapture by optical principles to direct and design a composition consisting of motion and alterations of color and free form designs; producing a stately procession of abstract patterns of a high order.

THE PURPOSE:

The purpose of this device is to provide aesthetic pleasure and or arouse interest in the beholder.

DESCRIPTION:

The device utilizes mechanical and optical principles and mechanical and optical components in directed order to produce a new display of an infinite series of designs in color, shape, light and motion. Embodied in a dimension of ever-changing varieties of color and hue. This colorful abstraction is visible to the beholder in animation.

FUNCTION:

A light source, by means of a parabolic mirror or parallel light-sources directs parallel rays through colorfilters onto the surface of a rotating reflection disk of free form. This surface is distirted. The reflected rays are scatterd, refracted thru colored filters, reflected by other surfaces and finally intercepted by a screen.

Operated in this, its simplest form, the pattern will repeat in a cycle, determined by the size of the surface and the speed of the rotation. It is also possible to adjust the device, than aninfinite number of non-repeating designs shall be generated. This is accomplished by utilizing the distortion of the surface by means of heat, stress, warping, pressure: however slight, to deform the area of reflection, creating a different distribution of color and light and resulting in a diversity of images.

By projecting these images through a projection device upon

the walls of rooms, illuminated murals in color and motion will be created.

It is possible for an advertiser to interpose a message, super-imposed on the continously changing image, or to interupt the motor mechanism for the display of the message against a static back ground.

While Mr. Wolder carried out his patent search, my father showed his machine to people he knew. The friends of my father's and the relatives with whom I checked all offered identical accounts of the interview at the Museum of Modern Art that resulted from one of these showings. My father met with several people, including some important figures. They were very interested in the machine and wanted him to leave it at the museum so that they could discuss it with others. He refused, out of a fear that they would steal his idea. The museum staff was unwilling to offer him anything on the spot. He left with his machine safely in his possession. (Did he really say, "What kind of dope did they take me for?" or did I imagine those words?) He did not return to the museum or even call the staff back, and, as far as I know, he did not try to sell or publicly display his machine again.

He first kept the light-machine on top of the large cabinet in the living room, bringing it down occasionally to show to visitors. He later broke it down to its component pieces, which he stored in a bedroom closet. This disassembly took place only a few months after the interview at the museum. When I was going through his study after he died, the only parts of the machine that I found were a few switches, an aluminum plate that might have served as a reflector, and the principal light, wrapped in newspapers dated October 12, 1961. Apparently he did not wait for a reply from Wolder that would have eliminated the risk attendant in leaving the machine with potential customers, either by offering my father legal assurances that his invention could be protected or by informing him that his idea was not original. I am fairly sure that he would have saved such a letter, had he received one, along with the description, sketch, and letter that he had sent Wolder. (My inquiries to the current partners of the firm to which Wolder had belonged did not yield any results, since their archives do not go back to the early 1960s, nor has Wolder's widow been able to locate any correspondence with my father among her husband's papers.) I do not know precisely what prompted my father to pack up the machine: he might have received a discouraging phone call from Wolder, asking for more money or suggesting that there would be delays in the patent search. Sensing his own aging in his brothers' deaths and his grandchildren's births, he may simply have despaired of his chances of achieving the fame that he craved. I think that my mother understood that this disassembly was a significant act for him. In her phrase "early retirement," she may have meant not only the end of his work in the fur trade in the early 1960s but the close of his artistic career at this time as well. She may also have been referring to his lack of creative production, to a kind of sterility, when she spoke of his menopause.

If my father had had more confidence or less suspicion, this machine might well have given him the big break he had long hoped for. For once he had anticipated a trend in art. His use of plastics paralleled other experimentation with new materials in that era of wholesale abandonment of oil paints for acrylics. The light-machine could have fit in with the color-field painting then just reaching wide recognition, especially Morris Louis's veil paintings, with the neon art that developed at the end of the decade, and, more generally, with the outburst of experimentation that marked 1960s art, following the dominance of abstract expressionism in the 1950s. The Museum of Modern Art did display a device by Thomas Wilfred called the Lumia, very similar to my father's light-machine, in 1964. Its soft forms, slowly moving and changing, drew large audiences in that decade of light shows, lava lamps, tie-dye cloth, and yellow submarines.

I cannot fully accept my father's suggestion that his decision not to leave his machine at the museum was a sign of his ability to size up people and situations, of the shrewd business sense with which the Orloves were gifted. I have tried to picture him at the meeting. Did he take the details that differed from his ordinary Brooklyn world — the fashionable dress, the elegant furniture — as auguries of success, or did they overwhelm him? Did he feel himself able to charm the museum staff, as he had often charmed artists and gallery owners, or was he bewildered, tongue-tied, in the presence of these more powerful individuals? Did he recall his brother Max's fear of having an invention stolen? As I thought about these different possibilities, I kept returning to the "disclosure" he wrote about his "device," with his naive excitement and his efforts to sound polished. He must have been entirely out of his element at the museum. Unable to construct and weigh alternative courses of action, he simply withdrew, and a few months later, in a discouraged moment, took the machine apart, never to put it back together.

*Light-machine*

## Chapter 10   C A R D S

My father's study contained few records with firm dates that would allow me to describe the diaryless years of crisis after the failure of the light-machine, the years following his retirement from work and art. I can trace one shift, the decline of his chess playing, through some dates in the advertisements on the backs of chess columns that he cut out of the *New York Times*. These clippings begin in the 1950s, after our return to New York from Chicago, and taper off in the years after 1960. He may have played less often with his principal partner, Adolph, whose health, which was never good, began to deteriorate. I think, too, that he found a replacement for chess. As I review my notes and scrutinize my memory, images of my parents' games of Scrabble come into view: it is the setting, the kitchen table at 845 East 14th Street, that allows me to date these images to the period from 1962 to 1965, after we had moved into that apartment and before I had left it to go to college. These were years when my father was around the house a good deal, with time on his hands. My mother and he became avid players of the game. I particularly recall the grand gesture that he would make after laying his tiles down. When he was satisfied with his move, he would sweep his arms open and rotate his wrists so that his palms would be nearly facing the ceiling, and then he would look up, gazing past my mother, as if he were waiting for an audience assembled behind her to burst into applause in admiration of his excellent vocabulary and his clever use of the various colored squares   279 that doubled or tripled the scores of letters or words. He would reach into the box to pick up his new tiles only after a long final look at the changes his new word had brought to the board. Eager for recognition, he did not solve crossword puzzles — unlike my mother, who usually finished the puzzle in the Sunday *New York Times* magazine section. She had a distinct Scrabble style as well, more private than his. She set her tiles down casually, often placing an *i*, *n*, *o*, or *s* upside-down so that the number that indicated its value in points appeared in the upper-left rather than lower-right corner, a disturbance of the pattern on the board that irritated my father. Even after making an exceptionally good word, she paused only briefly to note her triumph, at most uttering a pleased "ah" before counting up her points and writing them on a sheet (she was invariably the scorekeeper). She would then take her new tiles and settle down to wait, since he was usually the one who delayed in making moves. I can recall a few occasions when she picked up a book and began to read. She no longer needed to look at the board, having already planned several alternative moves while he was taking a stretch of time more appropriate to chess than Scrabble.

They both enjoyed winning and were not very good losers. She usually attributed low scores to poor tiles, clacking her tongue when she got a trayful of vowels or other low-point letters, and sometimes proclaiming, only partly with irony, "*mayne glikn*" [my luck]. He frequently became agitated when his scores were low, restlessly shifting his position in his chair. He sometimes blamed her rather than luck for impending failures. He would accuse her of complex machinations: she had made some word, composed entirely of low-point letters, with the sole purpose of blocking future moves of his.

Especially when the game was going poorly, one would sometimes refuse to accept the other's moves, demanding that the other take back the tiles that had composed the nonexistent word and lose a turn. The one who made a formal challenge had to look the word up in the dictionary, even though it would mean losing a turn if the disputed word did appear. Their dictionary, though, a medium-sized college edition, was not always the final arbiter. Each one could sometimes convince the other that the word did exist, despite its absence from this source. My mother would stand on her status as a native speaker and a longstanding reader of English, on her decades of taking dictation; my father, on his refinement and culture. Sometimes one could persuade the other to withdraw the challenge, a triumph worth more than the mere points that came with having the word accepted and the additional gain that would come if the challenger lost a turn. An unresolved dispute, though, could lead to great tension. My mother responded to such offenses with a glowering silence. My father more than once jumped up from the table and paced around the room, muttering to himself, frustrated at his failure to achieve recognition even in his own home. They would abandon the game, since they could not agree which player should lose a turn, and one or the other would make a great show of putting the pieces and the board back in the box. They might remain angry for hours or even for a few days, but never longer than that. One would eventually take the Scrabble set out and approach the other with a coy request for a game, and they would rush to the kitchen table. They became excellent players, with individual scores regularly topping 300. Though they might enjoy a game with visiting relatives, each was the other's favorite partner.

   In addition to games, my father took up foreign travel, another activity common to the recently retired. My mother and he spent the summer of 1964 in Europe, their first trip across the Atlantic since their honeymoon in 1930. If it had not been for his crisis, they might well have gone earlier. They certainly were free to travel during either of the two preceding summers, their first without any children at home for several decades. (Judy had married Paul in 1961; I spent the summers of 1962, 1963, and 1964 in upstate New York, the first two with Carol and Joe, the third in a science program for high-school students.) I also do not think that money was a problem, since they had some savings from the sale of the house on East 17th Street, and their two daughters were both out of college and married. Had the expense of sending me to college been a concern, they would have waited until I graduated from high school in 1965 to find out whether I would go to a public or a private college. At any rate, in the mid-1960s European travel was much cheaper than it later became, in part because the dollar was very strong in relation to the pound, franc, and lira. A guidebook popular with middle-class and middle-aged travelers as well as the younger Eurailpass-and-hostel set accurately promised to tell its readers how to see *Europe on $5 a Day*.

Though my father did not return to his diaries, he did keep a notebook on this trip, in which he jotted down thoughts and observations. The entries confirmed my sense that my parents had enough money to travel, since they stayed in comfortable, though not luxurious, hotels and occasionally ate meals in fancy restaurants. I checked on the pace of their sightseeing as well. They went to major tourist spots — London, Oxford, Stratford-on-Avon, Canterbury, Paris, Rome, Venice — stopping at churches, museums, gardens, and spending a few mornings or afternoons without visiting any sights, either strolling in the neighborhood near their hotel or remaining in their room, where they did laundry, read, relaxed, and, I suspect, made love as well, though I have no squares, circles, or other signs to confirm that activity, only the rather indirect evidence that my father reported feeling very well.

A few of the notes caught my interest. I read and reread a description of a walk that he took in an English village:

> Cypress trees. Heavily foliaged trees on hill, against gigantic, broodingly darkened thunderclouds, side lighted — etched out of the background in early morning wind. Massive clouds in varying illuminations, shading from white, dovegrey to wet slate. Ominous in the complete enclosure of the total circumference of horizons, flattening out the arch of zenith. Moving, scudding across the sky a celestial ocean of turbulent winds and darkened vapors.

Another passage that he had written in their hotel room in London took me longer to figure out. The unusually large and irregular letters confirm the suggestions in his notes: that he was writing in the faint light of the room while my mother was sleeping, not wanting to turn the light on and wake her up; that he, and perhaps she as well, had had a good deal to drink with or after dinner, possibly as a farewell celebration to their trip, then nearing its end.

> Blind sounds sparkling gaze
> The church bell's ringing does not tell what time it is, it announces at a new location in eternity. How rapidly the ¼ hours pass, at night, when I do not sleep, and the thoughts wander on reflective

paths, the tinkling of a small bell, suspended somewhere, spilling a series of sounds as I seek the silence that brings sleep.

The days pass, they run, they flee, rushing away, few are left of the allotted, of the holiday, is not every day of living a holiday. — and as the allotted account diminishes and loosens the intensity and awareness increases

My mouth is open, to breath the air

But why should eyes be closed to see the light.

The room is square, the door is shut — yet all the world is with me visiting.

Let me add my ignorance to yours, how slowly the pen moves, What do I know but what is past, yet why do I to know wish whats to be — Oh, why is Live but what it was. Why not what it is, so that the futures burden may be light. Why should the struggle be — between stability and whirling [illegible] which can be bought for 12 × 12 pence

What is this world, what is this sense, but a towel drying in the window, as the sun sets, because it must of the globes whirling in the firmament and my mind realing because 12 × 12 pence bought enough truth intoxication to reveal the truth to my temporary consciousness. To wash away, to make room for another wishes

Will then be there more ignorance in this so lovely world or shall we then have then added negligence to negligence to give us further evidence we know may know know, what is to our heritance and what is the totality of all, I love you, I love you, I love you all    I thrill to the intensity of consciousness, I near the edge of knowing alle, To know, to understand, to have    to give to those who are in need of understanding so that they too may give to more and more, to be free to free the others.

That first trip to England, France, and Italy must have given them a good deal of pleasure, since they took five more trips to Europe in the following twelve years, all of which followed the plan of the first one. They spent a month or two in the summer sightseeing in a few countries, usually staying just a few nights in each spot, remaining at most a week in their favorite locations. These later trips had high points as well: a long boat trip through the Norwegian fjords in 1966; a tour of a Greek temple in ruins in a stark barren stretch of the Mediterranean coast of Turkey in 1970; a stay in a small village in the Italian Alps in 1971; and visits to Israel after Carol and Joe moved there in 1973.

I have no source that documents my father's visits to Manhattan in those diaryless years with the detail and precision that his notes offer of the European trips. I did find a box filled with catalogs, brochures, and flyers from art exhibits that he attended, but this set of materials is incomplete, since he sorted through it before moving to California, selling the most valuable items and discarding others. The most that I can do is to date his peak gallery-attending years roughly to the period between 1964 and 1978, a span that accords well with his recovery from the failure of the light-machine in 1961. My own memories do not have reference points as precise as the kitchen table on East 14th Street. Because I am certain that he came with me to lower Manhattan when I interviewed for a summer job in the spring of 1965, I think that it was probably on that occasion rather than some other that we went to Canal Street. I accompanied him there after the interview, and he looked through the stores that sold odd lots from the small factories in the city: brass valves, toggle switches, rubber stoppers, and many other such items of hardware; he sometimes bought such items for small assemblages that he made. We were both browsing through the display of one of these stores when we neared a shelf on which were standing several dozen identical objects, metal hemispheres several inches in diameter, each with a white plastic handle. A label stated that these were ten-minute timers. I looked at him, and he grinned, rolled his eyes, and tilted his head theatrically. Without speaking, we knew we were thinking the same thing. We quickly wound up all the timers and darted out of the store and down the street. Not until we were a couple of blocks away did we start to laugh.

I can date somewhat more accurately his friendships with artists, and, in the case of Bernhardt Crystal, with an art gallery owner as well. When we moved to East 13th Street in 1958, my father met Crystal, who lived with his wife at the end of the block. Their eclectic art collection not only filled their house but, in the case of some of their sculptures, extended into their garden, enormous by Brooklyn standards, perhaps a quarter-acre in size. Crystal, as great a talker as my father was, welcomed his visits. They delighted in details: a comment of my father's on the position of the hand in an Indian temple carving, or on the rendering of a lion's mane in a Renaissance etching, would touch off a conversation that would last for hours. They also shared a distaste for the pop art then receiving a great deal of attention. They could speak at length of the shallow commercialism and gimmicky quality of the works that offended them: Warhol's silk-screened images of soup cans and of Marilyn Monroe, Oldenberg's mammoth plastic clothespins, Lichtenstein's blowups of comic strips.

Though my father occasionally stopped by Crystal's gallery when it was in midtown, on East 58th Street between Park and Madison, he became a more regular visitor after Crystal moved the gallery in 1963 to its downtown location on East 16th Street, just off Fifth Avenue. By this time my father's confidence had recovered sufficiently from the failure of the light-machine for him to engage readily in conversation not only with Crystal in his home but with whomever might walk through the door of the gallery — the customers, the other dealers, the artist friends of Crystal's. My father may have met one such artist, Marvin Cherney, a man in his thirties, when the gallery was still in midtown, but their friendship developed downtown, in 1964 or 1965. After a number of lengthy conversations, Cherney invited my father to model for him, more than thirty years after my father had last sat for a painter, Mike Lenson.

I had never taken very seriously my parents' remarks that Cherney was a well-known artist until I began to research his work. Not only was he mentioned in a standard bibliographical work, *American Artists of the Twentieth Century*, and listed in the permanent collections of such important museums as the Whitney and the Hirshhorn, but the library at the university where I teach has two catalogs of retrospective exhibits of his work, one held in 1970 and the other in 1980. The first of these catalogs contains a work, dated as having been painted in 1966, titled *Orlove*. The portrait is not a great likeness. Even though there are a few accurate details — the large, well-formed ears, the slight wispiness of the hair around the temples — the cheeks are wider than his, the neck thicker. The troubled expression, though, is very much my father's, one that I recall even though I have never seen it in a photograph. He could compose himself for the camera, but Cherney elicited this mood during the longer sittings necessary for an oil painting. The downward look of

the eyes suggests a troubled moment of reflection. My father sits just left of center, the top of his head near the upper edge of the canvas, as if he cannot find a comfortable spot for himself in the painting. His mouth is barely open, his lips slack rather than tense, as if he wishes to speak but does not know what to say. Cherney must have been pleased with this painting, because he made another one very much like it later in 1966. He titled this second one *Ecce Homo*, a common title for paint-286 ings, from the words spoken by Pontius Pilate when he brought out

Christ with the crown of thorns just before the crucifixion. My father in a tie and jacket might seem an unusual Jesus; Cherney may have chosen this title to underscore the qualities of suffering and gentleness that he captured in this second portrait. Cherney's widow recalls a third portrait of my father, entitled *The Philosopher*. Apparently it was sold before anyone took a photograph of it, since neither she nor the gallery that represents Cherney's work has a copy of it. There may be a few additional portraits or sketches, but probably not many, since Cherney died suddenly in 1967 at the age of forty-one.

Perhaps buoyed by Crystal's friendship and Cherney's interest, my father met other artists on his own. In 1965, the light-machine a few years behind him, he attended an exhibit of work by Marcelo Bonevardi and struck up a conversation with him. This first contact developed into a long friendship. Of all the people whom my father met after his return to New York in 1951, this artist was the only one whom he commemorated by making a box for his papers: M. Bonevardi in a quick cursive on the top of the box, M. BONEVARDI in larger block letters on the side, to mark the artist whose nine catalogs, six New Year's cards, and two reviews are contained inside. The biographical sketches in the catalogs give an outline of his life: born in Buenos Aires in 1929, raised in the provincial Argentine city of Córdoba, trained as an architect, he taught in the architecture faculty of the university in Córdoba, where he became interested in abstract painting. His works won prizes in several Argentine provincial cities and earned him the Guggenheim fellowship that brought him to New York in 1958, just past the zenith of abstract expressionism.

His "painting constructions," according to the *New York Times*, are "geometrically patterned low-relief sculptures, punctuated here and there by niches containing still-life groups of carved objects with a functional look but a magic spirit, . . . the product equally of necromancy and logic." The catalogs, running from 1965 to 1981, document his success as an artist. By 1967, the biographical sketches no longer include the group shows in which he participated, because there were enough one-man shows to make a respectably long list; by 1973, the catalogs become thicker (now bound rather than simply stapled) and include more color illustrations, even though Bonevardi's works, canvas constructions that include some wood and burlap, have natural tones — soft grays, yellows, and browns—a deliberate downplaying of color to emphasize texture and form; by 1980, the critical text accompanying the illustrations of Bonevardi's work has become longer and of sufficient import to be copyrighted.

The contents of the Bonevardi box pointed to a paradox that I sought to understand: the contrast between the apparent steadiness of this friendship on the one hand and the continuous upward trajectory of Bonevardi's career on the other. I could imagine that Bonevardi, still a new and rather marginal arrival on the New York art scene, would have welcomed my father's attention when they met in 1965, and I could understand why he would send him New Year's cards with brief greetings ("Dear Robert: Best wishes for the coming year! Marcelo"). I was a bit surprised, though, at how Bonevardi's success did not undercut the relationship. My father received invitations to openings of Bonevardi's shows at the Bonino Gallery, always with some inscription ("With my best regards! Marcelo," reads one from 1973). The catalog for an exhibit of Bonevardi's that traveled to the Museum of Contemporary Art in Montreal and the Quebec Art Museum in Quebec City in 1974 had a longer dedication: "To my very good friend Robert, with my best wishes, MBonevardi." The invitation to a major retrospective in 1980 was certainly not perfunctory, granted the scale of the event and the number of such invitations Bonevardi must have sent out: "Dear Robert; Warmest regards and I hope to see you, Marcelo," reads the card announcing the opening, and the catalog that accompanied it was also inscribed: "to Robert with my warmest regards MBonevardi." My father did attend that opening, held in the Center for Inter-American Relations, an institution that occupied an entire four-story structure at the corner of Park and 68th, a grand building designed in 1910 by the famous firm of McKim, Mead, and White, first a family mansion, then the Soviet mission to the United Nations before the Center took it over. The exhibit then continued on to the major modern art museums in Mexico City, Caracas, and Buenos Aires.

Since my father did not keep diaries during these years, I did not have access to a source that would reveal his more private thoughts. At most, I could take the absence of the diaries as a sign of his self-confidence. Nonetheless, I felt that I could understand the friendship from his side. Of great importance for him was his genuine appreciation of

Bonevardi's works. I believe that he would have liked them even if he had never met the artist. He would have recognized and respected the care that went into the smooth polishing of the wood, into the neat assemblage of different materials into a whole, and he would have been fascinated by the obscure mysticism of such titles as *Trap for a Nightmare*, *Short Calendar*, and *Angel's Habitat*. But he was not only an admirer of Bonevardi's works but a friend of his as well — a tie based, at least in part, on the similarities that my father recognized between himself and Bonevardi: both were immigrants to New York, both had a philosophical bent, both had a technical background (my father in toy design, Bonevardi in architecture) that gave them skills that they transferred to art. Another aspect of the friendship was my father's ability to accept, even to enjoy, the success of a man twenty-five years younger than he was. It took me a while to recognize that he had this ability, in part because it contrasted so sharply with the painful, almost intolerable, doubts about his self-worth that the more limited accomplishments of Michael Lenson, a man his own age, had provoked decades earlier.

For a while, expecting him to feel envy, not pleasure, in the face of Bonevardi's success, I toyed with the uncharitable notion that my father realized that it was only as a friend of an artist rather than as an artist that he would gain entry into the art world in New York, and that Bonevardi was a means to achieve this longstanding personal ambition. I decided later, though, that he was not using Bonevardi as a way to attend studio parties and exclusive gallery openings; he did save Bonevardi's New Year's cards, after all, as well as the invitations. There was no parallel in this friendship, it seemed to me, to the turmoil that Lenson had stirred up in him and that he worked hard to keep hidden. He simply enjoyed his visits with Bonevardi and welcomed the chance to have long conversations about art and life. The ability to have such pleasures was hard won, the consequence of having lived through the crisis of the years just before he met Bonevardi.

I had few documents to help me understand the friendship from Bonevardi's side. The notes that he sent my father suggested some depth of feeling, since they moved beyond cordiality into genuine warmth, but they were too brief to provide much detail. The one occasion on which my father introduced me to Bonevardi gave me only the most general of clues about the tie between them. The visit took place in my second or third year of graduate school, between 1970 and 1972. Whatever independent image I once had of Bonevardi's face is now so thoroughly submerged under the photographs that I have seen in catalogs that I cannot summon it up at all; I see the dark hair, the broad forehead, the penetrating gaze caught by the photographers rather than by my own eyes. But I do recall the visit clearly: taking the elevator up to the Bonino Gallery, my father nodding at the beautiful and elegantly dressed young woman at the desk, Bonevardi walking over to us, his firm handshake. He looked steadily at me, and my father listened proudly while we spoke in Spanish. We talked about our visits to Machu Picchu. Back in 1968, before the development of tourism in the 1970s and the rise of the Shining Path in the 1980s, rules had been lax. I told him how I spent a night in the ruins, which were lit by a waning moon that rose several hours after sunset, how I wandered up and down terraces before curling up to sleep in a corner of an ancient stone house. Emboldened by Bonevardi's interest, I announced to him that I also knew Quechua, which I had begun to study, and offered him a few sentences in this language that he might have heard a few times in his life, perhaps if he had walked into a kitchen in Buenos Aires and intruded on a maid talking with a cousin recently arrived from Bolivia. He then switched back to English and drew my father into the conversation. They were soon talking animatedly together. I took a step or two back and began strolling around the gallery, glancing at his canvas and wood constructions, and trying to build up my courage to speak to the receptionist, a woman about the same age as me, but, I was sure, far more sophisticated.

Interested in exploring the friendship from Bonevardi's perspective and knowing only that he sent my father some notes and that they conversed, I indulged even more in speculation: did Bonevardi miss his own father, back in Argentina; had he had some teacher whom my father resembled? I still was puzzled at the appreciation with which he received my father's expressions of interest even in the early 1980s, after the Museum of Modern Art and the Guggenheim had purchased works of his, and retrospectives had traveled to several countries. After some reflection, I realized that it was I rather than they for whom success was a great concern. Keeping in mind the genuine animation of the one conversation I had witnessed, I looked back at Bonevardi's catalogs and recognized many themes that he might have discussed with my father more fully or more passionately than with almost anyone else. They were both admirers of the Argentine writer Jorge Luís Borges, whose stories and essays I had always found a bit cerebral: the resolutions of his plots are too perfect, the references to Europe and Asia too erudite. A friend, Carol Simpson, once described Borges's writings as contrived, a word that struck me as appropriate and that, on reflection, suggests a quality that both of them, as makers of constructions, might well have found appealing. They certainly would have liked his theme of hidden patterns, coincidences, and recurrences. Bonevardi might have welcomed my father's comments on the cabala, which appears frequently in Borges's work. They may have discussed, for example, "Death and the Compass," the story in which three murders take place in spots that later are discovered to be the three corners of an equilateral triangle (linked mystically to the Hebrew letters *yod*, *hay*, and *vav*, the first three of the four letters in one of God's names), since Bonevardi's constructions, like my father's drawings, often contain this shape. There was a good chance, I decided, that my father steered Bonevardi toward the mystic titles he chose for some of his works, such as *Astrologer's Kite* and *A Scale for Premonitions*. The catalog of his international retrospective in 1980 states that "His Pythagoreanism is confirmed by the fact that he still plays with the Golden Section": did my father speak to him of links among religion, geometry, and cosmology, of the Greek ruins he and my mother had visited a few years earlier, of the facade of the City Hall in the Leipzig of his childhood? I now imagined their conversations as exchanges between equals, and it occurred to me that Bonevardi may have invited my father to his openings because he really wanted him there. There would have been many other people who could have chatted with Bonevardi on other themes — his breaking of the convention of the flat canvas, for example, and the connections of this move to the heavy layers of paint used by some abstract expressionists, to the convergence between Joseph Cornell's thickening of his collages by the addition of objects and frames and Louise Nevelson's flattening of her sculptures into cabinetlike assemblages of found or constructed objects. Very few of the visitors, though, would have had as intimate a knowledge and appreciation of Bonevardi's work as my father.

One day I called directory assistance in Manhattan and found a listing for Bonevardi, still at the same address in Greenwich Village as when he had written to my father. His son Gustavo, who lives in the apartment, answered the phone and told me that his father now spends nearly all his time in Argentina. Gustavo, who speaks regularly with his father, relayed messages back and forth between Argentina and California. It turned out that Bonevardi had kept the letters and notes that my father had sent him, and even the envelopes because he liked the flourishes and designs with which my father had decorated them. My father said that I shouldn't send them to you, Gustavo told me, he wants to keep all these things, but he did ask if you would like me to photocopy some of them for you; he knows where they are, and I could pick some out and take them to a copy shop. Gustavo selected thirty-seven of the eighty-odd items stored in an enormous envelope and mailed me photocopies of them.

The notes supported many of my ideas about the friendship. Some made explicit references to topics from their conversations, confirming my thought that they spoke about art a great deal:

vi/9 — 1970

Dear Friend,

The wall structure I had mentioned to you, is at Delphi, Greece.

The eighty-yards long terrace wall of the temple of Apollo, called the Pelargikon (6th Century B.C.) with its stones intricately fitted together, is covered with neat inscriptions.

The polygonal construction of the long wall, is an anti-earthquake device. Every angle or curve in each stone is fitted with extreme skill into the complimentary angle or curve of its neighbor.

The whole length of this superb wall is covered by some 700 inscriptions, a register of freed slaves, and a record of decisions by the Council who supervised the sanctuary.

It has given me much pleasure to see your work and your creation; in a small measure, I hope, I have shown my appreciation.

Only in the moment of creation do we bind the past to the future.

Yours
Robert

I was puzzled by the "Dear Friend," which struck me as impersonal. Since there was no other friend to whom this card could possibly have been directed, why didn't my father use Marcelo? He retained this usage for most of the correspondence.

7 Oct 1972

Dear Friend,

I think you might like to have a look at the books, I mentioned to you recently, and am therefore sending their titles to you. I look forward to a visit, but cannot set a date, and will phone you next week.

With best wishes,

Yours<br>Robert

| | | |
|---|---|---|
| Alex Marshak. | The roots of civilization. | |
| Peter Fingesten. | The eclipse of Symbolism. | |
| Emil Fredricson. | A mistress called Time. | |
| S. M. Robertson. | Rosegarden & Labyrinth. | |

I wondered whether these notes suggested an asymmetry in the relationship: perhaps my father felt that he could not take up the time of this important artist unless he could offer him useful information in return. But there is nothing sycophantic in my father's congratulations to Bonevardi:

ix/6/80

Dear Marcello,
Many good wishes
for the success-
ful showing of
your recent works
and those that will
follow.
Robert

A feeling of equality rather than dependence also comes across in shorter notes in which they arranged to see each other:

Dear Friend

Various intrusions of minor matters have prevented me from scheduling time for a visit to you. I hope to see you soon and will phone again when the calendar is clear.

In the meanwhile,

Kind regards

vi/24/1981                                             Robert

My father's self-assurance in his relationship with Bonevardi also comes across in his willingness to reveal his own creations. He made many of his own cards, with the message written on one side, the other side containing a collage. One shows two men playing catch with a clockface rather than a ball; another contains a Greek temple, next to which stands a pillar on which is mounted a hand with the index finger pointing skyward. These cards contain my father's reflections on art:

The physical works of Nature
are mysteries to us.
        Shall we, then, attempt less?
With love and passion & inspiration,
We'll make visible for others,
that share our time and those to come
What is hidden within us now.
        With warmest wishes,
    Dec.
1976−77                          Robert.

Silent thoughts are perchance seen,
When we are fast asleep; the sounds of words,
When we're awake, come to the mind at times,
When listening attentively,
To that faint inner voice.
Communication is established
with enigmatic oracles
and what had been a mystery before
will suddenly divulge its esoteric
message.
4/28/77                          Robert

In the first poem, my father joins Bonevardi in the "we" of artists; in the second, he was able to include himself as one of the "we" who can understand mysteries. Still other notes refer to the friendship itself. Some suggest that Bonevardi revealed a more troubled side of himself to my father:

Dear M.B.

Several unexpected errands have come up and as they'll fill my schedule I'll have to postpone my visit, I hope for not too long. I'll phone you week after next.

As time goes on I trust you will gain a new equilibrium of your own or by good news.

Yours

5/20/84   R.

I also found this note on the back of an undated collage showing snowy mountains with faint clouds in the background, on which are imposed some black and gray rectangles:

> **B**ecause you do not
> walk on surfaces,
> your pain
>
> is for you
> and many
> others who see
> a gain,
> **Alas** but true.

I was sometimes surprised by the openness with which my father expressed his affection for Bonevardi. On the back of a collage in which a cyclops stands, outlined against a sky with a clock rather than a sun, he wrote:

> To Marcello.
> with best wishes,
> brief visits
> are long remembered.
> 5/V/1976.   Robert.

The collages that my father sent to Bonevardi provoked a double reaction in me. On the one hand, I was curious, I wanted to learn new things from them, to use them to trace this friendship; on the other hand, I was satisfied by them as familiar reminders of the many other collage-notes that my father had sent to my sisters, to me, to other relatives as well. I had been the recipient of such cards after I left home in 1965 to enter college. They found me at American Express offices during the summer I hitchhiked through Europe, at the different apartments I lived in when I was in graduate school, at the post office (an old two-story adobe house, built around a courtyard) where I picked up my mail when I was doing my field work in Peru. I still come across these cards. I found one misfiled with the owner's manual to my washing machine, others mixed in with old photographs, and, most recently, one in a book that I looked at when I was preparing a lecture for an undergraduate class. When I opened the book for the first time in a number of years, I saw an item that seemed entirely new to me, a card that my father had made from one of his collages. He had glued a picture of an Eskimo soapstone carving of a goose onto a picture of a beach, making a simple design whose balanced shapes and colors appealed greatly to me. He must have taken the picture of the carving, on thin paper, from a magazine, most likely *National Geographic* or *Natural History*; the one of the beach, on a heavier stock, probably came from one of the travel brochures that he picked up at airline offices in Manhattan. Seeing the card again, I now wonder whether this contrast was deliberate, whether he intended it to underscore the effort of the carver to achieve the smooth lustrous finish of the sculpture, to suggest his own awareness of the permanence of nature and the fragility of art. When I first received it, I must have taken it more casually, reading its brief message — "Dear Ben, I look forward to your visit to Bklyn, now two weeks hence. Love, Robert" — after glancing at the collage, and then casually inserting it into the book to mark my place. At that time I took my father's collage making for granted. On each visit home I would see him in his study (first in my old bedroom at 845 East 14th Street, then in the small bedroom in the apartment a few blocks away to which he and my mother moved in 1981, at 410 East 15th Street — or, more precisely, 410 Marlborough Road, to use the alternative name of the few blocks of East 15th Street that lie to the north of Foster Avenue). He would dedicate some mornings or afternoons to cutting pictures out of magazines and storing them in a set of boxes, many more mornings or afternoons to assembling these collages. When a design satisfied him, he would pick up the upper picture, carefully spread paste on its back, and then lower it slowly over the background picture until it was set in place. After waiting for the few moments it took the paste to begin to dry, he would press on the middle of the top picture, using his index fingers for small images, index and middle fingers for larger ones, and then suddenly, firmly, sweep his fingers out to the edges of this picture, squeezing out any air bubbles and sealing the bond. He would then get up and walk at least a few paces around the room before returning to the table, picking up the glued images, and moving them to the shelf where they would dry further. A collage with only two elements would be finished, ready to attach to a card; a more complex one might have to return to his table on several successive days before its completion. He might finish two or three collages in a day, with breaks for cups of tea, a look at the newspaper, and perhaps a game of Scrabble or a walk to the library with my mother — a slow pace of artistic production, but a steady one. Since he made many more collages than he sent out, the stock gradually accumulated. There were over a thousand in his study at the time he died.

I eagerly began the task of sorting through the collages in his study. I sat on the floor and arranged the contents of a big box in front of me, a row of stacks, each with forty or fifty collages. A few items appealed greatly to me. One collage, dated 1/1/1983, is a haiku composed of fragments of text cut from newspapers. This Japanese verse form, written in three lines of five, seven, and five syllables, appealed to my father for its Oriental restraint as well as for the symmetry of its lines, which, like the suitcase combination of 818, add up to 17.

High   Coo

No Flight of Fancy
and rekindled memories.
Prune, Prune      ider Time

The title undercuts the notion of taking art too seriously. That is the impression that I am left with as well. I think of Time pruning away

excesses of fancy and memory to bring us back to the present moment
and the world around us. Perhaps, though, there were other thoughts
that he had in mind when he made the poem. Surely, his imprecision
was deliberate: does fancy fly by carrying us aloft or by running away?
Does the "no" refer only to this flight, or does it extend also to the
rekindled memories? And what might "ider" mean? It scans well, but
the only possible significance I have been able to come up with is an
anagram, dire. Could it have been a dire time that pruned superfluous
recollections and fantasies?

I was aware of such superfluities as I searched, with increasing impatience, for more flashes of wit. Had I simply happened to find the collages that I liked best early on? It might be, I thought, that I was unwilling to admit that my father's creative range was limited. He may
have known his collages well, I thought. He understood that a large set
of them could bore a viewer; that was why he mailed them out one at a
time, so that they might have a stronger impact on the recipient. He
might have already sent out the best collages so that the ones that remained were inferior or incomplete. I came across dozens and dozens
of collages of Northwest Coast Indian sculptures or stone heads from

Easter Island set against galaxies and nebulae. After seeing the first few of these, the others struck me as tiresome, even though they were carefully composed and skillfully glued. Fine: he was captivated with the idea that all people had a capacity for art, an ability to recognize the vastness of the universe: hadn't he already fully expressed himself? Didn't he find, as I did, something dull and ponderous in this repetitive presentation of single ideas?

I kept thinking that I ought to look through the collages, but I never set aside an entire morning for this task. I would spend a half-hour or so, turning over a few dozen collages, setting them in piles on my desk, before some interruption would come: a telephone call, a spider web in a corner of the room that I wanted to sweep away, the appearance in my mind of a memo from my department chair that prompted me to think that I should head into campus early. I would feel relief at being finished with the collages for a while and would replace them in the box where I had found them. On one of those days, as I put the box back on its shelf, I saw a small card slip out and flutter down to the floor. I turned my head to stare at it lying on the carpet, a piece of thick pale-blue paper, folded in half, a collage that I could not quite make out pasted on one side. I must have been careless when I put it away, I thought; had I left it on top of the box so that it slid down when I closed the box? As I bent over and reached my hand out to pick it up, I heard a voice say, "I'm sorry." It took me an instant to realize that it had been I who had spoken. I had no memory of the impulse to apologize, no recollection of speaking, only a tightness in my throat that came from having uttered words after a long silence without having made the usual unconscious initial relaxation of the vocal cords. For a second or two I froze in my half-crouched position, afraid that someone else was in the room, the other me who had spoken and who might come into view if I turned. The silence in the room seemed like the silence between echoes, and indeed it was that other voice, not my own, that I heard repeating the apology in my mind as I walked slowly back to my desk and sat down, as I got up again, as I picked up the card and set it gingerly on top of the box. I did not return to the collages for over a month.

When I began to look through them again at a calmer pace, I found myself more willing to skim through the images until I found ones that appealed to me. Here was a set with playful variation rather than mechanical repetition of a theme: the passage of time. Time is a burden for the Atlas who stands, back bent, bearing a clock rather than a globe, but not for the ballerina who leaps over a row of clocks on a stage. It is simply a presence for the Javanese puppet outlined against a sunset, with a clock rather than a sun in the sky; a marker in the large clock with twelve postmarks cut from envelopes on its face, rather than numbers; an ultimate truth, I suspect, at the center of a nebula in a starry sky.

I am not sure whether my father, in making these time-collages, recalled the watch whose crystal face he nearly broke in Sweden, nor do I know whether he intended the humor that I see in a few of them, such as the one in which a musician beats on a drum whose heads are clock-faces. There is no doubt, though, that he was deliberately comical in another series of collages, based on the number 17. These include a few pictures (a San Francisco cable car, bearing the number 17; a hockey player, seen from behind, the number 17 on his jersey); and snippets from newspaper articles: "ENTIRE 17th FLOOR" reads one; another, "HOPPING SUGGESTION," which is seventeen letters long, presumably had an *s* both at its beginning and at its end before he deleted those two letters.

Most of the elements in these 17-collages, however, are newspaper clippings. A few are headlines:

Dylan's First Album in 17 Months Is a Runaway Hit

PEKING SENTENCES 17 AT MASS RALLY

17 PICASSOS BRING $600,000 IN PARIS

Crackdown on Slugs in Subway Turnstiles Results in 17 Arrests

But most are articles:

The fight is all over in San Francisco, and the sculptor Isamu Noguchi's show will go on. What happened was a 17-day strike for more money at the San Francisco Museum of Modern Art by 31 unionized employees below curatorial level. The Noguchi show, "Imaginary Landscapes," was left crated across the bay in an Oakland, Calif., warehouse. No one would cross picket lines to deliver it, and no one was at the museum to receive it. But the strike is settled, and the Noguchi show will open next Friday, shortening its planned stay by about two weeks.

When not working, the interpreters relax in their lounge on the 17th floor of the Secretariat Building. In conversation, they switch languages with ease.

Four ice age relatives of the modern pig huddled together 17,000 years or more ago for shelter against the cold Arctic wind and blowing dust of what is now Kentucky's Fulton County.

The authenticity of at least 17 paintings in a Miami Beach art museum — many of them Old Masters — was questioned yesterday by the Art Dealers Association of America.

Officials refused yesterday to disclose how they had acquired the reminiscences, which were made at Mr. Khrushchev's dacha, Petrovo-Dalneye, 17 miles west of Moscow.

One shale sheet, showing 17 of the most common fish — called Knightia and about five inches long — was priced at $1,700 in a Jackson, Wyo., art gallery.
"Fossil fish are really becoming popular," said Tomi Wolff, who runs a rock shop with her husband in Jackson.
Ralph Wolff said that he has a "whole warehouse full" of fossil fish to sell in his shop.

Born in Rumania in 1914, Steinberg went to Milan when he was 17. The importance of architectural draftsmanship in his work cannot be overestimated.

A nationwide campaign is taking shape to save 17 beluga whales trapped in Arctic waters near the Beaufort Sea.

Hundreds or even thousands of shooting stars may be seen in an hour. There are 17 annual meteor showers, representing the debris left by as many comets.

Fischer literally destroyed Dely in 17 moves with White against the Sicilian Defense. He rained flailing blows against the enemy king and afforded it no cover.

A party of 17 Soviet explorers dropped in at a remote American station in the Antarctic the other day — and there was "much socializing, and a James Bond film," a radio message to the National Science Foundation reported today.

A lively morning was spent by 17 youngsters Saturday in the graveyard of one of the oldest churches in New York.

The boys and girls, aged 11 to 17, were on a field trip as part of a workshop in gravestone rubbing.

He made these 17-collages, some of them assembled into notebooks, over most of a decade. The earliest clippings are dated 1966. The last date appears in a notebook that he signed "r. s. revolo 1974," retaining his initials but giving himself a new surname, an anagram of orlove. Revolo, revolving, turning: turning the seriousness of his earlier monogram into a Scrabble-like play on words.

My father had given me a few of these 17-books soon after he made them. I kept them in the living room of my house in Davis and occasionally showed them to friends who came to visit. They enjoyed the absurd combinations of disparate objects and events that were included in these books and commented that my father must be "creative" or "imaginative." A visitor and I might take turns pointing out the sets that particularly caught our eyes: seventeens of meteor showers or millennia or chess moves or Soviet explorers. It is only now that I find myself pondering these books as wholes. How did my father want the readers of the 17-books to understand his efforts in establishing the obviously arbitrary connections among these seventeens? The books point in two directions. They show a disorganized, fragmented world, one with venality, suffering, and oppression as well as great natural beauty, but they also enact the capacity of the human spirit to make patterns out of this world. At times I thought I detected his disgust with the venality and trendiness of the New York art world in the juxtaposition of sales of Picassos with sales of rocks, in the mention of forgeries and striking museum employees. I now see these references, like the books themselves, as indicating the universality of a desire for art, a desire that he depicts more positively in the children who make rubbings of gravestones. Each of us, he proposes, may choose a personal theme, even as evidently meaningless as the number 17, and find order in existence. He celebrates this triumph of the spirit with lighthearted wit rather than with reverential solemnity.

Time, the number 17 — I wondered if there were other themes and found one in the photocopies that Gustavo Bonevardi had sent me. A few of the cards that my father sent to Marcelo Bonevardi had animals in them: a frog nimbly grasps reeds in its long slender hind legs so that it is suspended above a pond; an Eskimo carving of a whale rests on a sea represented by marbled paper. In the boxes of collages I found more elaborate constructions with animals: a horse leaps over a watch, much like the ballerina in the time-collage I had found earlier; a seated monkey, its mouth open in amazement, its hands raised to its temples, gapes at a nebula. I came across a whole series of collages based on the Indian cosmological belief that the world rests on the back of an elephant who in turn stands on a turtle. They range from the awesome (an enormous sea-turtle, swimming on the surface of a dark ocean, bears a majestic elephant who carries a globe, outlined against a starry sky) to the comic (the elephant is in a circus pose, balancing on one foreleg on the back of a smiling toy turtle).

The world resting on a toy animal: this collage brought to my mind how my father had struggled to keep his art separate from his work. He aspired to be an artist; he was compelled to be a worker. He earned money through the fur business, through the skills and connections that he received from his father and brothers. He felt art to be noble, work to be crass, especially the petty work in the toy trade. I had been struck many times by the irony of his work: he had been an artist for most of his working life, designing stuffed animals, making patterns. The circus elephant and toy turtle linked work and art in a way that was both self-conscious and playful. I took the ease and grace of these collages to mean that my father felt a vast relief when he abandoned the struggle to keep art and work apart, when he saw and accepted the presence of his art in his work, of his work in his art.

I became curious to find his earliest depictions of animals. I had come across a few pencil sketches of dogs that he had made in the 1930s, but these rough images, drawn on tracing paper, were almost certainly part of his work. The horse that he had carved for Carol in 1941, a sculpture of an animal, was just a single item, and, as a child's toy, still connected with his work. The earliest image of an animal from the notes that Gustavo Bonevardi sent me was a card from 1968, based on a Northwest Coast Indian mask of a sea-eagle. Some of the animal collages that I found in his study might have been a year or two earlier, but they were undated.

All at once I recalled an earlier moment when my father had entertained children with animals drawn on paper rather than sewn from furs or carved out of wood. In my mind I saw him seated in an armchair, two of his grandchildren at his side, telling them a story about the animals that he was sketching on a pad of paper. The children would have been Carol's third son, Rammy, and Judy's first daughter, Mira. They listened in rapt attention to his descriptions of the animals' adventures, breaking their silence only to giggle at the silly parts of the story. Rammy was about three years old and Mira two at the time, so this event would have taken place in 1964, toward the close of my father's crisis. He found an audience for these animal sketches, a smaller, more personal, and much more appreciative one than the large public audience that he had hoped would view his earlier work.

He accepted limitations, not only in the reception of his work but in his own skills as well. His inability to make realistic drawings had been the source of his deep sense of failure over his linoleum prints. He had kept it secret that they were copies of works done by others, principally Mike Lenson. No work, though, could announce its derivative nature more obviously than a collage — or point more clearly to his skills. Seeing the collage in which the heads of a drum were replaced with clock-faces, the viewer had to admire my father's ability to cut ellipses neatly out of the paper (the clocks were viewed from an oblique angle), to save enough such clockfaces to have one of the right size and proportion to fit into the drum, to paste the different pieces of paper neatly together.

Collages also played a central role in the one direct artistic collaboration between my father and myself in the 1970s. During my second year of teaching at Davis, in the fall of 1975, I received the exciting news that my doctoral dissertation had been accepted for publication. As I worked on the revisions of the manuscript, a thought kept coming to mind: I could ask my father to do the art work for the cover. The cover would be a sign, to myself and to readers of the book, that I was not exclusively an academic anthropologist but that I also had enduring personal ties. I also knew that he would be flattered, and I was fairly confident that he would produce an attractive design.

I checked with the publisher, Academic Press. They would be happy to look at some artwork from my father as long as it fit into their rather broad conditions — not smaller than 11 × 14 inches, not larger than 16 × 20, in black and white, suitable for photographic reproduction. Their deadline was a bit more than two months away. I called my father, who was delighted with the idea. We talked about the project, and then I sent him a letter with the details in writing. He had read a copy of the dissertation earlier and said that he was familiar with it. I felt confident that he knew the theme: in a remote mountainous region in southern Peru, small peasant communities and large haciendas had raised sheep and alpacas in the high grasslands above 12,000 feet, coexisting fairly well until the railroad arrived just before the end of the nineteenth century, driving up the price of wool and thus touching off land wars between the peasant communities and the haciendas that were resolved, somewhat unexpectedly, in favor of the communities, largely because the herding communities were able to establish social and political alliances with other groups — merchants, government officials, agricultural peasants in the few valleys low enough to support raising crops. The task that I had set for my book was to account for the peasants' triumph in a way that would fit both into anthropological theory and into the record of Latin American liberation — the stirring tale of Cuba, Chile, Nicaragua, and the other countries that were sure to follow the path to socialism. I was pleased with the way that my account of this region combined economic and ecological analysis with a Marxist sense of class struggle, and eschewed entirely the travel poster images of the Andes. No Inca ruins, Spanish colonial churches, or Indians in colorful ponchos for me, or at least not for my book, and therefore not for its cover. I expected him to know that the pleasure that I got from speaking Quechua, from sleeping out in ruins, from visiting shrines on mountaintops, was entirely personal, outside the scope of my academic work.

My father wrote me a number of letters in which he described his work on the cover. He made many visits: to the Peruvian consulate to request information, to the Brooklyn College library to consult books on mountain geography, to an exhibit of photographs of Peru at the Eastman Kodak Center in Manhattan. For several nights he looked at his slides from the trips that he and my mother had taken to the Alps and to the hills around Jerusalem. He seemed to find inspiration everywhere he turned. Mountain landscapes appeared in magazines, a program on shepherds played on the PBS television station, newspapers carried announcements of exhibitions of pre-Columbian woolen textiles. Even the drifts of snow piled up on the street reminded him of ranges of hills.

I grew anxious as the weeks passed. He sent me a card on which he had glued a photograph of some llamas sitting in front of a ruin and a clipping from the *New York Times* that asks why a publisher chose to give the most recent work by a major novelist "the year's worst jacket illustration." (The clipping reminds the reader, "don't judge the book, etc.," and concludes, "after the jacket is thrown away, this is a novel worth reading.") The sketch of mountains and clouds that he included in the card evoked the vastness of the grasslands and the intensity of the sunlight, and even made me recall the feel of the wind on my face, the satisfied fatigue of an hour's walk with villagers. The sketch, though, was much smaller than the dimensions that the publisher had suggested, and it had little bearing on the economic and historical themes of the book. Subsequent letters brought similar landscape drawings, a few with tiny figures of humans or animals, and then collages for which, I was distressed to realize, the drawings had only been working drafts. The collages were even more inappropriate. They had many different colors, their textures would be difficult to capture in a photograph, and, worst of all in my mind, they contained pre-Columbian images. He sent me two collages as his final efforts: one contained an enlargement of a pre-Columbian carving of an alpaca, posed in front of a mountain landscape with a large sun in the background, and the other showed three llamas standing in front of an image of a man taken from a painted pottery vessel found in some ancient tomb. I panicked: I thought that he might never come up with a suitable design, but I could not withdraw my offer to have him make the cover, especially after I had involved the publisher in the plan. I remembered the times when we would go to an art gallery, and he would break off conversation with me to talk to the owner or to a painter. Once again he was ignoring me, or, even worse, using me to gain recognition. I would be unable to show him that he was mistaken, that the publisher would not be willing to go to the expense of making a multicolored cover. On some nights I would lie in bed, unable to sleep, racked by fears: he would miss the deadline, he would not make the cover, the whole book project would somehow fall through, I would be denied tenure, I would have to move back to Brooklyn and stay with my parents. I would return to my old bedroom, the room he was now using as a study.

As I began to draft this section, the letters that I had written to him about the cover eluded my search. They were not in the boxes that I found in his study that contained the letters that I wrote between 1965, when I left for college, and 1986, when my parents moved to Davis. Those letters, usually two or three single-spaced pages and sent at intervals of a week or two, made up a large accumulation of correspondence that he had neatly filed by date, but the letters about the book cover were missing. Nor were they in files that he made of my papers — my public-school report cards and awards, the postcards and letters I had sent him and my mother when they were in Europe in 1964, my college term papers. I finally found them in a folder that contained the freshman orientation material I had received before going to college, as well as some postcards that my nephew Daniel and I sent to my parents after our week hiking in the Grand Canyon, an assortment of items based either on chance or on some theme of entering new places. The letter that I sent a week or so after receiving the two final collages particularly embarrassed me. It now seems to me that I tried so hard to mask my concerns that I ended up sounding awkward. Instead of writing to him on plain typing paper, as I usually did, I sent this letter on department letterhead. I must have been desperate to strengthen my position, and I was also eager, I admit with some chagrin, to patronize him.

Dear Dad,

I'm sorry that I didn't answer your letter sooner — these two weeks (last week and next week) are particularly hectic ones, since I have some additional lectures to prepare, and I also have some other small projects with deadlines coming up. I really am glad to see all the thought and care that you're putting into this project — your enjoyment and enthusiasm are just great.

I was glad to get the two designs you sent me. They're both very striking. I particularly like the repetition of the animal shapes, giving the sense of the herds, and the lines suggesting the landscapes. The pre-Columbian motifs don't fit in as well. I sent you a copy of the preface of the book, and a full text as well — in there I suggest that what's interesting about the book is that these people, living in remote areas, are very much influenced by the same forces as we are, that they're involved in the world market, that the national government affects their lives in a number of ways. (Chapter 10 really goes into that more than any other, and Chapter 6 is probably the strongest on the influence of the landscape.) So some pre-Columbian designs would suggest the opposite, that the book is about people who are still strongly affected by their ancient cultural heritage (which is also true, but not the dominant theme). It would suggest that the herders have remained the same since before the time of the Spaniards, whereas the book talks about the changes.

I really do like seeing the art, though I'll send it back to you with this letter so you can see what I'm referring to, but I would like it back to keep it for myself. The colors and the forms in the collage are great, it's just that they wouldn't show up in the kind of process the publisher has in mind.

Love,

Ben

This letter strikes me as so filled with muddled impulses and indirect statements that I cannot figure out what I really thought at the time. I can read almost every sentence as a denial. Did I feel that I owed him the apology with which I began the letter, an excuse for a short delay in replying? Did I really think that his "enjoyment and enthusiasm" were "just great," or was I impatient with his self-indulgence, with his use of me as an audience for his pompous monologues? I cannot be certain which interpretation is correct, just as I cannot tell whether I really wanted the collages back, or whether I was just trying to assuage any hurt that I feared my criticisms would have caused him. Perhaps I wanted to want the collages: I had to silence any unfilial doubts that I might have about his skill as an artist by expressing admiration and the wish to keep his works. At any rate, he did reply quickly, in just a day or two after receiving my letter, and he did understand that I wanted different art work.

Dear Ben,

I was very glad to receive your letter and to read your criticisms. Of course, I want to know your response, so that, if a design is used it will be in the spirit of your book. Your points are well directed. My thought of an ancient peruvian theme, was intended to show the background of the Peruvians of today, not that they were tied to their vanquished Past. However one cannot expect that the casual, although, interested reader will be able to reflect the image correctly — Subconsciously, I responded to this challenge by seeing a picture, and not a jacket for a book — I am not making any excuses, the project is a stimulating experience. I think about it, and follows the flashes of ideas — the ever-spreading circles, of the original impact, touch upon many other subjects, thereby widening the horizon far beyond expectations.

In looking for material, suitable for this work, I searched, among other things, in matters of landscapes — And have looked into and read sections of, LANDSCAPE as developed by the processes of normal erosion, by C. A. Cotton. The book describes the Geology of New Zealand — so the photographs in the book cannot be used — Your book is a scientific work, and cannot take a chance, that unsuitable material was used. After all, out of the many readers, there will be a few experts, who'd delight in finding errors — But I am taken by the terminology of this Science — antecedent rivers, anteconsequent gorges, subsequent divides, senile forms of landscapes, meandering, confluences, and many more, all containing very subtle reference to the element of Time — and this leads my thoughts onto philosophical paths — I won't go into this here, I have made notes for myself. You may say, & correctly at that, such response is digressing — It is all an exercise of sorts, as are the various sketches and little drawings I make, in order to see how to develope them further. And when, incidentally, I come up with a collage, which is not suitable for the purpose of my intention — still it has its good use — and would never have come into existence otherwise — I shall returns the (2) pictures you returned for reconstruction, and feel flattered that you want them — , plus a few more dummy designs — I'll look further. — I have more notes for letters, but I'll wait with them until the next letter.

with Love<br>Robert.

---

Despite his closing promise to send me some new drafts for the cover, I continued to worry. A week or so after the deadline, he sent me his final collage, along with his preparatory sketches. The background was a wallpaper sample whose uneven vertical stripes might suggest mountains and canyons; a geometric pattern, a highly stylized representation of an alpaca somewhat reminiscent of pre-Columbian art, was repeated four times, twice in dark brown glossy paper, twice in matte black. It would never work. I sent it off at once to the publisher, resigned to the fact that they would not find it appropriate and that my father would think that I was at fault if his design did not appear. I was confident that they would find some other art work for the cover.

The staff at Academic Press liked the collage. They shot a photograph of it but realized that it would neither reproduce well on the cover nor convey very much about the book. In a hurry for some cover material,

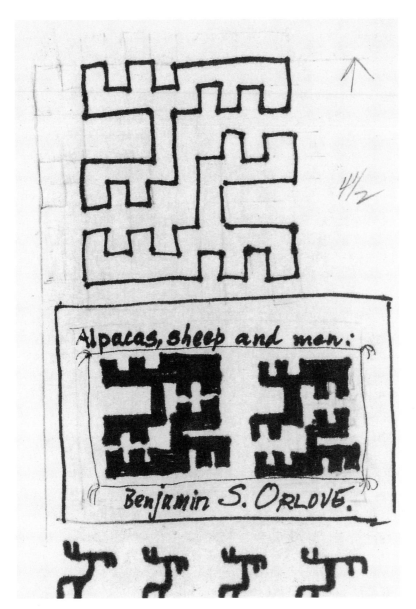

they looked through the photographs that were included in the book, and, without checking with me, selected one that showed a man holding a lamb whose legs were tied, apparently because it displayed a sheep or an alpaca more clearly than the other photographs. I was amused by the irony. This man was bringing the lamb to the district governor as a gift known in Quechua as *chaqo*, a kind of offering with undeniable links to Inca forms of tribute. In addition to its connection with the pre-Columbian past, this photograph is unlike the others in the volume for a second reason: it emphasizes the cultural distance that separated me from the local people. The people in my photographs are usually at work — shearing sheep, herding llamas, selling onions, carrying sacks of wool — they are busy, apparently unaware of my presence, looking not at me but at whatever their task requires of their attention. In the cover photograph, though, not only does the man pose stiffly, obviously at my request, with an ambiguous smile on his face, but on the right edge of the picture, a boy, slightly out of focus, also appears as he leans forward to peer into the lens. He was one of the few children in town who never took my presence for granted; instead, he would often follow me around, waiting for me to do something unpredictable and amusing. He often intruded in my rooms and in my conversations with other people, and here he had permanently intruded on the cover of my book.

I told my father at the time that these photographs were a way in which he was present in the book as well. If I had not heard him speak of photographs on many occasions, as he took snapshots or showed his own slides, I would not have absorbed as fully the basic rules that allowed me to take competent pictures (keep the picture simple; check for balance of form and tone; pay attention to the location of the horizon), and the editor probably would not have approved the inclusion of thirty pictures, a very large number for an anthropological monograph. I am now willing to admit something that I did not recognize then, that these photographs were crucial to the book, since they relieved its otherwise dry and analytical tone. I think, for example, that there must have been a good number of readers who got through long paragraphs about the effects of changes in transportation systems on wool prices because they could also look at a photograph of a train, shot from a distant hill, in which the two locomotives and twenty-seven cars appear as dark silhouettes against the light tones of the dry grassy slopes of mountains whose peaks reach several thousand feet above the tracks, much as the discussions of political centralization were rendered more palatable by the photograph of the man, the lamb, and the fuzzy nosy boy.

Nonetheless, the staff at Academic Press found a way to include the collage. The portion of the book jacket that covered the spine of the book included not only the book's title and the words Orlove and ACA-

DEMIC PRESS, printed in black on a white background, but the stylized alpacas as well, much reduced and printed in a dark shade of gray that happens to be very close to one of the natural tones of alpaca wool. They are attractive in their own right, they relieve what otherwise would be a harsh contrast of black and white, and, in a second irony, people look far more often at them than at the cover of the book because the book usually remains on the shelf with only its spine exposed to view. A note on the front inside flap of the book jacket carefully assigns credit:

*Cover photo by Benjamin S. Orlove*

*Spine design by Robert S. Orlove*

*Jacket design by Dawn S. Stanley*

As I think back to that time, I realize that I had been more eager to see his name and work included than he was. His contribution to the jacket and the book pleased him, but he would have been content if the design had been omitted. In his letter to me, he had termed the project "a stimulating experience," one that allowed him to explore a wide variety of images and thoughts; he no longer craved recognition and success, as he had in the past. I can also see other echoes of the past that I missed at the time. His decision not to use a photograph of New Zealand because "out of the many readers, there will be a few experts, who'd delight in finding errors" reminds me of his efforts to conceal that many of his linoleum cuts were copies of Lenson's work. The tension that I felt over the deadlines in preparing a design to submit to the publisher brings to mind the harsher disputes when earlier generations of Orlove men engaged in business dealings. I am far more aware of the significance of the lateness with which animal motifs appeared in his art, and I am struck by his ability to use them to explore the Indian cultures that fascinated him. Only now can I fully appreciate how pleased he was that I had chosen anthropology as a field of work. The cover not only expressed his satisfaction that I was able to travel and to encounter other cultures, it showed his gratitude that I had found a way for him to take part in these explorations as well.

My parents also found other ways to show that they were pleased with the course that my life was taking. In 1974, when I moved to Davis, I rented an apartment. The following year, I heard of a house that was available for sale, a two-bedroom house from the 1940s with front and back porches and a big mulberry tree in the yard. Its price was brought within my range by its location near the railroad tracks and by the proximity of Mexican families, student cooperative houses, and an auto parts store, features that gave it a certain charm in my eyes as well. When I called my parents to tell them that my loan had been approved and that I had signed the papers to make the sale final, they were quick with their reaction. May you have many years of health and happiness in the house, they said, may only good things come to you in your new house. I was able to get out a few words of thanks, but I nearly lost my composure. Their phrases astonished me. These were not mere good wishes but actual blessings, a form of speech so archaic that I was taken by surprise. As I thought about this conversation in the following days, I came to see that my parents had not spoken casually. Nothing could be more important to them than that I should be settled, that I live in peace in my home, and no other words could convey these feelings more powerfully.

They came to visit me in this house a year later, in 1976. Recalling how much they liked traveling in Europe, I was concerned to take them to the sights in northern California. They did enjoy the trips to the Sierra Nevada, the coast, and San Francisco. They preferred, though, to remain in Davis. They wanted to visit the university where I taught. My father, familiar with his own study and with many other studios and shops, noted with pleasure every detail of my office: my name outside the door, the view from the window to the Quad, the full bookcases, the sturdy file cabinets, the sleek IBM Selectric typewriter. My mother welcomed the chance to chat with the secretaries in my department, to confirm her sense that I went each morning to an office with a friendly atmosphere, a place where work got done, where nobody could get away with trying to be a big shot. Their greatest pleasures, though, came in my house. The Pacific Ocean mattered less to them than a cup of tea in my kitchen, and no entertainment, no excursion could equal a game of Scrabble with me, a conversation in my living room.

During this visit, they could not have failed to notice my double bed. Did they wonder when, or whether, this single son of theirs, then in his late twenties, would ever get married? As I reflect back on those times,

I find a number of contradictory elements. Surely they would have wanted me to be married, to see any children I would have before they grew much older. Yet I do not recall any of the prying or hinting like the parental pressures of which my other single friends complained.

On different occasions my parents had met several of my girlfriends, and they treated them cordially rather than with the warmth — or mistrust — that might have come from people eager to marry off a son. When I would ask them directly for their opinions, I got only diffident responses. I haven't spent much time with her, my father would explain, I can't really tell. She seems nice enough, darling, my mother would say, how do you like her?

That was the most difficult question. From my unclear responses to it, as well as from other clues — hints in letters, the difficulty of finding me at home some weekends, and so on — my parents sensed, I believe, that a few of my relationships had settled into the vague ground between seeing each other and living together. No name exists for this state, yet I saw it in my friends' lives as well as in my own: the man and the woman have a toothbrush and some clothes at each other's places, they rarely spend a night apart, the future and the present of their tie are uncertain. In my case, at least, this stage could last six months, a year, eighteen months on one occasion, before stagnation turned into decay. The relationship would lack resolution at its end as it had lacked definition throughout its duration, though I would be left with a sense of disappointment and loneliness that would last through the years, a time of neither celibacy nor promiscuity, until another such relationship began. Did my parents recognize this pattern, did they know it lasted for my first eight years in my house as it had lasted throughout graduate school? It seems to me impossible that they could have failed to notice the contrast between my sisters' early marriages (at twenty-one and nineteen) and my prolonged bachelorhood. Would they have attributed this difference to the sharp changes in mores that occurred after the late 1950s and early 1960s, when my sisters married? Would they have been able, as I was, to entertain the hypothesis that my mother, the stronger of my parents, gave my sisters a model of self-assurance in a marriage that my father could not offer me? Or was I simply special, the traveler, the professor, unique and beyond judgment? My parents' lack of con-

cern may have come as well from the pleasure and comfort that they took in their youngest child's familiar visits to their apartment in Brooklyn.

Whether from fate, from my parents' blessings, or from my growing self-knowledge and self-acceptance, this pattern ended. It was not just that my tie with Judy, a woman I began to spend time with, grew more quickly and more steadily than the others; it is rather that some combination of my readiness and our being right for each other allowed me to care for her more fully. How easy to look back and say that we met in 1982, that we married in 1983, that our first child was born in 1984 — but that is the vision of hindsight. Those two years were long, full times of their own, not simple steps that were to be passed through on the route from bachelorhood to family life. My parents, though, appeared to have known from the beginning that this future awaited us. They may have sensed Judy's warmth and practicality from their first meeting and hoped that we would stay together. They must have liked the way that our romance made a good anecdote. Judy graduated from Madison, another high school in Flatbush, the year that I graduated from Midwood. We crossed paths briefly in Brooklyn the following summer, introduced by a high-school friend of mine who met Judy at college. Judy remained in New York when I went off to Boston, California, South America, and we did not see each other again for sixteen years. In 1982, when Judy took a trip to San Francisco, the same mutual friend suggested to each of us that we look up the other. And so we finally met in California in our thirties, despite our having grown up in the same neighborhood. *Bashert*, "meant to be," our aunts sighed at our wedding. My parents' knowledge that Judy and I would make a life together, though, came from other sources as well: from the same directness with which they wished me "good things" in my new house, from the same confidence that their words could help send these things to me. Home, love — those were what they had together, what they wanted for me.

The alpacas on the design for my book jacket and the collages of mountains that my father had never seen with his own eyes remind me of other journeys that he imagined, journeys that he enjoyed even more than the trips he took to Europe and Manhattan after his retirement. Among his papers I found a dozen or so postcards on which he had written fanciful messages and addresses, and for which he had made the stamp and the postmark as well as the card. One, which he sent to me from Brooklyn, might seem a statement of the simple, almost banal, notion that life is good. The globe, the clockface, and the word YES! are the same size and shape, and the girl on the stamp is smiling; the address has a comic play on words (POINT OF DELIVERY Leads to From A to Z). This card, though, is a bit like a puzzle, with many elements to figure out. Some points are purely personal: the 11226 in the postmark was my parents' zip code in Brooklyn, and only people who knew him would understand that the decision to include the numbers 1–17 in a column was not arbitrary. Other items, still linked to his life, come close to general knowledge. The words on the stamp, perhaps the message that the girl in the car is delivering, are ICH LIEBE, which mean "I love" in German. The date on the stamp, 1 April, is April Fool's Day, but it does not seem to suggest a trick but merely an association with being spring-like, youthful, carefree, the same qualities in the cartoonlike drawing of the girl and the car.

Even the points that do not necessarily require knowledge of specific facts about my father are still quite idiosyncratic. Accustomed to the coded messages in the letters between my father and his brothers, and familiar as well with the hours he spent looking at racks of Scrabble tiles, I was prepared, for example, to unscramble the ERHE in the postmark to make its anagram, HERE. I took the list of numbers as a hint, and counted the number of times that he repeated in another column the letters *Re*, twenty-six, a connection with the address, Leads to From A to Z. The play on words became more serious, more touching: the point of this delivery was that the message of the card did range over everything possible. The postmark specifies one place and time; the message reaches to the whole world, to the entire passage of time, and also to me, to his affirmation of our close understanding of each other.

In other cards, he wrote more words and lines. In the card reproduced here, for example, he inscribed not only the postmark ("toponym" means place name; "circinus" is a term for a pair of compasses, perhaps the one with which he drew the circle for the postmark itself) but also a message and a scrawled address, # 17, on an illegible street in an illegible city. This writing is so similar to the fanciful documents and speeches in cartoons by Saul Steinberg that, I believe, the resemblance is intentional. In 1973, the date in the postmark, Steinberg had not yet made the single work for which he is now best known, the much-imitated cover of the *New Yorker* in 1975, which shows the world as seen from Manhattan, with distinct individual people, cars, and buildings running from Ninth Avenue to the Hudson River; across the river is a brown stripe labeled Jersey, and then the USA, a flat green surface with a few mountains and some place names written in, beyond which lies an unnamed surface of blue water, with China, Japan, and Siberia as low hills on the horizon. Nor had Steinberg had the major retrospective of his work, which opened in 1978 in the Whitney Museum before touring in the United States, Britain, and France. My father, though, had already become a great admirer of his, seeing his work in smaller galleries and in published collections. The depictions of documents, postmarks, and envelopes in Steinberg's work in the early 1970s may also have influenced his cards.

The message is reminiscent of comments that travelers send home. (I have filled in the covered portion of the message as best I can.)

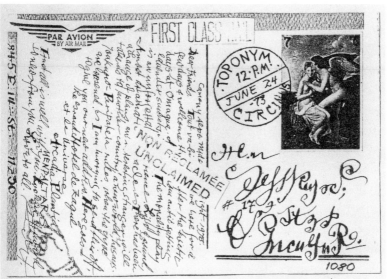

Camony Alps Mids[*ummer'sn*]ight 1973
Dear Friends, Tout va bi[*en. We a*]re here for a
few days of wellcome t[      *a*]fter the hectic
days at Omagua. A[      *f*]rom antic setting
lavender sunsets [      ]The morality play
is an unforgetta[*ble expe*]rience. Light & sound,
A most dramat[*ic spect*]acle. — There has been
a change of plans, an interesting stranger will
take us to another country, "a new world" he said.
You know — Peripateia rules, when the gyre
are loosened. — I am hurrying to send this off
to give you our new address. Here goes=
    Le Grand Hotel de Zague
        et le Univers
        Arcadia Plantia
        MENPALTARS
Trust all is well with you. Looking forward
to news from you. Love to all. Robert
845 E. 14 St. 11230

I was able to figure out only some of the toponyms. The address from
which he wrote, Camony Alps, remains unclear, though it suggests     319

mountains. The Omagua are a group of Amazonian Indians in Peru, and perhaps a link as well to his many visits to the American Museum of Natural History, with its numerous exhibits of such Indians; Zague, I presume, comes after Zigue; Arcadia suggests a quiet, simple rural paradise — or is Arcadia Plantia a suggestion of arcade plants, greenhouses? I recognized MENPALTARS as PLANET MARS, and 11230 as the Brooklyn zip code of the time.

Even without a complete deciphering, though, the sense comes through: a celebration of the world in its diversity and unending possibilities of newness, an evocation of spontaneity and openness. He proposes peripateia, walking from place to place; he suggests that one loosen the fixed patterns of the circular gyres. At midnight on midsummer's eve, as one day changes to the next, as spring becomes summer, my father leaves his planned path. To get to the universe, to arcadia, to new worlds, he zigs to the Grand Hotel de Zague. Much as the interesting stranger takes him to a new world, so may the angel on the stamp take the young woman with whom he speaks. The "Friends" to whom the postcard is addressed also seem to make such spontaneous changes in plans; they, too, have left whatever undecipherable place they lived in, without a forwarding address, so the postcard is *non reclamée*, unclaimed.

Other cards also recount such imaginary journeys. "Dear Friend," one card begins, "We are taking, here today, a well earned rest before continuing the long ascent to INNENSEE." The toponym refers in German to an inner lake but is also a pun in English, suggesting insight. Another reads, "Always looking for distant intersections, where footnotes for thoughtful meanderings are found." One card bears the postmark PLOMTENGS but is dated VIII–17–1977, Selmptong. It begins "Dear Ben, Being here at the Chalet Ibid & Passim is a pleasant prospect for a time. Our guide Herr Hy Decker brought us safely across the Geplonmst Glacier & promises more meandering tomorrow towards other domains." "Ibid" and "passim" are notations in footnotes that mean "in the same place" and "in many places," respectively; Hy Decker is the philosopher Heidegger, whose difficult works my father often checked out of the Brooklyn College library. Geplonmst resembles the German *geplumpst*, which means what it sounds like: "sat down with a thud." (As far as I can tell, the other anagrams have no specific meaning, though Plomtengs strikes me as having a Nordic tone, while Selmptong could be the capital of a small Buddhist principality in the Himalayas.)

The card continues, "It is an orientation in time that sends us, via temporary evocations to the final residence. I shall go out on the balcony and look at Mt. Molpsteng & Stelpmong. Everybody is just standing about with their hands in their pockets. fi fa. Und jetzt FYI to be off and to rummage in other sections. For more Metaphysical Schnapsshots. Con amore, yours, Robert." More anagram-mountains, more musings, and a drink or two after finishing the card, consumed either by the Robert on the balcony of the chalet or by the one in the study in Brooklyn, high-deckers both.

Around the time that I began to outline this chapter, I spoke on the telephone to an old friend of mine from Brooklyn, Mark Chenven, who also lives in California now, in San Diego. I mentioned this book to him and described the imaginary postcards. He laughed and told me how the cards reminded him of my father. "Whimsy" was the word that came to Mark to describe what he remembered most clearly about him. It was a scarce trait among fathers when we were growing up, one that had struck Mark in his teens and early twenties when he visited my house most often. But whimsy might also seem a paltry quality by which to be remembered. It lay far below the heights to which my father had aspired earlier in his life, when he hoped that his works of art would embody the nobility of the human spirit. The cards did not have beauty, only charm; lacking wisdom, they had only wit. Or, to be more accurate, their wisdom lay in their wit, a wit that was generous rather than cutting, graceful rather than clever. Their playfulness had not come easily. His struggle for self-acceptance had been a long one, bound up in his failure to find a public audience for his work. In the calmness that came when this struggle was resolved, he found a second acceptance, an acceptance of death: he mentions "the final residence" in one card and shows an angel in another (and he may even allude to the angel of death in the mention of the "interesting stranger" who will lead him off earth). These cards show not the obsession with time that appeared in many of his earlier collages but rather an acceptance of the transitory nature of life, an acceptance that comes from a whimsical celebration of the imagination.

This whimsy remained with him to the end. He continued to make cards and collages in his last years in Brooklyn, when he nursed my mother through her emphysema while his own health declined, and even after his move to California. Once when I visited him and my mother in Davis, I brought them a finger painting that my son Jacob, then two years old, had made, some blue and green patches. On a visit a few weeks later, I saw the same finger painting on their wall. My father had used it for a collage. The line of animals (a horse, a teddy bear, two penguins, an elephant) that march across the lower half of the painting makes a blue streak look like the horizon and turns the green and blue spots into bushes. Above this blue horizon, a bird glances down as it flies by, and, up in what is now a sky with blue and green clouds, a sun-face of hammered gold from some ancient civilization looks thoughtfully into the distance.

He made imaginary postcards in Davis as well. One card, on a sheet of heavy black cardboard, has no words, only pictures. It shows a red mailbox, two stagecoaches with horses, perhaps mailcoaches, and a large cursive *B* cut from a newspaper. He might have intended to send it to someone whose name began with *B*, to me, to Bernhardt Crystal, to Bonevardi, or he might have meant a pun, the message a simple command: "be." The address is written in a florid scrawl of thick white marks: some Roman and Cyrillic letters, one Hebrew letter (a *tzadik*), and some letters from an entirely imaginary alphabet. I can date this card because it includes a strip from a newspaper: Sunday, April 5, 1987.

Less than two months later he entered the cardiac intensive-care unit of a hospital in Sacramento, after he had a severe heart attack. He remained quite weak but gradually recovered his strength. After the first few tense days, some of my visits with him were pleasant in a way that I had not imagined time in hospitals could be. We spent hours drinking tea, reading newspapers, discussing the books and mail that I brought him. The doctors began to plan his discharge from the hospital in the second week of his stay. On the twelfth day, the nurses gathered with my mother and me when we were visiting him. They gave the three of us detailed instructions for what foods he would be able to eat at home, how far from the apartment we might expect him to be able to walk when he first returned. Late that evening, I received a call from the hospital, telling me to come at once. He had had another heart attack, a serious one, and the nurses were not sure if he would survive through the half-hour that it would take me to drive to see him. When I arrived, he was alive, very tired, but calm. I pulled a chair up to the bed and sat next to him. We talked for a while and then both drifted off to sleep. He was sitting up awake when I woke up the next morning, and was still very weak. I asked him how he felt. He said, with a smile, "Very surprised to be alive." The nurses were surprised as well. We conferred some more and soon acknowledged the obvious: his recovery was set far back, the date of his discharge from the hospital might be long postponed. After a half-hour or so, I told him that I would go to have breakfast in the hospital cafeteria, then head home and come back later that day to see him. As I was finishing my breakfast, I heard my name on the loudspeaker—I was being paged to return to the intensive care unit. I ran back and saw him lying prone, his mouth open. I am not sure whether the sound that I heard was his gasp or mine, or whether I imagined it entirely, and I do not know if I arrived as he died, or moments after.

As the first anniversary of his death began to approach, I spoke with my mother and my sisters about the inscriptions that we would put on his gravestone. We agreed on having his name and dates in English and Hebrew. My sisters and I thought that we might add something more, and I asked my mother whether there was anything that she would add. I was nervous: would it take her a long time to find the right phrase, would she propose something too long to fit onto the stone? She hesitated for a brief moment before saying, yes, she knew what she wanted. I recall her precise words: "A gentle man." She paused, smiled, and continued, "He was a gentle man, you know," her voice quavering slightly on the last two words. I was relieved that she had been able to find a brief phrase quickly, and I liked the phrase as well. At the time, I was impressed with my mother's ability to express several meanings in a simple phrase: he had a true nobility that came from his individual character rather than from his birth, he had a gentlemanly elegance of expression and bearing, and, most simply, she had missed his gentleness since he had died. As the years have gone on, I find more and more in those three words, and I cannot believe that these meanings are accidental. In the months after my father died, my mother must have turned this phrase over and over in her mind, as she often sang a line of a favorite song to herself, noting the different facets of meaning that the phrase contains, but not mentioning it until I asked her about the gravestone. These words are gentle themselves. They gently undercut the claims to nobility that the Orloves had made in suggesting their descent from famous rabbis, in seeking to found a lineage of prosperous family businesses. They gently praise the feminine attributes that my mother had recognized in my father, often with bitterness, and they balance the feminine adjective, "gentle," with the simplest of masculine nouns, "man." My mother's brief phrase gives unity to a life that often seemed composed of dislocations, of fragments, of incompletions. It gives this unity not by describing the totality of his accomplishments but rather by showing the underlying qualities of his presence: his compassion for other people, his whimsical humor, the calmness to which he long aspired and that he finally achieved. It took my mother less than a year to find a few words with which she could speak publicly of her acceptance of his death. Being who I am, I have needed several more years than she did, and many more words.

The Anti-Warrior: A Memoir
*By Milt Felsen*

Black Eagle Child: The Facepaint Narratives
*By Ray A. Young Bear*

Fly in the Buttermilk:
The Life Story of Cecil Reed
*By Cecil Reed with Priscilla Donovan*

In My Father's Study
*By Ben Orlove*

Journey into Personhood
*By Ruth Cameron Webb*

Letters from Togo
*By Susan Blake*

A Prairie Populist:
The Memoirs of Luna Kellie
*Edited by Jane Taylor Nelsen*

Taking Part:
A Twentieth-Century Life
*By Robert Josephy*

Tales of an American Hobo
*By Charles Elmer Fox*

Unfriendly Fire: A Mother's Memoir
*By Peg Mullen*

The Warsaw Sparks
*By Gary Gildner*